Selling Our Souls

Selling Our Souls

THE COMMODIFICATION OF HOSPITAL CARE
IN THE UNITED STATES

Adam D. Reich

Princeton University Press
Princeton and Oxford

KH

Library of Congress Cataloging-in-Publication Data

Reich, Adam D. (Adam Dalton), 1981–
Selling our souls : the commodification of hospital care in the United States / Adam D. Reich.
pages cm
Includes bibliographical references and index.
ISBN 978-0-691-16040-5 (hardcover)
1. Hospital care. 2. Hospitals—Business management. 3. Hospital care—Cost effectiveness. I. Title.
RA971.3.R35 2014
362.11—dc23
2013034451

British Library Cataloging-in-Publication Data is available

This book has been composed in Minion Pro

Printed on acid-free paper. ∞

Printed in the United States of America

10 9 8 7 6 5 4 3 2 1

5/30/17

For Ella

Contents

Introduction 1

PART ONE *PubliCare Rebuffs the Market* 19

CHAPTER ONE *Health Care for All* 26
CHAPTER TWO *Privileged Servants* 48
CHAPTER THREE *Feels Like Home* 59

PART TWO *HolyCare Moralizes the Market* 71

CHAPTER FOUR *Sacred Encounters* 78
CHAPTER FIVE *Good Business* 95
CHAPTER SIX *The Martyred Heart* 109

PART THREE *GroupCare Tames the Market* 123

CHAPTER SEVEN *Flourishing* 127
CHAPTER EIGHT *Disciplined Doctors* 147
CHAPTER NINE *Partnership* 171

Conclusion 189
Acknowledgments 199
A Note on Methods 201
Notes 205
Bibliography 213
Index 221

Selling Our Souls

Introduction

The hospital has a paradoxical place in U.S. society.[1] It is central to the nation's economy, yet many of us are uncomfortable with what is implied by a market for hospital care. The hospital remains a last resort for the poor and desperately sick. It is a place where most of us were born and most of us will die. And it is a place to which we often turn in our moments of greatest physical uncertainty and emotional vulnerability. We have intimate connections to hospitals and strong feelings about them. Perhaps as a result of our ambivalence about the market for hospital care, the vast amount of money that changes hands as a result of this care rarely changes hands *within* the hospital itself.[2] As the hospital historian Rosemary Stevens observes, hospital organizations continue to "carry the burden of unresolved, perhaps unresolvable contradictions."[3] Such contradictions, between the mission of hospital care and the market for it, are the focus of this book.

The United States is unique among modern industrial nations in the extent to which it has relied on the market to determine the organization and allocation of hospital (and all health care) services. By "market" I mean, most basically, the principle of exchange for profit or gain. The market has played an important role in the organization of the American hospital since at least the first decades of the twentieth century. Still, over the past forty years, public health concerns, professional autonomy, and charitable impulses have given way even more dramatically to a focus on profit making and the bottom line.[4]

Since all hospitals today must compete for the dollars that accompany patient utilization, all are under pressure to engage in similar practices, such as reducing the amount of free care they provide, investing heavily in capital improvements,

1

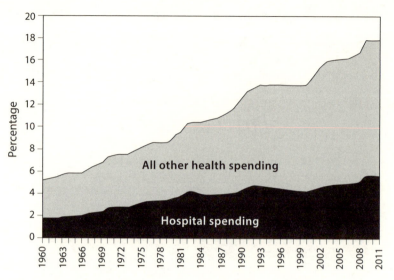

I.1. ▸ Health expenditures as percentage of GDP, 1960–2011.
Centers for Medicare & Medicaid Services, 2012.

increasing their provision of profitable services, negotiating more aggressively with insurance providers and physicians' groups, and using staff more efficiently.[5] The local ties that made some voluntary hospitals "community" organizations have also frayed: most hospitals are now connected with large state or national hospital systems, derive very little money from local foundations or charitable giving compared with government or private insurance reimbursement, and spend much more money on capital investments than on supporting any kind of community program.[6]

Health spending has continued a seemingly inexorable increase as a proportion of gross domestic product, reaching nearly 18 percent in 2010. This rise can be seen both as a cause and a consequence of the ascendance of market actors and market logics across the health care industry.[7] And while hospitals are only one facet of the burgeoning health care sector, they remain a central player. Throughout the period from 1960 to 2011, hospital spending has made up a consistent proportion of health spending (approximately one-third). Hospital spending was responsible for 5.6 percent of gross domestic product in 2010 (see figure I.1). The medical advances that have occurred over this period—from dramatic reductions in infant mortality to the successful fight against cardiovascular disease—remind us that growth in health spending is not inherently problematic if these increases lead to improvements in health.[8] Nevertheless, cross-national comparisons suggest that while Americans spend much more on health care than other industrial nations, we do not get much for this additional spending.[9]

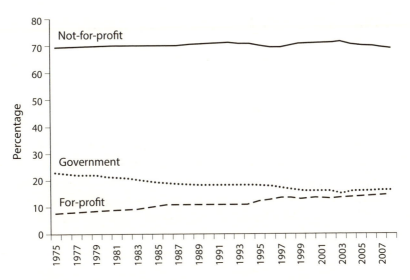

I.2. ▸ Percentage of short-term hospital beds by type of control, 1975–2008.
American Hospital Association, Hospital Statistics.

Market actors wield tremendous power within the hospital industry, but they are not the entire story. Despite market pressures, between 1975 and 2008 the percentage of hospital beds under the control of not-for-profit organizations remained virtually unchanged at around 70 percent (see figure I.2).[10] In a broader health care environment dominated by for-profit insurers, Big Pharma, medical-device manufacturers, for-profit physicians' groups, and other such entrepreneurs, the hospital might seem a last redoubt of the not-for-profit ethic. And despite similar market pressures confronting all hospital organizations, there continues to be a surprising amount of variation in contemporary hospital practice—both across different geographic areas and across different hospitals within the same communities.[11]

Moreover, the development of the hospital market has been mitigated historically by a variety of institutional rules and norms that buffer hospital care from the market's worst excesses.[12] The recently passed Patient Protection and Affordable Care Act, or "Obamacare," intervenes in the market along these lines, changing the broader rules of the game by—for example—increasing access to health insurance for the currently uninsured and incentivizing evidence-based medical practice and quality outcomes. (For more about this legislation, see "Conclusion" in this book.)

So while market forces and market actors have become increasingly important to contemporary hospital practice, the commodification of hospital care in the United States remains uneven and incomplete.[13] At the same time that hospitals compete in a competitive marketplace, many hospitals—and the people within them—work to sustain social values that sit in uneasy tension with this market.

Welcome to Las Lomas

In order to understand these contradictions, we must look not only at the broad sets of rules and regulations through which the market for hospital care is structured but also at the meanings, practices, and people that make up the hospital itself. This book is a detailed study of three hospitals within the same medium-sized city of Las Lomas. Each hospital was founded in a different era of American medicine to serve a different kind of patient and solve a different sort of problem. Today, these historical legacies frame each hospital's ongoing struggle with a different contradiction in the commodification of hospital care, as each works—imperfectly—to reconcile the social values on which it was founded with the imperatives of the competitive marketplace. (For a detailed discussion of methods, see "A Note on Methods" in this book.)

Located within a few miles of one another, PubliCare, HolyCare, and Group-Care serve as the only major hospital facilities in the larger 500,000-person county. Each is a part of a different not-for-profit health system (PubliCare previously had been the county's public hospital but was privatized in 1996). Each considers the other two as its primary competitors for the county's pool of insured patients. The three hospitals offer many of the same services, and they face many of the same market pressures. Despite these similarities, however, they are in many ways worlds apart.

Katherine Taylor, a nurse manager at GroupCare, had strong opinions about all three. We spoke together while sitting on flimsy plastic chairs on a small patio just outside GroupCare's basement cafeteria. Taylor remembered getting into the nursing profession because of a desire to care for people in difficult times. She had a particular "affinity for children," she said, and assumed she would become a pediatric nurse. But this same emotional connection she felt with kids ultimately made pediatrics overwhelming: "Because I love them so much . . . [it] was really hard for me, to deal with my emotions around it." And so—like many other nurses I would come to meet in the city—Taylor had found ways to manage her emotional vulnerability at work. She realized that she either would have to "shut down" or would have to find another area of hospital practice. Taylor found the intensive care unit: "I have a very fast-working brain, so it was just the constant stimulation: information, machines, critical patients. It kept me on the edge of my seat for the whole twelve hours I was working. So that was really enticing for me."

She would escape her vulnerability in the pediatrics ward via the frenetic hum of critical care.

Taylor had been working in Las Lomas for the last fifteen years as a critical care nurse and nurse manager. During this time she had been employed at each of the three hospitals. PubliCare, she thought, was remarkable for the "mutual respect" among the doctors and the nursing staff there: "It was a rare moment at PubliCare that we would have a physician be rude, obnoxious, disrespectful—any of that." But this egalitarianism, she thought, sometimes digressed into a kind of sloppiness: "The nurses would sit at the nurses' station and laugh at the physicians, talk about things that I was, like, 'Oh! Ugh! What?!'" People dressed "a little flowerier and funkier" than she was used to. And while the care was "pretty good," she did not think it was "exceptional." No one seemed particularly concerned with national hospital standards: "Compliance . . . wasn't really part of what they talked about at PubliCare." Taylor worked her way into a more managerial role at PubliCare and helped oversee an inspection during which the hospital almost lost its accreditation. But she liked the place and loved the people: "The people are delightful. Physicians were delightful. . . . It had this great personality, but it really needed to rise up to the level of, you know, clean, competent." The manager before she arrived was "a real hippie."

At HolyCare, in contrast, "everything was impeccable—I mean, uniforms were impeccable, your presentation was impeccable, your conversation was impeccable." She appreciated the professionalism of the place and took pride in the fact that "we were giving exceptional care." But the care came at a cost among the staff: "There was a lot of negativity, a lot of disciplinary stuff, people going through your charts, and, like, if your 'i' wasn't dotted, you'd get a conversation." The staff at HolyCare often wound up feeling like "Big Brother is watching," she told me. Strict standards of professionalism came with a lot of "hostility," both among the nursing staff and in their relationships with the physicians: "the standard egotistical, degrading, demoralizing" stuff, she laughed.

Most recently she had come to GroupCare, though she had been somewhat reluctant to make the move given her "preconceived notions" about the place. At this point in my interview with Taylor her voice dropped to a conspiratorial whisper. Before arriving at GroupCare she had heard that it was "kind of the meat market of health care," a reputation she said was partially deserved. Granted, GroupCare did much more in terms of preventative care than either of the other hospitals: "You know, you have a child with asthma, they've got a program, they've got all kinds of resource for you. So that's fantastic." But the inpatient hospital experience was different. GroupCare had "substandard people working for them," Taylor thought. Physicians would refuse to call nurses back. Staff would fight in the middle of the floor. And while Taylor approved of the organization's massive investment in electronic medical records and other integrative technology, she sometimes worried about what happened to patients as a result: practitioners "were so focused on the computer that patients' lights were going off, their alarms were going off," and no one was noticing. The computerized system was "fantastic for pulling out data," she thought, and allowed the organization to streamline its operations, but it did not always serve the individual patient. Things had "come a long way" since her arrival, she assured me, and the care was getting better. But the process of change at GroupCare had felt "like war."

Morals and Markets in Medical Care

Taylor described dramatically different hospital organizations. That differences exist is not particularly surprising. It is something of a commonplace that there continues to be enormous variation in contemporary U.S. hospital practices—both across different geographic areas and across different hospitals within the same communities.[14] But while this variation has been well documented, it remains poorly understood. From where do these differences spring? What are the underlying repertoires of practice and meaning that help to sustain them? In Las Lomas, I will show, these different cultures of practice emerge out of each hospital's attempts to grapple with a different contradiction inherent in the commodification of hospital care.

A contradiction implies a problem, which begs the question: Why might it be problematic for us to buy and sell hospital care? While no one, so far as I know, has spelled out these different problems as they pertain to the hospital, sociologists, philosophers, and other thoughtful people *have* suggested three separate reasons why the commodification of certain goods and services might cause problems.[15]

THE PROBLEM OF SOCIAL RIGHTS

First, scholars have made the normative argument that turning some things into commodities depends on the denial of social protections or social rights. As a result, commodification is unjust, or coercive.[16] In different forms, this idea is prevalent throughout economic and moral philosophy.[17] In *Why Some Things Should Not Be for Sale: The Moral Limits of Markets*, for example, the economic philosopher Debra Satz argues that there are "universal features of an adequate and minimally decent human life,"[18] and that the commodification of certain things—from child labor to the vote—makes this life impossible. For her, any conception of social rights must necessarily place boundaries on what can be for sale. The philosopher Michael Sandel makes a similar point in a book with a similar title (and identical subtitle), *What Money Can't Buy: The Moral Limits of Markets*. Paying for access to congressional hearings (through a company that hires people to wait in line), for example, creates an unjust inequality in political influence;[19] paying poor women to sterilize themselves may have long-term economic benefits but it denies these women the right to their own bodies.

The political philosopher Michael Walzer relates this same idea more specifically to medical care: "Doctors and hospitals have become such massively important features of contemporary life that to be cut off from the help they provide is not only dangerous but degrading."[20] He continues, "Needed goods are not commodities."[21] In order for hospital care to be turned into a commodity, according to this argument, it must be denied to those people unwilling or unable to pay for it. Yet this denial constitutes an erosion of basic social protections and the denial of basic social rights.

THE PROBLEM OF DEBASEMENT

A second, separate argument against the commodification of certain things is that it may undermine or debase the very value of these things.[22] Whereas the problem of social rights implies that some things *should* not be bought and sold, the problem of debasement implies that some things *cannot* be bought and sold and still retain their integrity. Were we to try to buy friendship, the argument goes, this purchase would erode the very meaning of "friendship."

Perhaps most famously, this line of argument has been pursued in relationship to altruism and the blood supply.[23] Richard Titmuss found that a system of blood allocation based on *donations* was associated with blood of a higher quality than a system in which donations were coupled with financial incentives. The commodification of blood, he argued, eroded the social values and social institutions through which it was otherwise given and received. To the extent that blood was treated as a commodity it became degraded. Even Kieran Healy's compelling critique of Titmuss's findings maintains that market incentives can "crowd out" other sources of motivation.[24] This idea makes sense intuitively and finds support across a broad range of other studies.[25] When we do something we understand as being an expression of generosity or citizenship or honor or love, an offer of cash compensation for it can undermine the value we thought we were expressing. Even if we did not object to buying access to congressional hearings on the basis of inequality, Sandel points out, we might object to it on the grounds that it erodes some value essential to democratic governance.

Just as hospital care might be understood as a social right, it might also be understood as this kind of social and moral good. Hospital care is often a deeply emotional experience for patients and their loved ones, and it depends—at least to an extent—on professionals' and other workers' vocational commitments. Private hospitals are still often classified as "voluntary hospitals," a phrase derived from their origins in philanthropy or religious charity. Well before the hospital was able to provide much in the way of medical cures, those within it were able to offer spiritual guidance and emotional support. And even today, many of us look for emotional connection and support from those with whom we interact in the hospital. The surgeon may need to regard us as a piece of meat when we are under the scalpel, but we want to be seen as a *person* before and after an operation. To the extent that hospital care is commodified, the hospital might be unable to foster noneconomic values central to care itself.

THE PROBLEM OF UNCERTAINTY

Third, distinct from the denial of social rights or the problem of debasement is the danger of malcoordination and anarchy caused by uncertainty in the value of some things.[26] If the other two problems concern the potential *effects* of a market for certain things (on people's rights or on the integrity of the things themselves), this problem concerns the difficulty of *establishing* a market in the first place. If the other two problems concern the relationship between the market and other social values, this third problem concerns the market on its own terms.

It is well established that doctors often do not know the medical value of the services that they provide.[27] Indeed, for most of medical history, doctors have been remarkably *incompetent* in a technical sense.[28] Despite huge investments in recent years in medical research, information technology, and evidence-based medicine, there is still (and will always be) much uncertainty in the diagnosis and treatment of particular conditions.[29] More profoundly, the value of health—and by association, hospital care—is remarkably difficult for people to assess in a rational and calculating way, meaning that weighing costs and benefits in relationship to it is fraught. This is not to say that people do not put a price on these things implicitly or explicitly.[30] But it is challenging for people to weigh preferences in relationship to them.

Finally, even when practitioners know the value of a particular intervention, patients often do not. Commodity exchange presumes a market of buyers and sellers with equal amounts of information. But patients are almost by definition dependent on the authority of doctors to tell them what they need[31]—what economists call *supplier-driven demand*. Patients' uncertainty makes them unable to discern between different choices. Combined, these sources of uncertainty mean that a market for hospital care can never approach the conditions that economists assume to exist when they discuss "markets" in the abstract.

The Contradictory Commodification of Hospital Care

For philosophers like Debra Satz and Michael Sandel, the dangers posed by commodification mean—quite simply—that some things should not or cannot be bought and sold. This is pretty much where their arguments end. Economic sociologists such as Viviana Zelizer and Kieran Healy have gone further by working to understand why and where people draw the distinctions between moral and immoral economic activity, and how people use "different payment systems and exchange tokens to express and define different social relations."[32]

Within this "moralized markets" school, the normative claims of previous theorists—whether critics or defenders of markets—are themselves subject to analysis. The important insight is that moral-market understandings and practices, or "relational packages,"[33] serve to maintain social ties and distinguish different sorts of relationships from one another. Where Sandel emphasizes how industries such as life insurance threaten to degrade the value of human life,[34] for example, Zelizer documents instead how life insurance came, over time, to be understood as a way of *sanctifying* death.[35] Where Satz discusses the ways in which sex work undermines women's right to equal standing,[36] Zelizer shows how the distinction between gifts and payments helps us sustain the distinction between girlfriends and prostitutes.[37] Where Titmuss argues that market incentives debase the altruism necessary for a healthy blood supply, Healy demonstrates how different economic motivations have different effects within different environments and how all organizations are constrained by the types of economic motivation on which they rely.[38]

This moralized markets school has done much to illuminate the creative capacity and agency that people have in their economic activities. People work hard to live connected lives, to reconcile their economic activities with their values. And yet, at the same time, this perspective has been less attentive to the broader institutions—sets of rules, practices, and understandings[39]—that, on the one hand, constrain individuals' moral-market understandings and practices and, on the other, constitute the material and symbolic environments within which moral-market understandings and practices exist.

First, while actors may have a degree of agency and creativity in their moral understandings of market activity, they exist within already-moralized worlds. The moral frameworks they elaborate and maintain do not arise out of thin air but rather were shaped historically, institutionalized in the organizations in which they participate and the social positions they inhabit. History, in this sense, should not be understood as a static starting point from which all future events can be read off in path-dependent fashion. Rather, history is embedded in the structures of formal organizations, shaping (but not determining) the way that the organizations and actors make sense of and act in the present.[40] Different moral positions can thus usefully be traced to different institutional trajectories and histories, though they live on in the understandings and practices of the actors who inhabit the organizations today.

Second, actors' efforts to understand and structure their economic activities so as to preserve important social distinctions take place within an evolving institutional environment in which market logics are increasingly powerful. At the level of individual actors, Zelizer is certainly right that an ideal-typical market—anonymous, self-interested, utility-maximizing buyers and sellers making one-time transactions based on full information—is a fiction. Yet, at a more macro institutional level, this market ideal remains a *powerful* fiction with real social consequences. Margaret Somers and Fred Block, for example, demonstrate just how powerful this idea continues to be in their study of welfare reform in the 1990s.[41] Indeed, the notion of markets as "self-regulating natural entities" that "must be set free" continues to guide much of social policy in the United States.[42] We live in a time when this understanding of markets seems particularly powerful, a time, as Marion Fourcade and Kieran Healy put it, of "undeniable growth in the commercialization of certain goods and services, notably in the areas of domestic labor, care work services, and human goods."[43]

Zelizer admits that she has focused more intensively on "interpersonal interaction" than on the relationship between micro- and macroprocesses.[44] The question, then, is how individuals' moral-market understandings and practices relate to the broader organizational and institutional contexts within which they exist. As Fourcade reminds us, "if people produce meanings through the use of goods and money, they (to paraphrase Karl Marx) do so out of circumstances not of their own choosing."[45] It follows that while people may be *trying* to lead connected lives, they may not always be able to achieve them. And so we should not only be looking for "good matches" between economic activity and social values, as Zelizer does, but also for *bad matches*.[46] We should be looking for situations in which people try and fail to connect their values with their economic activities, for situations in which people use thin moral scripts to justify their economic activities, and for situations in which market actors seem to generate a self-referential conception of morality—a morality of efficiency.[47] We should be looking not only for connected lives but for *contradictory* lives, as individuals and organizations work imperfectly to reconcile their values with broader forces out of their control.[48]

As I argue in what follows, hospitals founded in different periods in the history of U.S. medicine arose from different institutional foundations, embedding an emerging market for health care in different sets of social relations and different understandings of care. Different hospitals implicitly addressed different problems with the market for care, like those outlined above. (1) Early hospitals in the United States were indistinguishable from almshouses, and guaranteed the poor a basic (if limited) right to care. As the primary source of state relief in many communities, they simultaneously were intended to dissuade a burgeoning working class from reliance on poor relief. (2) By the beginning of the twentieth century, the private hospital had emerged as an organization catering to a new clientele of paying patients. In order to distinguish itself from the public hospital,

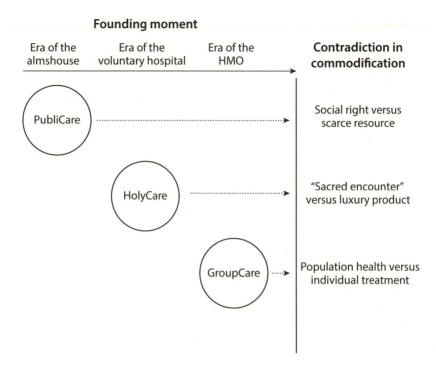

Founding moment

| Era of the almshouse | Era of the voluntary hospital | Era of the HMO | **Contradiction in commodification** |

PubliCare ....→ Social right versus scarce resource

HolyCare ....→ "Sacred encounter" versus luxury product

GroupCare ----→ Population health versus individual treatment

I.3. ▸ Hospital founding moments and contemporary contradictions.

and in order to convince a wealthier clientele to leave their homes for medical care, this new kind of hospital emphasized the dignity of the patient and the individualized treatment he or she would receive within it. Thus, at the same time the private voluntary hospital made possible a market for hospital services, it did so by emphasizing how much it was like an upscale home—and downplaying its own commercialism. (3) Finally, in the last decades of the twentieth century, medical costs began to spiral, and new constituencies—from middle-class patients to the employers who insured them—began to call into question the autonomy and authority of the medical profession. In this environment, a new form of health organization gained prominence that promised to rationalize the provision of medical care, reducing medical uncertainty and reining in medical spending through risk management across established populations.

Today, actors in hospitals confront different contradictions between these previously institutionalized values and intensifying market pressures (see figure I.3). (1) At PubliCare, a hospital founded to provide care as a right for the poor, actors confront the contradiction between health care as a right and health care as a scarce commodity. (2) At HolyCare, a hospital founded to highlight the emotional and vocational dimensions of care, actors today wrestle with the relationship between these vocational commitments and the *marketing* of "caring"—

I.4. ▸ Contradictions in contemporary hospital practice.

	PubliCare	HolyCare	GroupCare
Founding orientation	Social right . . .	Sacred encounter . . .	Population health . . .
Market contradiction	Versus scarce resource	Versus luxury product	Versus individualized treatment
Morals and markets within organization	Insurgency (bottom-up)	Frame (top-down)	Incorporation

a patina of spirituality and authenticity encouraged by administrators and presented to the public, which threatens to reduce these vocational dimensions of care to little more than rhetoric. (3) At GroupCare, a health care organization founded to rationalize care across a population of patients, actors wrestle with the tension between the flourishing of each individual patient and the well-being of the population as a whole.

These contradictions have implications both for the way that each hospital relates to its patients and for the social relations within the hospital—among actors who relate to moral-market orientations from different standpoints and with different motivations.[49] In other words, the contradictions can be seen in each hospital's efforts to make its mission consistent with its participation in the market for care, and also within each hospital as different constituencies relate differently to the moral project elaborated by the organization as a whole (see figure I.4).

PROTECTING RIGHTS: REBUFFING THE MARKET AT PUBLICARE

At PubliCare Hospital, many practitioners were committed to the idea of providing care as a social right to the poor, a legacy of the hospital's history as a public institution. These practitioners worked against the interests of the upper administration of the hospital, who had been trying since the facility's privatization to make the organization financially viable. The providers of care thus waged a kind of insurgency against the financial interests of the hospital administration. Among these practitioners, the market was viewed as a threat to the hospital's mission and was kept—as much as possible—at the periphery of medical practice. Physicians at PubliCare were not incentivized to practice in any particular way, and conversations among practitioners used the language of duties and reciprocal obligations.

Yet care at PubliCare was also distinctive for its disorganization and inefficiency. Doctors, nurses, and ancillary staff worked side by side with relatively little role differentiation among them when compared with the other hospitals.

Many practitioners discussed being resourceful in the face of a lack of resources, but practitioners' resourcefulness as individuals was accompanied by a significant amount of organizational inefficiency.

PubliCare rested on a backward-looking traditionalism and was plagued by perverse incentives and unintended consequences. By providing care as a right, PubliCare to some extent prevented the commodification of hospital services. Yet as its practitioners provided care as a right, they subjected the poor to other sorts of moral evaluations and indignities. And the hospital operated with such high levels of inefficiency—due both to patients' boundless needs and to the organization's inability to reconcile the right to care with the market for care—that it was always on the brink of collapse. While practitioners had been able to sustain a degree of care for the poor and uninsured at PubliCare Hospital, the long-term viability of their strategy was questionable at best. The hospital had been losing money ever since it was privatized in 1996, and it seemed likely to close in the near future. Nevertheless, the hospital's historical commitment to the provision of care as a right gave practitioners some degree of leverage over hospital administration through the channels of local government and public opinion.

OVERCOMING DEBASEMENT: MORALIZING THE MARKET AT HOLYCARE

At HolyCare Hospital, administrators, hospital leaders, and a few select categories of nursing staff expressed most clearly the hospital's mission of preserving the moral and spiritual dimensions of care, but they worked to do this *through* the market rather than in opposition to it. HolyCare was the most explicitly mission driven of the three hospitals in Las Lomas, given its close connection to the Catholic Church and its conscious investment in its Department of Mission Integration and Spiritual Care. Yet this spiritual mission served as a framework that made possible some of the most clearly entrepreneurial behavior among the three hospitals—both by the organization itself (in relationship to the medical environment) and by its medical staff (in relationship to their patients and the hospital). Since its inception, the hospital's focus on the emotional and spiritual dimensions of care was designed for a wealthy clientele—a constituency seeking a personal touch along with medical care.

At HolyCare, the hospital's attention to the spiritual dimensions of the patient experience allowed care to be sold as a sort of luxury good. Like many private facilities of both religious and secular origins, the organization emphasized the social and emotional significance of care at the same time it sold this care to a wealthy clientele. The extensive chaplaincy program, like the oak chairs in the facility's cafeteria, helped to give patients the feeling of personal attention and comfort that made the organization resemble a fancy hotel.

Paradoxically, this patina of spirituality allowed the doctors at HolyCare to behave as entrepreneurs: their professional roles merged almost seamlessly with their roles as economic actors. Unlike the doctors at either PubliCare or Group-Care, most of the doctors at HolyCare did their own billing, meaning they were paid based entirely on the number of paying patients they saw. According to doctors at the other hospitals, the doctors at HolyCare tended to maximize the treatment they gave in order to make money. Within the hospital, doctors at HolyCare were conscious of competing for those patients who paid the most. Outside the hospital, doctors based at HolyCare also seemed more likely to convert their professional expertise into financial gain. For the doctors themselves, however, this market orientation to medicine felt consistent with (and in some respects made possible) their commitment to the delivery of high-quality care.

Whereas staff roles were relatively undifferentiated at PubliCare Hospital, at HolyCare there was a clear demarcation between the medical staff and the nursing and ancillary staffs. Administrators highlighted the sisters' historical ideal of sacrifice in order to secure an obedient and subservient workforce. Ancillary staff members were encouraged to be "good stewards," subordinating their own interests for the interests of the hospital, and wages at HolyCare tended to be lower than at either of the other two hospitals. When workers made claims for organizational power, they were most successful when they made these claims on a moral, rather than economic, terrain.

Despite accusations among other doctors in the county that those at HolyCare overtreated their patients in order to increase revenue, many practitioners at all three hospitals said that they would rather be treated at HolyCare than anywhere else. Not only was it the nicest-looking hospital of the three (several interviewees compared it to a hotel), but it also had the reputation (unsubstantiated by any third-party monitoring agency) for being the facility where patients received the highest-quality care. HolyCare historically had been quite financially successful because it framed the market in moral terms.

REDUCING UNCERTAINTY: TAMING THE MARKET AT GROUPCARE

GroupCare, an integrated health management organization, sought to overcome the uncertainty inherent in medicine through an extensive bureaucracy and technical infrastructure. Whereas the mission at PubliCare was insurgent, espoused by practitioners against the market; and the mission at HolyCare was ideological, espoused by administrators to moralize the market; the mission at GroupCare was *integrated* across the facility's administration, its physician staff, and its nursing and ancillary workers. Through bureaucratization, standardization, and the creative use of technology, several different constituencies worked together to tame the market.

In the name of scientific medicine, GroupCare generated protocols based on the latest medical evidence, and it conducted small experiments with changes in procedure that—if successful—were diffused across the entire organization. Given its focus on an efficient use of medical resources, more resources were invested in ensuring that patients managed chronic health conditions and avoided the hospital than were invested in acute care. Within the hospital, there was an emphasis on avoiding costly medical mistakes and on eliminating redundant tests and interventions.

Because GroupCare depended for its survival on patient-members, however, it had to balance its own conception of efficiency with the desires of patients themselves. Patients, in turn, were expected to play an active role in their health. Membership satisfaction scores and surveys were used to incentivize doctors and change procedures, and members were encouraged to take part in hospital-sponsored educational seminars and fitness classes.

Doctors at GroupCare seemed to understand themselves to some extent as line workers, sacrificing professional identity and entrepreneurship for the security and stability of a nine-to-five job. With that said, the organization worked to discipline doctors in such a way that their professional identities could be reconciled with bureaucratic subordination. Relations between doctors and staff were rule-bound: doctors and staff shared some degree of power, as they did at Publi-Care. Yet where this egalitarianism was informal and relational at PubliCare, at GroupCare it was formal and bureaucratic. Workers were fully incorporated into the organization's decision-making structure through a strong union and innovative labor-management partnership.

GroupCare, as a planned economy, certainly offered the most promising long-term possibility for containing the commodification of hospital care. Yet it did so in part by excluding the uninsured, who received less care at GroupCare than at either of the other two hospitals, and in part by reducing health to a set of discrete, quantifiable variables and reducing health care to a series of technical interventions. The system's bureaucracy also left room for the emergence of a class of bureaucrats who used it for purposes other than the perfection of scientific medicine. And since there are (and will always be) limits to the reach of evidence with regard to medical practice, the system was only able to prescribe behavior within relatively narrow parameters.

Most problematic, however, was that the organization did not explicitly grapple with the extent to which it inevitably *rationed* care in the process of rationalizing care—thus concealing difficult organizational decisions about the economic value of life and the relationship between the individual and the broader constituency of GroupCare members. In both the organization's practices and in the ways that practitioners discussed their work, the health of each individual member was conflated with the health of the membership as a whole.

An Outline of What Follows

The core of this book consists of detailed case studies of PubliCare, HolyCare, and GroupCare. Most broadly, as I have argued, each case should be understood as a historically rooted response to an ongoing contradiction in the commodification of hospital care. In order to highlight this history, I begin each case with a brief historical account of the hospital's founding moment. I do not claim that these histories are responsible for shaping the attitudes and practices of the people within them. It seems equally likely that practitioners with different ideas about the market for hospital care decide to work at different hospitals. In other words, I use the cases not to explain *why* hospital care varies so much as to explore the dimensions of its variation—to understand the different constellations of ideas and practices by which actors in each hospital work, imperfectly, to reconcile their social values with their economic activities.[50]

Furthermore, while all hospitals must navigate the problems with the commodification of hospital care, the three responses highlighted here are not evenly distributed across the contemporary landscape of U.S. hospital care. While the model offered by PubliCare is obsolescent, GroupCare seems to offer a plausible pathway for health care's future. HolyCare, with its emphasis on individualized treatment and its premium on professional autonomy, continues in most parts of the country to be the dominant model through which hospital care is delivered.

After situating each case historically, I examine three dimensions of care, corresponding to three separate chapters per case. First, I explore the contradictions embedded in each hospital's conception of care. At PubliCare, care is understood as a social right, and practitioners consistently treat the most marginalized patients in the city for a variety of medical and social problems. Yet practitioners consistently confront both the boundless needs of their patients and the limited resources they have to respond to these needs, thus placing them in a perpetual state of crisis and disorganization. At HolyCare, care is understood as a "sacred encounter." But while this hospital does attend more explicitly to the emotional experience of hospitalization, many who work there have come to see this attention as a disingenuous marketing ploy—particularly as the Sisters of St. Francis who traditionally owned the hospital have handed over authority to lay leaders. At GroupCare, care is understood as maximizing the health of its prepaid membership in the aggregate. Yet many practitioners within the organization conflate the good of the membership as a whole with the good of each individual member, leaving unaddressed the inevitable tension between the two.

Second, I explore how each organization structures the work of its physician staff. In days past, the hospital was considered the doctor's workshop, offering him (and it was almost always a "him") the tools and personnel to do his work, but guaranteeing him professional independence as well. And while the hospital is no longer so subservient to the medical profession, the work that doctors do within the hospital remains central to its functioning. But what is this work, exactly? What do doctors do, how do doctors understand what they do, and how do these tasks vary across different organizational contexts? I argue that we can productively understand professional work as akin to what Viviana Zelizer calls a "relational package."[51] In their everyday work, doctors interact with their patients, with their medical colleagues, and with hospital staff and administrators. They also work according to a particular system of financial incentives and under certain rules governing the way they go about making and documenting medical decisions. Finally, they work with certain understandings of what it means to be a doctor—with a set of ideas about the nature of the medical profession, the nature of medical knowledge, their ethical obligations, and their status privileges.

Different hospital organizations foster different kinds of relational packages. At PubliCare, doctors try to uphold an ideal of the profession as an altruistic and cooperative community apart from the market. At HolyCare, in contrast, doctors' professional identities seem to serve as a cloak of legitimacy for their own entrepreneurship, just as the hospital's spiritual emphasis helps to mask its market participation. At GroupCare, doctors' work seems to have been disciplined in such a way so that their professional interests become consistent with subordination to the bureaucracy as a whole.

Third, I explore how the delivery of care is organized among the different constituencies that work within it. Hospitals are large, highly differentiated bureaucracies that depend upon a great degree of coordination and continuity across different departments and different occupational groups, and at different times of day. They are also places in which power is allocated unequally across different roles. The question here is how the different sort of market problem each hospital faces relates to the way in which work is organized and power distributed within it.

At PubliCare, the division of labor was less precise than it was at the other hospitals. Practitioners discussed with pride their resourcefulness despite a lack of resources. Yet practitioners' resourcefulness as individuals was accompanied by a significant amount of organizational inefficiency. Where staff roles were relatively undifferentiated at PubliCare, at HolyCare there was a clear demarcation between the medical staff and the nursing and ancillary staff; staff members were encouraged to be "good stewards," putting the hospital before themselves. Finally, at GroupCare, relations between doctors and staff were bureaucratic and rule-bound: doctors and staff shared some degree of power, as they did at PubliCare. Yet, where this egalitarianism was informal and relational at PubliCare, at Group-Care it was formal and bureaucratic.

Within each hospital, people work imperfectly to manage the relationship between social values and the market for hospital care, but they do so very differently in different organizational contexts—working, respectively, to rebuff, moralize, or tame a market that each regards as potentially undermining its core social commitment. This book tells a story about the contradictions inherent in a market for hospital care; the methods different hospitals use to try to manage these contradictions; the different historical trajectories driving differences in contemporary hospital practice; and the perils and possibilities inherent in different models of care. It is a story of the different souls of modern American medicine.

PART ONE

PubliCare Rebuffs the Market

A s was the case throughout the United States, hospital care in Las Lomas began in the almshouse, tied deeply to the needs of the dependent poor. Hospital care emerged at a time when the categories that would come to distinguish different sorts of dependency from one another—physical and mental illness, illness and old age, disability and poverty—had not been firmly established. And it emerged at a time when the curative capacities of an embryonic medical profession were questionable at best.

The early U.S. hospital can usefully be understood as sitting in opposition to the market, in three related ways. First, institutional care was intended primarily for sick, poor people unable to participate in a burgeoning market economy. The fact that most people of all classes were reluctant to turn to the hospital was in some sense deliberate, a strategy by which community leaders could distinguish the truly needy from those able-bodied poor who could turn to the labor market for their subsistence. As the historian Charles Rosenberg writes, "the hospital's patients were seen as genuinely needy almost by definition and less likely than recipients of free food or fuel to be impostors, for none but the ill and desperate would willingly seek the dubious comforts of a hospital ward."[1]

Second, what little market there was for physicians' services took place almost entirely *outside* the hospital. Certainly, hospital appointments became coveted status markers among ambitious members of an emerging medical elite, and a minority of medical students learned their trade by treating the poor in voluntary or municipal hospitals. But paying patients almost always received their care at home; and physicians were almost always prohibited from collecting professional fees in the hospital—even from those patients who paid the hospital for their care.[2]

Finally, the labor force within the early hospital consisted mostly of recovered patients who, according to Rosenberg, "differed little in background from their charges."[3] Most of these workers were recruited informally, lived within the hospital, and gave the organization an anarchic feel. As a house physician at Massachusetts General Hospital put it in 1857, "There is no system or order & no one knows precisely his duty or keeps to it."[4] Paternalistic impulses and some scientific ambitions were certainly present in the nineteenth-century hospital, but by and large the market was not.

The first hospital in Las Lomas was established in 1859 in the center of town as the second story of the small city jail. According to a local paper, the lower story of the building consisted of "six dark cells, a room for the jailer, and one for petty offenders," while the upper story was "arranged to accommodate, as comfortably as possible, such indigent persons as may need the assistance of the county, in their sickness."[5] Between 1860 and 1867, the years during which records are available, use of the small hospital grew substantially—from only nine admissions in 1860 to sixty by 1867. All told, between 1860 and 1867, 201 admissions and 37 deaths were recorded. Syphilis, a venereal disease suggestive of moral turpitude, was the most common disease recorded among patients, while the most common cause of death recorded was consumption (or tuberculosis).

The county board of supervisors soon came to regard the facility as inadequate for medical care and, because of its central location, a risk to a public increasingly concerned with contagion. The hospital physician reported, "A more unfavorable location could not well be conceived of, either for the protection of the sick within, or the well without." The board of supervisors ordered a new stand-alone hospital to be constructed in the northern suburbs of town. This hospital was completed by 1866 and consisted of two stories, with separate wards for male and female patients. While no doubt an improvement from the previous facility, this organization was still a far cry from the hospitals with which we are familiar today. A reporter visiting the new hospital in March 1868 was "highly pleased with the neatness of the surroundings" but nevertheless noted "the necessity of having a dead-house." As it was, "when of the patients dies his body is placed in the passage-way, where the sick cannot help but see it—anything but a pleasant site—and which does not tend to the improvement of the remaining inmates."

A report from the hospital physician emphasized moral as opposed to medical concerns.[6] Of utmost importance, he wrote, was a "suitable library . . . for the use of patients . . . as a most wholesome governmental measure, because even in sickness, idleness breeds dissatisfaction and mischief." Similarly, a reporter in 1872 highlighted the facility's social, rather than medical, purposes. After a "careful examination," during which the reporter spoke with patients "when none of the officers were there," the only complaint he heard was "in regard to the regulation which requires only two meals a day to be supplied." The hospital was still, by and large, indistinguishable from a homeless shelter or nursing home; the facility offered medical care, moral training, and basic subsistence simultaneously.

This second facility was similarly short-lived. Both the hospital physician and the board of supervisors had expressed concern about the need to distinguish among different categories of the sick and dependent. There was also worry that this second hospital—which only recently had been on the outskirts of town—had already been enveloped by the expanding city. According to one local history, neighbors had been "passing petitions asking that [the facility] be relocated outside the city limits, citing its odors, the danger of contagion and the loitering of ambulatory patients."

During the 1870s, then, the county began to shift its care for the poor to a site even farther from downtown: a hundred-acre farm where PubliCare Hospital now stands. It was here where the county consciously undertook the work of distinguishing various categories of dependency. In 1874, the board of supervisors first bought the property to serve as the county farm. The poor would be sent there, while the sick would stay at the hospital. In 1882 it was reported that there were thirty "inmates" at the county farm, while twenty-five still remained at the hospital. A farmer, hired by the county, grew vegetables that could feed the residents of both facilities and be sold as cash crops to help defray the costs. His wife served as the matron of the almshouse, tending to its occupants. As early as 1877 the county had built a "pest house" on the property of the county farm to isolate those with contagious disease, while the board of supervisors began to plan for a new hospital on the same grounds.

Over the course of 1887, a new hospital facility was built on the land. A newspaper article on May 14 of that year gushed with pride about it: "If there is any one thing more than another of which [the] county may justly be proud and to which her citizens may point with pardonable pleasure it is her public institutions . . . far from being least, her new County Hospital, which is made the subject of this article." The reporter continued,

> As the brow of that long and tedious hill is reached and the low, long roofs of
> the farm buildings, come into view, the pathetic lines of Will Carleton's poem,
> with which all are familiar[,] are brought vividly to mind. It is certainly "Over
> the Hills to the Poorhouse," but the scene presents none of the aspects of the
> bleak and desolate places about which we read in the old New England tales.

The article went on to describe the "gleaming white walls of the new Hospital building," the "brilliant green of the window-blinds and shadows cast by the ornamental framework of the verandas which afford delicious shade on three sides of the building." The new hospital boasted a dining room, kitchen, and sitting and reception rooms; multiple wards for both male and female patients; an operating room "located with a view to securing a true and even light"; offices for doctors and a room for the resident steward; and, throughout, "the latest improved ventilating aparatus [sic]." Standing apart from the facility was now a dead house, also to be used as a "dessecting-room [sic]." The reporter concluded that the "building is an ornament to the county, a compliment to the Board of Supervisors and a sanitarium most propitious in its location and purpose."

Throughout this period, the board of supervisors appointed a single county physician responsible for the patients at the hospital. This physician was paid an annual salary to tend to the indigent, though he continued to see paying patients in their own homes. The steward and matron, meanwhile, lived on the premises and took care of the nonmedical concerns of patients and almshouse residents. The boundaries between almshouse and hospital were porous.[7] As late as 1928, reports from the county physician discussed patients who were transferred from the almshouse to hospital or hospital to almshouse. In December 1928, for example, thirteen men from the hospital (out of forty-five discharged) were transferred to the poor farm, while seven men from the poor farm (out of fourteen discharged) were transferred to the hospital. The line between illness and delinquency was also somewhat blurry. In 1894 the county built a two-room building on the property to serve as a "discipline home." A reporter described its purpose:

> Occasionally some old inmate or feeble-minded persons stray off in search of the fountain of eternal youth or walk to the nearest saloon where bitters are dispensed, and some times [sic] get arrested for vagrancy, which costs the county good money. Such stray sheep have to be punished in some way, and it is proposed to confine them in the two-room house with a high fence around it as a salutary lesson.

These facilities may not have been "bleak and desolate places" like the poorhouses of the big cities on the East Coast, but they were still very much a part of movement away from "outdoor relief" or welfare benefits characteristic of the second half of the nineteenth century. As discussed by historians of social welfare and hospital care, early public institutions were erected often with the explicit purpose of deterring the "able-bodied poor" from seeking welfare payments.[8] The almshouse and early municipal hospital embodied the "[i]irreconcilable contradictions"[9] in the early modern welfare state between the provision of basic rights and the fear of generating dependency. As a historian of Las Lomas put it, the county was "proud of the fact that they took good care of the poor people. At the same time, it's not exactly something that the Chamber of Commerce is going to advertise. So they've always been of two minds."

The question of moral hazard is one as old as state social welfare programs. If the state provides too much in the way of social entitlements, the perennial argument goes, then people will lose all sense of work ethic or personal responsibility.[10] The movement away from "outdoor relief" towards various types of institutional care in the United States was meant to provide for the poor without enabling the pauper.

Staying Public while Going Private

PubliCare had thus been a place of last resort since its founding. In the 1990s, however, the county decided that it could no longer bear the financial burden of care for the uninsured and underinsured. Nevertheless, there was widespread optimism among county officials and local health care executives that, under private management, the *right* to care could actually be made consistent with the market for care. This optimistic vision was articulated most explicitly in a study of public-to-private hospital transfers spearheaded by the Henry J. Kaiser Foundation—a study that included PubliCare among its cases. The foundation wrote:

> To preserve the institution for indigent patients, for whom it was the provider of last resort, those responsible for the public hospitals decided it was necessary to operate the institution for *everyone*—that is, to use the market to make the hospital financially viable by attracting not only patients who cannot afford to pay, but also those who can.[11]

In the case of PubliCare, the report concluded, local government did not have the resources to make the capital expenditures necessary to attract paying patients; the hospital was too small an entity to negotiate with organized insurers and physicians' groups; and the hospital under public governance was at a disadvantage because hospital leaders were "forced to develop and implement long-term competitive strategies in a public forum . . . and their competitors [could] sit in on their planning meetings."[12] Turning to the market could actually help the county live out its commitment to the poor more fully.

The board of supervisors decided to lease the hospital to Westside Health Corporation, a large statewide not-for-profit health care company. At the time of the hospital's privatization, many local residents worried that the move would undermine the hospital's mission of providing care to the poor and make the hospital less publicly accountable. A community coalition led by the area's largest public-sector union organized a ballot initiative calling for a public vote on the plan. Despite this opposition, however, the county board of supervisors was set in its decision. A county supervisor said of the opposition, "They might think that they are going to win. But if they win, they lose. The hospital just won't make it much longer." When the petition had secured enough signatures for a referendum, the board tried (albeit unsuccessfully) to challenge the validity of the ballot measure in court, arguing that the management of the hospital was "too complicated and time-sensitive to turn over to the electorate." A vote finally occurred almost eight months after the hospital was privatized, at which point voters decided by a three-to-two margin to continue the lease.

Despite public concern, some practitioners at PubliCare felt more hopeful about the privatization—at least when compared with what had preceded it. One ER doctor was particularly critical of the hospital's prior public governance, attributing its failures to a combination of incompetence and deliberate neglect. First, he suggested, the hospital's insulation from the market meant that it was fiscally irresponsible—in a socialized system, he asserted, "no one takes responsibility." He described how at one point it was discovered that millions of dollars' worth of workers' compensation reimbursements had not been received because the county had not hired the staff to do the paperwork. This was emblematic of the county's incompetence. Yet the doctor also believed that the county had deliberately underfunded the public hospital "because the theory in those days was [that] the public [should] not compete against the private sector." Private medical interests in the county had thwarted public investments: "Anything that we asked for . . . like social services, or an improvement to the OB wing . . . was lobbied [against] by the private sector. . . ." While many other doctors, at the time of the transfer, were concerned that Westside Health was "going to kick out all of the homeless and uninsured patients because [Westside was] a big corporation," this doctor thought that at least Westside Health had "dedicated themselves to doing this." In his mind, the public mission of the hospital had never been embraced fully by the county: "The county [was] not supporting this hospital; they [didn't] want this hospital." The only alternative was for the hospital to try to sustain its mission as a participant in the private market.

When the county decided to privatize the hospital, the board of supervisors had sought to be discerning about buyers. It refused a proposal from a large for-profit corporation—according to the Kaiser Foundation report—because the "hospital's medical staff was afraid [it] would 'turn the hospital upside down to make a buck.'"[13] And it believed it had found in Westside Health a corporation that could pay attention to the bottom line while remaining committed to the hospital's public mission. In turn, Westside Health was interested in taking over the facility because the company "had a relationship with a physician group in the area, but no local hospital; the lease of PubliCare Hospital was a way to get into the local inpatient market."[14]

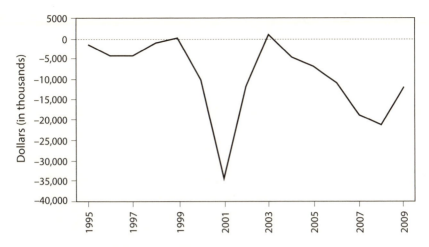

P1.1. ▸ Net income at PubliCare, 1995–2009.
California Office of Statewide Health Planning and Development.

The conditions of the lease were articulated in a health care access agreement, in which Westside Health committed to working "cooperatively and in good faith" to ensure that all residents of the county had access to a "full range of women's health services (e.g., preventive care, birth control, sterilization, pregnancy termination procedures, labor and delivery) and treatment of HIV/AIDS and other communicable diseases." Importantly, Westside Health also committed *not* to "seek additional sums from [the county] to subsidize the cost of Services provided to beneficiaries" of government programs like Medicare and Medicaid.

An underlying assumption, made by both Westside Health and the county, seemed to be that the facility's financial crisis could be remedied without sacrificing the organization's public mission. With enough up-front investments and organizational efficiencies, the organization could return to the black. Yet in spite of millions of dollars invested in upgrading the hospital to attract paying patients, PubliCare Hospital had been losing money (excluding capital expenses) under the management of Westside Health in all but two of the fourteen years since the lease had been signed (see figure P1.1).

And while there were several possible explanations for why PubliCare Hospital continued to lose money despite its new investments and new management, the contradiction between the right to care and care as a scarce commodity—a contradiction manifested both in organizational policy and in practitioners' understandings and practices—is a central part of the story.

CHAPTER ONE

Health Care for All

Sandra Lacks, a social worker at PubliCare Hospital, was an African American woman in her forties, with braided hair tied in a bun behind her head and an authoritative stride. While growing up in a poor section of Boston, Lacks had been introduced to a social worker that "took a liking" to some of her writing and entered her into a citywide speaking contest. Lacks won the contest, and the social worker helped secure a scholarship for her to attend a prestigious East Coast boarding school. "She saw more of me than I saw of myself," Lacks told me. Making sure Lacks got into boarding school was the social worker's way of "pulling [her] out of the ghetto." That social worker's commitment stayed with Lacks: "I remember when she did it, it touched me so much, and it really changed and started where my life had began. And I decided at that point I was going to be where she was; I was going to help people out, just like she helped me out. Ergo, social worker."

At PubliCare, Lacks worked across all departments of the facility to help patients find resources or to provide them with emotional support. The morning of our interview, she was trying to find funding for a homeless diabetic in need of medications; working to find a placement for a chronic alcoholic who had walked away from the multiple facilities Lacks had previously found for him; figuring out what to do with a schizophrenic patient who had broken down the door of her parents' house and run down the street naked; attempting to find care for a developmentally disabled woman whose mother had been in the hospital for a month ("I'm working to make sure that her daughter is safe on the outside, even though her daughter's not a patient"); and helping to arrange burial services for a baby who had died in utero at forty weeks, while providing comfort for the grieving mother. Every few minutes Lacks's telephone would ring, and she would dash out of the break room where we were speaking to answer it.

At the other hospitals in Las Lomas, social workers had narrower responsibilities—either they were in charge of a particular dimension of the patient experience, such as discharge, or they were responsible for a particular department in the hospital. At PubliCare, however, "it's not one particular assignment, it's everything." This suited Lacks: "It breaks up the monotony, knowing that you're not always dealing with alcoholics, you're not always dealing with death and dying. . . . You get to change up a little bit, which reduces the burnout."

Lacks saw social dimensions to cases that others would have treated purely as medical problems. One morning at PubliCare, for example, there was a patient who had contracted hepatitis using intravenous (IV) drugs, and the disease was gradually destroying her liver. The patient was shaking and feverish and seemed constantly on the verge of tears. The doctor did not think there was much that the hospital could do for her aside from continuing a course of IV antibiotics, and so he was trying to figure out how he could discharge her to a specialized nursing facility that would administer IV antibiotics despite her history of drug use. Within the next few hours, however, Lacks spoke to the patient. She learned that both of the patient's daughters had died early deaths—one of a seizure at the age of fifteen and the other of sudden infant death syndrome as a baby. She suspected that some of the patient's fragility was due to undiagnosed post-traumatic stress disorder and recommended that the doctor refer the patient to psychiatry. The doctor was hesitant, assuming that the psychiatrist would not want to see the patient before her medical issues were cleared. But Lacks was adamant: "Just write the order, I'll take care of psychiatry," she said. The doctor relented.

Lacks told me that her commitment to the poor and underprivileged was widely shared among the doctors and staff at PubliCare: "We fall under the true motto of health care for everyone. We really try to follow it." Lacks sometimes also worked shifts as a social worker at HolyCare Hospital. Despite the similar job descriptions she had at the two facilities, she found the work quite different. At HolyCare, Lacks's role was primarily that of a discharge planner, coordinating care for patients as they left the facility. At PubliCare, on the other hand, she felt able to use different aspects of her social work training and got to spend "a lot more time with patients." At PubliCare, "If we really need to advocate [for patients] and they need to be here, we're going to keep 'em here. [At HolyCare we] get 'em out no matter what." Lacks felt that her work at PubliCare allowed her to live out her ideals: "I know why I'm here. I know what my purpose is. I don't know what my purpose is [at HolyCare]. . . . My purpose over [there] is to move 'em out, get 'em out, get 'em out. My purpose here is to treat them, you know?

Not just them, but the whole them. [At HolyCare it's] a medical model. There's a difference." When HolyCare recently asked Lacks whether she would move there full-time, she refused: "Never in a day would I ever work [at HolyCare] full-time."

But the generality of Lacks's job inevitably had its drawbacks. For example, while GroupCare and HolyCare offered palliative care programs, which helped patients with terminal diseases discuss their treatment options and prepare for death, PubliCare Hospital had nothing like it. Lacks and other social work staff would do what they could, but they only had so much time. For terminally sick patients, a charge nurse said with a resigned shrug, "We just wait for them to die, we don't care about them living well with pain." A nurse joked sardonically about a case in which a husband "blew his brains out" in front of his infant son while the mother was at work. The mother came to the hospital and "we gave her Ativan to calm her down. That's palliative care, right?"

Doctors at PubliCare would often be left to talk with terminal patients or their families without any specialized assistance. On one occasion I observed, a doctor took aside the grown son of a woman who had just had a major operation. The son mentioned that he already went through the painful process of keeping his father alive on a feeding tube for nine months and that he was not planning on going through the same thing again with his mother. As we prepared to leave the room, the doctor signaled his approval offhandedly: "So you learned with one parent not to torture the other." Such a conversation almost certainly would not have happened with a trained palliative care physician.

Lacks embodied both the promise and paradox of care at PubliCare. On the one hand, practitioners' deep commitment to the provision of care as a right gave the facility a special character. On the other hand, these same commitments seemed to go hand in hand with a lack of role differentiation or organizational structure that left the organization in a constant state of disarray and in financial peril. While PubliCare was more willing than the others to engage with the problems of the poor, this very engagement seemed to corrupt it in the eyes of wealthier, paying patients, making it even more difficult for the hospital to stay in the black.

The Right to Care

Among practitioners across the three hospitals in Las Lomas, those at PubliCare struggled most with how to reconcile a right to health care with care as a commodity to be sold. A manager exemplified this tension when she spoke of the challenge: "We're viewed [as an indigent hospital], even though we try to not to be." Restating her position later in the interview, she said: "Somebody has to take care of [the indigent], and we're proud to do it, but we don't want to only be seen

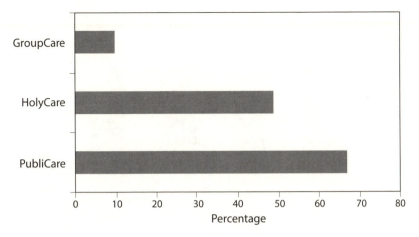

1.1. ▸ Percentage of emergency room visits by patients with no insurance or indigent insurance, 2009.
California Office of Statewide Health Planning and Development.

as, 'Oh, that's where all the poor people go.' We want everybody to use us. And we still want to do our part [for] the indigent." She expressed pride about the hospital's public orientation at the same time she sought to distance herself from it. Even one of the hospital managers responsible for utilization management— whose job was focused on ensuring the hospital was not giving excessive amounts of unreimbursed care—expressed a commitment to the right to care: "I am an old 'sixties person, and I believe that everybody deserves care. . . . I don't care what your income bracket is. And I believe that everybody deserves the same level of basic care. . . . I believe it's our obligation to pay for that for everybody within our community." It was difficult for her to balance this commitment to justice with her job responsibilities.

The hospital's ongoing commitment to the poor was nowhere more evident than in the hospital's emergency department. Since the passage of the Emergency Medical Treatment and Active Labor Act (EMTALA) in 1986, federal law has mandated that emergency rooms stabilize all patients who arrive, regardless of their ability to pay. The law thus guarantees a basic amount of care to everyone, citizen or noncitizen, in any emergency room in the United States. But despite the formal openness of all three emergency rooms in Las Lomas, the percentage of uninsured or underinsured patients arriving at PubliCare's emergency room was always higher than those arriving at either HolyCare or GroupCare Hospitals (see figure 1.1).

Furthermore, the emergency room at PubliCare treated the largest number of nonemergency patients in the county,[1] and by far the highest *proportion* of nonemergency patients, in spite of being the smallest emergency room of the

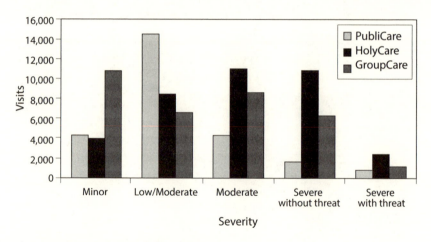

1.2. ▸ Emergency room visits by severity, 2009.
California Office of Statewide Health Planning and Development.

three hospitals (fifteen stations as opposed to nineteen at HolyCare and seventeen at GroupCare; see figure 1.2).

Those who frequented the emergency room at PubliCare Hospital were thus more likely to be poor and uninsured or underinsured and were more likely to use the emergency room for conditions that were not of acute medical importance than those who were seen at either HolyCare or GroupCare. As one ER doctor put it, a fair amount of what PubliCare Hospital saw in its emergency room was "stupid, clinic, why-are-you-wasting-my-time stuff. You never say that, but I'll tell you [at] three in the morning you're more inclined to ask that than you are at three in the afternoon."

In explaining the overrepresentation of the poor at PubliCare Hospital, many pointed to the hospital's legacy as a public facility. According to some, the poor relied on PubliCare simply because they always had. One nurse administrator at GroupCare pointed out that for many years PubliCare Hospital was "county supported, county owned. And that's just where [the poor] went. . . . And since that's where they've always gone, that's where they always go." An ER doctor at PubliCare also suggested that the poor's reliance on PubliCare had historical roots. When PubliCare was the public hospital, "certain people who could afford it [went to HolyCare], and certain people who could not afford it [went here]." In recent years this stratification had become less formal, but it had not disappeared: "We're a little bit more politically correct today, so we won't say it that way, but it still goes on." A second ER doctor at PubliCare said, "There's definitely a whole contingent of the county hospital population that comes here because that's what they are used to."

But while poor patients' habitual use of the facility likely explains some of the disparity, this explanation obscured the ongoing role that physicians and other health practitioners—at PubliCare Hospital and at other hospitals in the area—played in the poor's disproportionate utilization of PubliCare. After all, it had been almost fifteen years since the facility's privatization, during which time hospital administrators sought in various ways to remind potential patients that the hospital was now privately run.

Indeed, it seemed that a particular *approach* to care among practitioners at PubliCare helped to reproduce the hospital's poor clientele. An ER doctor at PubliCare recognized that the unemployed had "been made to feel like the emergency room at [PubliCare] is the place they should come and can come and also not be treated poorly." "On a mechanical level," he suggested, the other hospitals "could probably take care of everything that we take care of here." But "what might be lost in the translation is the feeling that patients who've been coming here a long time are comfortable coming here, and we get back stories of being treated poorly when they go elsewhere." A second ER doctor at PubliCare affirmed that indigent patients "go down [to GroupCare] and don't feel welcome. . . . I think they're treated like second-class citizens." Those working at PubliCare Hospital seemed proud that they created an environment in which poor patients felt welcome. Yet this had been a cause of consternation among administrators at the hospital, who were all too cognizant of the financial costs of such utilization by the poor.

PubliCare administrators had encouraged the county to take steps that would allocate poor patients more evenly across the three hospitals. As part of one such effort, the local emergency medical services (EMS) agency developed a point-of-entry plan that divided up the city into three geographic areas. All else being equal, if an ambulance picked up a patient in a particular part of the city it would be directed to take that patient to a particular hospital.[2] Nevertheless, this system did not change the distribution of patients significantly since, as one nurse at GroupCare put it, "the first [criterion] on the point of entry plan is always [the] patient's request." A nurse in PubliCare's emergency room said, "If a patient requests us, [the ambulance] will cross all those [geographic] lines to come to us." Those who felt more comfortable at PubliCare hospital seemed able to find their way there.

Practitioners at the other two hospitals in the area had come to depend on PubliCare for negotiating the problems of the indigent and underinsured. Many at PubliCare seemed ambivalent about this, simultaneously begrudging the unfair distribution of indigent care and taking pride in their ability to handle the tough cases. A nurse at PubliCare recalled an incident in which a "fifty-one fifty"—a patient on involuntary psychiatric hold—had been brought to GroupCare, but "the nurses didn't know how to handle [him]." At the time, PubliCare did not have any beds available. But those at GroupCare "called [PubliCare] every single day to get that patient moved out of there." The nurse concluded, "We know how to take care of these people, you know? And they don't. They get all flustered and lost."

Because of PubliCare's capacity to deal with difficult patients, several practitioners at PubliCare implied, ambulance drivers sometimes overrode the point-of-entry regulations altogether. A social worker at PubliCare suggested that, despite regulations, when ambulance drivers picked someone up who is "down and drunk," they often say to themselves, "We can't take him to HolyCare or Group-Care, we better take him over [to PubliCare]." A case manager told me that the day before our interview she had seen a homeless man being picked up by the police at the local farmers' market. While HolyCare was the designated hospital, she remembered thinking to herself, "That's my new project for tomorrow." Sure enough, she was negotiating placement for the man on the day of our interview. Like other practitioners at PubliCare, she spoke of the poor's dependence on the hospital with a mixture of regret and pride: "I think it's just been a stigma or a stereotype, or it's just how it's always been that they come here. And they're used to it here. . . . They know it here; they're comfortable here; we know them; we know how to handle them, I think, quite well."

A nurse administrator at PubliCare remembered a paraplegic patient who "refused to poop anywhere but in his pants" and would always come to the emergency room for his care. No matter where the ambulance drivers found him, they would always bring him to PubliCare. "And finally we looked at the paramedics, and we're like, 'You know, this isn't fair.'" She continued, "You know, the county hospital often is the dumping ground. And even though we're *not* county, we've always been county and we've always had that label."

Others at PubliCare went further, implying bad faith on the part of practitioners at other hospitals. Since HolyCare was the "base hospital" for local EMS services, communicating with the ambulances as they transported patients, one ER doctor at PubliCare suspected it deliberately directed a disproportionate share of the uninsured or underinsured to PubliCare: "There was a little conflict of interest there," he chuckled. Several nurses and social workers at PubliCare also discussed how workers at GroupCare would try discreetly to transfer their uninsured or underinsured patients to PubliCare. A manager recalled how the social workers at GroupCare would sometimes call her saying, "We have one of your patients." She would respond, "Is it a Westside Medical Foundation patient?" referring to PubliCare Hospital's associated physicians' group. The social worker would respond, "Well . . . no, the patient's unfunded." She would tell the GroupCare social worker that it had the responsibility to care for the patient. But social workers at GroupCare would sometimes call multiple social workers at PubliCare, she said, "shopping for an answer" that would let them transfer. A discharge planner at PubliCare had also witnessed GroupCare trying to transfer unfunded patients and told me it was "basically illegal." She had to coach her colleagues not to take these patients when GroupCare came asking.

Likewise, some health practitioners in the other emergency rooms, and even within some primary health clinics, encouraged the uninsured and underinsured to come to PubliCare Hospital in order to receive specialty follow-up treatment. For example, according to many practitioners, the only way for uninsured or Medicaid patients to get orthopedic care was for them to show up at PubliCare's emergency room to see the orthopedist on call (many specialists did not accept Medicaid patients because reimbursements were so low). One nurse explained that she sometimes saw discharge orders from HolyCare Hospital's emergency room that read, "Go to PubliCare's ER to have your cast changed in two weeks." At any given time within the emergency room at PubliCare, two or three patients likely were there for what nurses wrote on the patient board as "ERFU," shorthand for "emergency room follow-up."

Social Medicine: PubliCare as Almshouse

Ruth Malone aptly described the emergency department in today's health care system as having a "hidden role as a public 'almshouse,'"[3] which certain marginalized populations depend upon not only for medical care but also as "a place to receive 'help' much more broadly defined."[4] She argues that the problem of overutilization of emergency services must be couched within the broader question of "how and where we as a society and as individuals care (or fail to care) for those who cannot or will not care for themselves in socially sanctioned ways."[5] As other institutions of social welfare have folded, the demands on hospital care have only increased. Nowhere were these issues more pertinent in Las Lomas than at PubliCare Hospital—not only in the emergency room but throughout the facility.

Patients at PubliCare Hospital often arrived there as a last resort. One ER doctor put it bluntly: "The patients who come here are at the bottom of the barrel, they have nowhere else to go. They don't have a primary care doctor. They've burnt their bridges with their family, many of them. The social system has had it up to here with them. The cops drop them off here; they don't even take them to jail anymore." A nurse administrator recalled how the prison would sometimes release critically ill inmates onto the streets after their sentences only to have them end up at PubliCare. She recalled a case of a sex offender with dementia "whose last memory was that he had lived in Las Lomas. . . . And the prison put him on a bus and sent him back [here]." The police found him wandering outside of a church and brought him to PubliCare. "We had a terrible time finding a place to put him," she recalled.

Another group of uninsured patients treated the hospital's emergency room as a primary care clinic. An ER doctor said, "Many people have no primary care provider, other than the emergency room. So we do see an inordinate number of people that could be taken care of in the office. They can't seem to get into an office or don't know how to, or they have nothing better to do than wait five hours to be seen." One patient I observed—an African American woman with sickle-cell anemia and several other health complications—had been seen in the emergency room by the same physician for approximately fifteen years. The joke in the department was that the doctor could do his dictation on her from memory without referring to her chart.

Many uninsured or underinsured patients waited to come to the emergency room until they were quite sick. According to one nurse, many patients at PubliCare's emergency room wound up "being really, really sick people . . . because they didn't have the money, they didn't have the insurance, so they stayed home until it was . . . almost too late." Another ER doctor echoed this sentiment: "A lot of people are much sicker because of their lifestyles and because they wait a long time before they seek medical care." It was thus often difficult for practitioners to disentangle patients' medical and nonmedical needs.[6] As one nurse manager said, "I find that a lot of times when the social things fall apart, then it builds on the medical things falling apart. First the social things fall apart and then the medical things fall apart. And you'll find that forever." When a poor person could not afford her medication, or an elderly person did not have family or friends nearby to help him shop for groceries, the line between illness and other forms of social distress was unclear.

PubliCare Hospital had become a sort of clearinghouse for the desperate and despairing. As one ER doctor put it, "I don't know the numbers, but it's a rarity to see someone who has even has a job, actually." As a part of the health care access agreement that Westside Health had signed with the county, PubliCare Hospital was still responsible for medical clearances for the county jail (for which the hospital was to be reimbursed at approximately 80 percent of billed charges), as well as for several other county services—like screenings for victims of sexual assault and blood alcohol tests for drunk drivers. A nurse in the emergency room explained, "The emergency room can be 90 percent medical clearances for jail drunks and fifty-one fifties. . . . We may not have one sick or normal person in our ER." Stories abounded within the emergency room about the travails of psychiatric patients. In the past, for example, one of the examination rooms had had a lock on its door, in order that patients receiving gynecological exams could be given some privacy. The lock was removed, however, after a nurse accidentally put a psychiatric patient in the room and returned to find that the patient had locked the door and hung herself. Another patient had tried to stab herself with a syringe, so syringes were no longer kept in the evaluation rooms.

Given the hospital's close relationship with those living on the margins, one ER doctor told me how she had taken it upon herself to stay up to date with street slang: "[I] try to get the latest jargon with the drugs and the verbiage, because I can't keep up with it. They come in and tell me these things, and I don't know what they're talking about. I'm trying to keep myself educated. Keep trying to stay streetwise. Because we interface a lot with the cops." It was sometimes difficult even for the medical practitioners to know whether a case was medical or more suited for the mental health or criminal justice systems. On one occasion a patient was wheeled into the emergency room after he was found passed out in a Laundromat, only to become combative in the ambulance en route to the hospital. Finding the patient only partially conscious and in restraints in the psychiatric room, the doctor did not know whether to send him to psychiatry for evaluation or to send him to jail.

The tension between medical care and social control within the emergency room was illustrated even more forcefully one afternoon when a patient started yelling from his room, "I'm fucking cold!" One nurse said, "I'll get him a blanket." Paying no attention to the nurse, a doctor said, "Get him some Ativan," a popular anti-anxiety medication. And the charge nurse, disregarding both of the others, rushed into the man's room saying, "Would you like to go to jail? One more outburst from you and that's where you're going!" Different practitioners understood the patient's outburst differently—as a request for help, an indication of mental illness, and an act of aggression.

On another occasion a woman was brought to the emergency room because she had been loitering in a grocery store for more than twenty-four hours. Her blood pressure was dangerously high, but she was refusing to take her medications. The doctor was flustered, because she felt she could not transfer the patient to psychiatry before the patient's blood pressure was under control, but her refusal to take her blood pressure medication seemed to be a part of her psychiatric illness. "Should we go get the water board?" one of the technologists joked.

It was a challenge for the hospital to discharge those patients at PubliCare Hospital who came from such difficult social situations. Insured patients not only had access to medical resources, a case manager explained, but were also more likely to have "a stable home environment to go home to" and within which to receive follow-up care. As a charge nurse in the emergency room said, patients were often not sick enough to be admitted to the hospital, so she had to figure out "where are we going to go with this, socially." One uninsured patient had recently come to the emergency room in kidney failure and needed emergency dialysis. But since outpatient dialysis centers would not accept patients without funding, and since the hospital was not licensed as an outpatient dialysis center, the patient had to get treated in the hospital for six weeks while case managers worked to secure insurance: "He was walking the halls, he was sitting in the patio. I mean, essentially we were room and board."

On occasion, the hospital would also take in "social admissions," in which patients were admitted "until [it] can be sorted out how they can take care of themselves." A critical care doctor expressed frustration at the tremendous amount of resources the hospital spent dealing with social problems. One patient, who had been in the intensive care unit for a month, could have gone home if only the hospital could find the necessary equipment for her to take home with her. But since the patient had no insurance, and since she had "stiffed some of the [equipment] companies . . . nobody want[ed] to deal with her." Instead, she was left to "sit[] in the ICU. . . . It's incredible." A hospitalist[7] was treating a man who had been hospitalized for seven months because no one else could be found to care for him. The hospitalist remarked to an ancillary worker that he often felt he was directing traffic more than practicing medicine.

A Special Breed

Many doctors in Las Lomas had done their training at PubliCare Hospital's prestigious family practice residency program, so many were familiar with the patients there. Remembering this period of their training, several oscillated between nostalgia and revulsion. One family practice doctor at GroupCare remembered how "a lot of patients were coming in for reasons that would be other than medical." And since "you're trained as a medical student and a resident to treat medical problems . . . it drives you a little bit apoplectic." While this doctor "applaud[ed]" those who "had a stomach for" an environment like PubliCare, he did not think he had the patience or skills for it himself: "I'm good at diagnosing disease, I'm good at coming up with treatments and working with people to impress upon them the importance, but I'm not good at that other stuff."

Those at PubliCare agreed that there was something unique about those who chose to work there. One nurse at PubliCare suggested that "GroupCare nurses pick GroupCare because they're not subject to" the social needs of patients. Another charge nurse, who had worked at both PubliCare and GroupCare, said that there was "more impatience at GroupCare" with indigent patients. She herself said she enjoyed the "variety of patients [at PubliCare] . . . the people that have hard times from the community, as well as the private patients." This seemed connected to her own sense of egalitarianism: "That's a huge challenge to remember to treat everyone the same, respectfully, and I think it's a really healthy environment to work in." Overall, she thought that practitioners at PubliCare were united by a commitment to giving everyone—no matter what the background—the same quality of care: "You have an indigent patient on one hand and then you got little grandma from Oakmont on the other side with all her diamond rings. . . . Everybody is treated the same, and that's what makes this place so unique." This nurse also implied that caring for the indigent was particularly rewarding. The poor in particular "appreciated [the care] so much," which made the work "very, very gratifying."

An ER doctor at PubliCare also emphasized the importance of treating people equally, but for him this meant abstracting from the patient's social situation to focus narrowly on the patient's illness: "One of my mentors told me, he said, 'Okay, here, we do just medicine here, just medicine.' And I got that finally. He said, 'Don't bring your social biases, your judgments, your picking and choosing, don't bring your opinions to this ER, just do medicine here and you'll get along fine.'" This doctor went on to acknowledge that "there were some docs who, for one reason or another, got really, really angry and could not tolerate being in the emergency room with the kind of patients that we had, which were many times abusive, they were intoxicated so they were hard to deal with, they were manipulative, all of that kind of stress." Those were the physicians who were unable to let go of their judgments.

Several physicians and nurses at PubliCare seemed to direct their frustration with patients at the medical system more generally. According to one nurse in the emergency room,

> I think mentally you can work through it by understanding that a lot of time people have no choice. They have tried to go to the clinic, they can't get into the clinic for four or five, six weeks, they've tried to call their doctor and their doctor sent them to us. . . . It's not just the people not being responsible. . . . So you might as well get your head around that.

This nurse stressed the importance of not shaming those who came to the emergency room "because the implication of that is that they did the wrong thing, and then the next time they're not going to come to you. . . . Once we have somewhere for them to go, then we can tell them where to go, but we don't have that answer." An ER doctor felt frustrated "because for every step you try to take forward for the patient there's two steps back." She would write prescriptions and then realize that Medicaid did not cover them so the patients were not able to get them filled. The patients would then wind up back in the emergency room.

But despite these frustrations, many staff members took pride in the Sisyphean work with which they were engaged. When I asked one social worker how she handled those patients who returned to the emergency room again and again—called "frequent fliers" in hospital parlance—she answered flatly:

> You start again. What are you going to do? You start from the beginning. . . . You cannot deny people medical supports. . . . If they're homeless and they've

got pneumonia, we clear them up and they go right back out and sleep up under that same tree that they got pneumonia from the last time. We can't say, 'Oh, no you can't come in here, 'cause we told you to get a place to sleep,' when the reality is there is no place for you to sleep, and you're doing the best that you can. . . . We can't say no. We've gotta treat you.

Practitioners at PubliCare offered types of assistance that included a whole array of social services. As a doctor put it, "Okay, this person has nothing to eat and so why not give them a sandwich, you know? Or they have nowhere comfortable to sleep, so why not keep them a couple more hours?" One nurse administrator discussed how the emergency room would sometimes feed and board homeless people "if we're not too busy." The emergency room also had "a whole closet full of clothes and we give out, . . . God knows how many socks and things like that." During the holidays the hospital would "give out toys to kids," and they always had a stash for children to use while their parents were being seen. If the hospital ran out of spare clothes, nurses would give homeless people whatever they could find: "You know how many blankets we've sent out of this place for homeless people?"

A nurse in the emergency room acknowledged that the needy had come to expect "this place to be . . . their shelter, their food source." The hospital would sometimes offer taxi vouchers to patients without a ride home and would provide car seats for new mothers without the money to buy them. Nurses would bathe patients who were unable to wash themselves. These sorts of services were almost unheard of at the other two facilities.

Moral Distinctions

Many who practiced at PubliCare felt strongly that one's ability to pay should not determine one's access to hospital care. But practitioners still had to make decisions about how to allocate resources. And so many practitioners, consciously or not, had developed moral distinctions by which to differentiate those who deserved care, whom they were happy to treat, from the undeserving, whom they shunned.

Several practitioners at PubliCare emphasized the moral hazard of providing *too much* support to patients. One nurse described how neighboring HolyCare Hospital justified its own stinginess towards the indigent by saying, "This way they won't come back here. . . . If we give something for free, then they'll keep coming back wanting more." And while she asserted that "we don't think that way" at PubliCare, she acknowledged that there had been pressure from administrators to cut back on such handouts: "We get in trouble all the time because of the budget." On one recent occasion the head of the linen department at the hospital was passing by the ER entrance as nurses were putting a blanket around a patient and discharging him: "I observed this one," the administrator said. "You're not going to be able to talk your way out of it." Another nurse in the emergency room seemed to agree that they were creating perverse incentives by offering resources too easily: "It's gotten to the point where people abuse taxi vouchers, and every time they come here they take an ambulance and expect a taxi voucher home. And they're comin' in because they have a hangnail."

And so, despite their belief in care as a social right, many practitioners at PubliCare simultaneously suggested that the facility's generous provision of care to the poor had undermined some patients' sense of personal responsibility. Dr. Brittney Sampson was an ER doctor at PubliCare who made this argument most forcefully. Now in her late fifties, Sampson had grown up and gone to school in Boston before doing her medical training in Washington State. She had moved to Las Lomas because it looked like a nice place to live, and she had worked in almost all of the emergency rooms in the area before settling on PubliCare (although she still worked the odd shift elsewhere). Like other physicians at PubliCare, Sampson had a folksy air about her, though in her case it was moderated by some residual East Coast grit.

Sampson was forthright about her frustrations with the moral hazards at PubliCare. She recognized that PubliCare Hospital had a "role and an obligation" to take care of the indigent, but she was worried about the effects that the free provision of care had on the poor. She recounted the case of an eighteen-year-old with two children who lived in a shelter. Because she was obese and sleeping on a cot in the shelter, the woman was having back pain: "She called an ambulance because her pain was so bad to bring her to the emergency room to get her pain medication." Sampson asked whether the patient had tried ibuprofen, and the patient said she could not afford it. "I said, 'Do you know how much this ambulance just cost you to go from the shelter to PubliCare? About fifteen hundred dollars.'" The patient responded, "Medi-Cal [California's Medicaid program] will cover my ambulance ride." The patient asked for pain medications, which Sampson prescribed, but the patient also asked for free ibuprofen. Sampson told the patient to "take your cigarette money and buy your ibuprofen." The patient then wanted a taxi voucher to get back to the shelter. "I said, 'No, you're going to have to figure out a ride.'" The patient then responded that she wanted an ambulance back. "I looked at her and I said, 'The state is bankrupt, there is no money.' They don't get that. She looked at me like I had three eyes."

Sampson felt that "there's so many people in society that we enable." Because of entitlements like Medicaid and food stamps, she felt, "There's no reason for [people] to have to work." She was frustrated that people could receive disability insurance for bipolar disease "even if [it] . . . was induced by [their] methamphetamine abuse." She was angry that someone could get a lung transplant even though "he smoked all his life." She was fed up that patients would "use their money for potato chips and cigarettes and ask me to write a script for them for ibuprofen so that the taxpayers can pay for that." On one occasion a woman came into the emergency room needing an MRI. The patient said that she weighed 325 pounds, but a tech was afraid she might actually exceed the 350-pound limit on the hospital's MRI machine. Sampson told me that the newer machines could handle patients of up to 450 pounds. She then said, offhandedly, it was sad that instead of getting people to lose weight, companies develop machines to accommodate heavier patients. "Where's the ownership?" she said. "These people, there's been so many handouts for so long they're so used to it. . . . There is a sense of entitlement, and I hate that. . . . As an ER doc I cannot turn anybody away. They may owe fifty thousand dollars to the hospital and I cannot decline services to them." Alcoholics would wander into the emergency room and "you have to keep them there until they can walk and sober up. . . . And you kick them out of there, they're down at the bar and the local grocery store buying booze before you can blink an eye."

Sampson suggested that people's right to care should be contingent on their taking responsibility for themselves: "I'd be happy to give you health insurance, or provide your health care, but you gotta stop smoking. You gotta stop shooting heroin. You gotta stop snortin' the cocaine. You gotta lose weight." A doctor at GroupCare Health contrasted his experience at GroupCare with his residency at PubliCare Hospital. At GroupCare he still saw some patients who were "not taking care of their health" and "wanting me to fix their health." He continued, "I'll take care of them, but we have some parameters how to do this. . . . You need to follow my plan, if you can't follow my plan, then you need to find somebody else to go see." At a place like PubliCare, it was almost impossible to hold patients accountable in this way. As an organization of last resort, there was nowhere else for patients to go.

And while Sampson was the most forthcoming with me about the resources wasted on those she considered irresponsible, many others recognized that they sometimes felt their kindness was "abused." One nurse administrator discussed a patient who had a colostomy bag, "and every time it comes off, he will not try to learn how to put it back on. So he comes in incontinent of stool probably eight times a week for us just to clean him up. . . . So that is terrible misuse." A critical care doctor at PubliCare suggested that some patients in kidney failure would cross from Mexico to California emergency rooms to get treatment. Another emergency room doctor at PubliCare worried that some were "taking advantage of the goodness of the system." When people receive Medicaid, she suggested, "you should give them a little talk . . . to feel their own responsibility."

But when were patients taking advantage, when were they truly in need, and to what extent did this distinction even make sense? Sandra Lacks recognized that the "word was out on the street" that "all you have to do is go [to PubliCare Hospital] and they'll give you food vouchers," and that some patients had come to take advantage of it. She acknowledged that it was a type of "game playing," but in her mind it was "also survival. You do what you gotta do to survive out there." Was the Medicaid patient who came to the emergency room because there was a long wait at the clinic being manipulative? To many, the answer was unclear. One ER doctor told a story of a woman who brought her daughter to juvenile hall saying they had been fighting, when in fact she did not have insurance and wanted her daughter's urinary tract infection to be treated while in custody. On the one hand, this doctor pointed out, it was "gaming the system." On the other hand, could anyone blame her? Even Sampson herself was not uncaring. She volunteered in a local women's clinic, and in person she treated almost all of her patients with respect. At the end of one shift, a homeless man was about to be discharged when the nurses brought him a hot meal from the kitchen. Sampson smiled the biggest smile I had seen on her the whole day and said, "Isn't that nice. This is the best meal this guy will probably have all week."

Doctors at PubliCare were thus informal gatekeepers for the community's social welfare system, a role for which many felt ill equipped. One doctor, reflecting on his training at PubliCare, discussed how it seemed that "the medical care system was one of the few areas where [the poor] could seek out some entitlement." Doctors were required to sign work-release forms for those insured on the job, for example. This doctor remembered "struggling with" patients who wanted two months off for a sprained wrist when a few days would likely have sufficed. Doctors were also wary of those seeking pain medications in order to sell them on the street. As one doctor who had trained at PubliCare put it, "there's no teaching in medical school that tells you how to deal with the Vicodin addict that's going out and selling the prescriptions and coming in with incredibly ingenious and heartfelt stories of why they need more pain medications."

When patients were privately insured, their motivations for seeking care were rarely subject to much scrutiny. With those who sought care as an entitlement, however, doctors were constantly suspicious of being manipulated, even as they defended the poor's right to treatment. On several instances, one particular ER doctor would walk out of patients' rooms saying something like, "He's playing us." A second ER doctor discussed how patients would often only start groaning once she entered the room: "A huge amount of gaming goes on, a huge amount. . . . It can make you cynical, for sure."

One homeless woman was brought to the emergency room having been hit by a car in the parking lot of the local homeless shelter. The doctor and charge nurse thought it was a case of "poor me, poor me," and that the woman might be trying to "turn it into something" like a lawsuit. A case manager at PubliCare discussed a girl she had just seen who "didn't want to leave [the hospital] because she liked her IV pain meds. . . . It was like I had to get a forklift and pry her out of that bed to get her out of here." This case manager thought patients like this young woman were "institutionalized." She "knows the drill, and she knows exactly what to say" to stay in the hospital.

Some inmates from the local jail would come to PubliCare and "fake seizures so they wouldn't have to go back to the jail." While I was observing, there was an inmate from the jail who had been admitted to PubliCare for kidney problems. During a utilization meeting it came to light that the man was afraid of going back to jail and had convinced one of the nephrologists (a "pushover," according to the hospitalist) to let him to stay a few more days. The hospitalist said that someone was going to have to tell the man he was discharged and then walk out of the room without discussion; a case manager said the police would probably have to take him away "kicking and screaming."

Vocation and Disorganization

Many practitioners at PubliCare discussed a need to be resourceful in the face of a lack of resources—both the lack of resources that the hospital faced and the lack of resources their patients brought with them. One nurse said that it was her and her colleagues' vocational commitment and creativity that kept the organization running: "There's great nurses here that can do more with nothing than I've ever seen people do." In place of missing doorstops, nurses would tape doors to walls; in place of pins to latch tubing together, nurses would sometimes use needles and tape.

Doctors, nurses, and social workers were also quite resourceful about finding treatments and placements for uninsured or underinsured patients. One case manager said with a smile, "We get pretty good about coming up with creative discharge plans." Sandra Lacks, the social worker, considered herself a "researcher of resources." If she had not been a social worker, she said, she would have been "an inspector over in Scotland [Yard] . . . 'cause I like figuring stuff out." Given her wealth of knowledge, she saw herself as the "point guard of everything that happens within this county. Anybody who wants to know anything . . . regarding any resources, they'll start with me." But the way she spoke of her role was also indicative of the facility's overall lack of coordination. Whereas an organization like GroupCare had systems in place for different sorts of patients, each new case at PubliCare became a Sherlock Holmes mystery.

Several practitioners discussed the relationships they would build and games that they would play with other social service providers in order to secure placements for their patients. When practitioners at PubliCare interfaced with the broader medical community there seemed to be a sort of gift economy in which ongoing relationships, implicit understandings, and moral codes took the place of explicit transactions.[8] For example, one case manager described how she would send insured patients to particular nursing homes if those homes had also agreed to take the uninsured and underinsured. While I was observing her, she made at least two different "deals" to secure placement for those without good funding. With a worker from a local nursing facility, she explained, "We'll joke around and he'll be like, 'You're gonna help me out?' And I'll say, 'I'm gonna help you out.' It's kind of fun." Later on, she seemed to make a slightly more formal exchange: if one home would take a Medicaid patient, she promised she would send the same home her next Medicare patient (which reimbursed the home at a higher level). Laughing, she said, "It's a game." More generally, she explained her philosophy about placements: "We do the best that we can for the facilities that help us out." In turn, she tried to avoid some of the "fancier places" entirely:

> Not that I don't like them, I just know that they only want their cash cows. They want the fully funded seventy-five-year old with the hip replacement who's going to be there two weeks, so they'll get maximum benefits from Medicare and then they'll go home with a simple discharge plan. They don't want Joe Blow homeless guy who just had a BKA [below knee amputation], who . . . needs IV antibiotics for six weeks, oh and by the way, I don't know where he's going after that.

Lacks discussed how the resources to which she had access were oftentimes a product of the relationships she had established: "You do a favor for them, they do a favor for you. . . . That's the way it works." Reciprocal obligations—"a favor for a favor for a favor"—meant that she was able to do a lot for patients without much in the way of financial incentives on her side: "It ain't got nothin' to do with resources. If it was resources, honey, all of us would be in the poorhouse, 'cause there's no resources." (In a sense, of course, we *were* in the poorhouse.) The difference between successful and unsuccessful social workers, she said, was that successful ones were "seasoned," had "been around for a while and they've learned the game." A case manager also referred to the relationships she had built over time "with facilities . . . and with certain people." She told me that most people at PubliCare had trouble with a particular equipment company but she knew "this one guy. . . . And he bends over backwards to help me." At an oxygen supply company, another man she knew would break protocol and bring a patient a tank before funding came through. When other companies came to her, marketing their businesses, she would respond, "Well, you don't help me out."

At PubliCare Hospital, individuals worked creatively on behalf of patients, but did so with very few formal systems in place. Each of the other two hospitals had a different approach to such placements. HolyCare Hospital would fax a patient request to all of the facilities in Las Lomas and transfer the patient to the facility that made the best (or fastest) offer; GroupCare, in turn, contracted with facilities in advance, "buying beds" that were reserved for their patients. In other words, while HolyCare relied on an impersonal market transaction, and Group-Care on bureaucratic arrangements, PubliCare relied on the resourcefulness and relationships of its staff.

For many practitioners at PubliCare, this informality seemed to be part of how they understood their mission. Indeed, many seemed to juxtapose caring with efficiency, and suggested that pressure to streamline services threatened the very mission of the hospital. One charge nurse said, "PubliCare has the heart. [It has] a great heart, and the people there don't care about billing, they just want to take care of patients well. And they will do that. But they will not charge you for it. So it's a little crazy." Another nurse discussed how it would be "taboo" for her or her managers to ask her peers to conserve on costs because they would assume that management "just wanted to save a buck." And so the same spirit that motivated practitioners to provide health care as a right sometimes seemed to stand in the way of basic organizational efficiencies.

Indeed, the level of disorganization throughout PubliCare Hospital far exceeded anything at either of the other hospitals. On one morning I arrived in the hospitalist office just before Dr. Alex Polyakova was about to begin his rounds. The office fax machine was out of paper and seemed to have been for some time, because when Polyakova replaced it a stack of perhaps fifty faxes came spewing out. These faxes consisted mostly of lab reports on patients for which the hospitalist department was or had been responsible, but Polyakova seemed at a loss for what to do with them. Under normal circumstances he would just recycle them, he said, but he decided to keep them in order to show them to an administrator as an example of organizational inefficiency. Such oversights abounded. Down in the emergency room, for example, the nursing board had been built in the early part of the twentieth century with a lighting system. Nurses could turn on a red light beside a name if the doctor needed to take action on patient, and doctors could turn on a green light beside the name if the nurses needed to take action. But as far as I could tell only one doctor and none of the nurses used the lighting system at all.

Throughout the facility, Westside Health was making a slow and painful transition from paper records to electronic ones. During my research, hospitalists were using at least two different computer programs—one for patient care and one for billing—in addition to the paper records, and charts were constantly misplaced. According to one hospitalist, neither the electronic records nor the paper records were complete, meaning that practitioners had to refer to both in order to construct a comprehensive patient history. Inexplicably, results from blood sugar tests were not kept in patients' records at all but rather in a separate room behind a locked door. In the emergency room, one doctor was particularly notorious for leaving charts in patients' rooms or in the wrong boxes, sending various personnel scrambling to find them. The lack of reliable electronic records meant that tests were often duplicated unnecessarily, and some doctors jokingly discussed their biggest medical challenge as having to read other doctors' handwriting.

On one occasion in the emergency room, a patient looked closer to death than any patient I had previously seen—pale, dehydrated, and gaunt. For over two hours the doctor and nurses puzzled over his condition and tried to get his blood pressure to rise; it was only then that someone realized he had had a procedure in the hospital the previous day in which he had lost a lot of blood. With a more streamlined record system like they had at GroupCare there would not have been this confusion. At GroupCare, there was one comprehensive electronic records system on which all the staff had been trained. Each doctor interfaced constantly with the system or could be reached on a single cordless phone. At PubliCare things were much more haphazard. One hospitalist whom I shadowed carried with him two cell phones (an iPhone that did not get reception and a cell phone for calls), a cordless phone, a beeper, and an iPad that he used for e-mails and to look up medical information. Despite his dependence on these various devices, he joked, "To err is human, but to really screw up you need a computer."

Practitioners at PubliCare Hospital seemed to have reacted against the specialization that has come to define modern American medicine, each focusing instead on the patient more holistically. Doctors would do procedures out of their specialties; nurses at PubliCare would "act more like doctors" than nurses elsewhere, according to a physician. PubliCare Hospital was the only hospital in Los Lomas to hire family practice doctors alongside board-certified emergency physicians to staff its emergency room. These family physicians would often spend more time with emergency patients, sitting down next to them, for example, while the ER doctor typically would stand. One family practice doctor in the emergency room said of a hypothetical case, "This patient really could do those tests as an outpatient, but they may not get there, so I'm going to do them now." Another family practice doctor who worked in the emergency room said that she treated the "whole person, the whole family situation. . . . I mean, those are the things a family practitioner gets bogged down thinking about, and ER doctors are like, 'Stop using that [drug]—okay, next.'"

But again, this lack of specialization had its drawbacks. When patients treated the emergency room like a family practice clinic, it could be argued, they wasted the emergency room's resources. And when everyone tried to do everything, some things got short shrift. For example, until recently the nurses at PubliCare had been responsible for hospital billing. According to a charge nurse, "We used to be taking care of patients, running ragged . . . and before we turned in our chart, trying to click a few boxes for billing—well, you can imagine how much billing was missed."

The Mission against the Market

At PubliCare Hospital, the mission of health care was widely understood to be at odds with the market for care. Practitioners would offer resources to needy patients—from free Tylenol to blankets to meals—that sapped the hospital of supplies. The very provision of health care as a right, according to many practitioners, risked creating moral hazards: the fifteen-hundred-dollar ambulance ride for the two-dollar ibuprofen. Moreover, the *belief* among practitioners that the mission of health care was inconsistent with the market seemed at times to become a justification for disorganization and haphazard care. Practitioners, each of whom seemed deeply committed to patients' care on an individual basis, seemed to resist attempts to standardize or streamline the ways in which care was delivered as if rational organization was itself threatening to health care's public mission.

But the mission and market were even more starkly at odds with each other in terms of the hospital's desire to attract paying patients. The poor and underinsured at PubliCare, who made up a large proportion of the hospital's patient population, were a repellent for many of the wealthier patients. One ER doctor's wealthy neighbors had compared going to PubliCare Hospital with "waiting in the Greyhound bus station, [since] everyone's speaking Spanish." This doctor said that it was hard to get the fully insured patient to use PubliCare, or even to get doctors in private practice to send their insured patients to the hospital: "It's prettier over there at HolyCare. I mean the rooms are nicer, the nurses wear little caps." He continued, "I don't see any real difference in the treatment, but you know as one medical marketer told me, 'Perception is everything.' I told him, 'Jeez, I hope not.'" Among the privately insured, the presence of the indigent implied an inferior quality of care. One nurse said bluntly:

> If you had a choice to stay in a room that may or may not have heat or air conditioning, that might be within a foot of some homeless person, or to go stay at HolyCare where everything's shiny and new and looks better, then as a paying customer, where are you going to go? Are you going to go to McDonald's or are you going to go to somewhere nice, you know?

In keeping with this argument, a nurse administrator described a time when a student from a nearby private high school was brought to the emergency room after having been hit in the face by a baseball. At the same time, right down the hall from this "very well-insured, wealthy family" was a prisoner who was so disruptive that he required four police officers with him. The mother was "sitting in the hall with her high-school-age son hearing this prisoner cuss, swear up and down." The mother filed a "huge complaint" with the hospital.

Westside Health sought to attract paying patients to PubliCare Hospital by establishing a state-of-the-art cardiac care center, by investing millions in renovating the old facility, and by promoting the care that patients received at the hospital. Throughout my research there was a large banner displayed outside the hospital entrance on which five gold stars symbolized the high rankings Publi-Care Hospital had been given by a quality-ranking agency (an online video featured practitioners and workers dancing around the hospital waving the stars). As one department manager put it,

> It's not known, because we don't have as much as money to advertise as Group-Care or HolyCare. We're a five-star hospital in cardiac services. . . . We also just won a quality award for not having ventilator-assisted pneumonias or central line infections for more than two years standing, which is really hard to do. So people don't perceive us as thus, they perceive us as the county hospital and that's all we do. But actually we provide really good, quality care here, and we're really good at the things we do, and not to say that GroupCare and HolyCare don't, but we did get those awards; they didn't.

But it seemed that Westside Health had underestimated the extent to which the legacy of PubliCare Hospital would linger in the minds of practitioners and patients alike. As a social worker put it, the people at the hospital approached the new hospital administration "from the old mindset." The hospital "never changed; it's just the name got changed. The people were still the same. They're the same people that have been here for thirty, forty, fifty years." As one case manager put it, "It still has that stereotype. I think it's the building, the location, I mean everything about it. It's still considered the county hospital." A nurse manager acknowledged that despite the good care it provided, it still had the feel of an old county facility: "There's still a lot of old prejudice. . . . We are an old facility, it's not pretty." Westside was unable to turn the old public hospital into a moneymaker. According to one ER doctor, "From the taxpayer's point of view, the county did well on that contract. From Westside Health's point of view, um, luckily this was not their only hospital."

CHAPTER TWO

Privileged Servants

In an address to graduates of the prestigious family practice residency program at PubliCare Hospital in 2000, Dr. Dan Brenner—a leader of the program—decried the influence of the market in modern medicine, suggesting that it corrupted the vocational calling of medical practitioners. By way of analogy, he asked the audience to imagine a health care executive making cost-saving recommendations to a symphony orchestra after watching the orchestra play: "All twelve violins were playing identical notes at the same time. Such duplication could be eliminated with a cost savings of 92 percent in the string section alone." If physicians allowed the market to "constrict our current concept of care to such qualified terms as 'managed' care, or merely care as 'commodity,'" he continued, "then we've really turned something once noble into something tacky, and made 'care' just another . . . four-letter word." He urged residents to remember: "'to care' is derived from the same roots as caritas (meaning charity), carino (affection), caru (to love). In the largest sense." Access to care should be "everyone's right."

Similar themes were interwoven throughout many of Brenner's essays. In one piece, he emphasized that he preferred the word "patient" to other terms (like "client" or "consumer") because its root, *pati*, means "one who suffers." Several of his most meaningful experiences as a doctor—written down for residents to read and reflect upon—had taken place when he ministered to dying patients at their homes.

In another piece, Brenner wrote even more explicitly about the market for health care: "Our medical heritage, passed on from the professors who taught us . . . was that the practice of medicine, at its purest, is guided by science and driven by compassion. Money matters. But it has distorted the methodology of our science and has distracted us from the motive of our practice." The market, he suggested, was antithetical to care, something the medical profession needed to counteract. He considered himself and his colleagues in the family residency program "medically countercultural; some are closet revolutionaries." Brenner wrote that today's residency students "remind us that the real measure of our work is not what we get paid for it, but what we become by doing it. We are, after all, privileged servants."

Brenner and many other physicians at PubliCare saw care as a right. In turn, they seemed to conceive of the practice of medicine as a vocational calling or public service. This was an orientation towards medicine that was reinforced by those who took part in the family medicine residency program. Brenner explained, "I thought when I got out of the Peace Corps that I would never again have the opportunity to work with a group of people as committed and as dedicated and hopeful for effecting change in the world as I did in the Peace Corps. But I was wrong. The group of people that come through this program are equally committed." This public commitment was widespread among current and former residents. A family practice doctor who had been through the residency program and worked occasional shifts in PubliCare's emergency room discussed how her medical work was connected to her commitment to social justice—although she sometimes questioned her capacity to effect change through medical practice:

> It's very easy [to get frustrated] when you are doing stuff that feels kind of rinky-dink on a day-to-day level. It's like, you know, doing pap smears and checking people's cholesterol level is, you know, to feel so unimpressive. . . . I periodically get super pissed off, and I think I'm just going to go off and [work in] public housing and try to make the world a little bit better that way.

She was unconvinced that "medicine is the best place to actually address health disparities" and sometimes believed that "bike lanes and more accessible healthy food would [make] a million times more difference than I do every day." Still, there was something deeply satisfying about her work: "I have this person who's right in front of me and they are the one that I really want to help. And there is something magical about the relationship that, you know, you can actually make a difference." She thought she shared these commitments with other family practice doctors, particularly in Las Lomas: "Most of primary care doctors that you meet [here] will have a fairly strong sense of trying to save the world." Another doctor said that he came to PubliCare Hospital because he was "already aligned with" working towards the public good.

In an interview, Brenner explained that he thought "we took a step in the wrong direction when we commercialized medicine, when we made it a commodity, and we corporatized it." While there "has to be enterprise in medicine," he went on, "we've lost sight of the real reason that we practice medicine. . . . I think physicians . . . [are] privileged servants." A hospitalist at PubliCare Hospital thought the profit motive should be removed from medical practice altogether: "I wish we could weed out, in medical school, the guys that are entrepreneurs and are in it for the money." One way to attract the right people to medicine was to take the money out of it: "By not having it [be] a lucrative field, you get rid of one group of people."

More than doctors at either HolyCare or GroupCare, doctors at PubliCare understood their professional identities in vocational terms. By their own accounts they had come to the profession for reasons of public service and had tried with some success to live out these ideals in their everyday work. They thus evoked a forgotten tradition in the sociology of professions—one in which professions were understood to be a bulwark against the spread of capitalism and a model of altruistic community towards which all workers might strive.[1] For others outside PubliCare, however, these doctors seemed an obsolescent old guard clinging to professional autonomy at the expense of patient care and organizational efficiency; a group of misfits and layabouts who were living in the past.

And the honorable sentiments expressed by many doctors at PubliCare belied other perhaps less honorable practices. Some doctors seemed to prefer working with the poor at least in part because these patients were less likely to question their authority. Others seemed committed to PubliCare because PubliCare was the most likely to leave them alone, letting them practice in the ways they always had. Patients' multifaceted problems and a lack of resources created an environment of disorganization and improvisation, which some doctors were able to use as cover. The hospital's commitment to providing care as a right thus served as a broad discursive and organizational frame within which doctors with different sorts of values and interests, from the beneficent to the banal, were able to find their place.

A Vocational Ethic

In the middle of rounds one morning, Dr. Polyakova paused for a moment to reflect on the tumultuous real estate market. He and his wife had helped their son buy a house not long before the housing bubble burst. But he was not too perturbed. There were two ways to think about buying a house, he told me. One way was to treat the house as an economic investment. By this logic he and his wife had done miserably. But the other way to think about it was as an emotional investment, a place in which their son could build a life. He preferred to think about it in those terms. This was not so dissimilar from his understanding of the medical profession. He believed that "if it's not a calling, if it's not something that you really want to do, you shouldn't be in it." He joked, "I always said I'd do it for nothing, so the government and insurance companies took me seriously."

The county's small family practice residency program—no longer run by PubliCare Hospital but still centered there—helped to preserve what one hospitalist called the "ethic" of the organization. "No one ever got rich or famous by being a family doctor," said Brenner, "So they're not in it for that." He continued, "The choice of family medicine is an act of social commitment and probably political courage. . . . And maybe financial insanity." At any one time there were more than thirty residents who took rotations in the hospital and at a clinic across the street (although the residency program had recently branched out to include some rotations at HolyCare and—to a lesser extent—GroupCare). Any patient admitted to PubliCare from the emergency room without insurance or without a primary care provider would be assigned to a resident, who would follow up with the patient at the residency program's clinical offices across the street. Doctors and nurses in the emergency room would also sometimes lean on the residents to follow up with outpatient cases. Many of the most beloved family practice doctors and health care leaders in the area had gone through the program and stayed in Las Lomas afterwards. As one graduate of the program quipped, "When you finish residency, you are so exhausted, you can't even contemplate moving to a different city."

After residency, some family practice doctors left PubliCare for greener pastures. But many of them appreciated the way they were able to practice medicine there. Polyakova discussed how, at PubliCare, he was able to "really see the people a lot. . . . Half the time I'll just stop by the room, sit down, and just talk to them in the afternoon." He had previously worked at HolyCare Hospital, and admitted that he would "make more money" there. But there he would have as many as twenty patients to look after in a day, whereas at PubliCare he had only between ten and twelve: "I can see everybody at least twice per day [here]."

Several doctors at PubliCare also had experienced working at GroupCare. Many echoed the sentiments of one ER doctor who said he "felt a little bit like a cog in the machine" at GroupCare. A second ER doctor, who had done shifts at GroupCare, bemoaned how much time he spent behind a console there: "I'm just the kind of guy who, when someone finds out that they have cancer, I sit at the bedside and I put my arms around them, because they need that. There's no time for that at GroupCare, they're busy, you've got to go back to your computer." A third ER doctor said that GroupCare "really is cookie-cutter in many respects." A fourth doctor, who had practiced briefly in GroupCare's OB department, also discussed GroupCare's standardization as a sacrifice: "Pretty much everybody gets an epidural, the midwife comes in, and you have your baby, and you never see [the doctor] ever again." All these doctors suggested that working at GroupCare meant sacrificing the personal care and professional discretion that they valued at PubliCare. The fourth doctor went even further by describing her *political* opposition to working at GroupCare. Despite her belief in the efficiency of an integrated system, like the one used at GroupCare, she said, "I went into this to address health disparities and make poor people's lives slightly better. . . . I think it would sort of go against my conscience to work for The Man."

Doctors at PubliCare also valued the professional independence they were able to maintain there—even though this independence came at personal cost. Don Clinton, for example, an intensive care doctor, was at the time of our interview almost solely responsible for staffing the closed intensive care unit at PubliCare, meaning that he was on call nearly all the time. He had been unable to attract other intensive care doctors to PubliCare because of the department's twenty-four hour shifts, which meant that he had to work many more of them than he otherwise would have had to. The sleep deprivation was sometimes difficult (some doctors "get crazy" when they lose so much sleep, he said), and it was "difficult to have a family when you're tied up at the hospital all the time." But he liked the level of responsibility: "I see every patient and I manage every patient in the ICU." There was no single person responsible for the ICU at either HolyCare Hospital or GroupCare. At HolyCare, all of the intensivists had office practices as well. At GroupCare, the intensive care doctors only worked during daytime hours and handed off responsibility to the hospitalists at night. At PubliCare, Clinton was indisputably in charge.

Clinton was an employee of the Westside Medical Foundation, and his salary was based on working at least 122 twenty-four-hour shifts a year (though Clinton worked significantly more than this). Hospitalists at PubliCare were also employed by Westside Medical Foundation and paid based on the number of shifts they worked, with small financial incentives offered for admissions and discharges. Within the emergency room, the arrangement was slightly different. The doctors there were part of a small, independent group that had secured the ER contract with the hospital. The contract was formally held by one of the old-time doctors, but eight of the full-time doctors were "partners" in the group, splitting proceeds from billing and paying several other doctors to cover occasional shifts. Unlike those working directly for the Westside Medical Foundation, all of the ER doctors were compelled to buy health insurance on the individual market. Several of them had bought high-deductible plans, figuring they could take care of themselves or one another unless something serious came up. According to one part-timer, the group as a whole was "fiercely independent, willing to sacrifice benefits for I don't know what—freedom and flexibility or something."

What was common to these doctors' financial arrangements at PubliCare was twofold: first, their pay did not vary much depending on how they practiced medicine (different from doctors at HolyCare Hospital, who billed on an individual basis); and second, there was relatively little oversight over the ways that doctors practiced medicine (different from doctors at GroupCare Hospital, whose salaries were accompanied by detailed records of physician practice patterns). Doctors were oriented to their patients not through their pocketbooks, as they were at HolyCare, nor through an extensive bureaucracy, as they were at GroupCare. This is not to say that financial incentives and bureaucratic oversight were entirely absent but rather that these countervailing powers over doctors' clinical judgment were much weaker here than they were at the other two facilities. Professionalism here implied a freedom to practice at the pace one preferred, using wide clinical discretion.

That Old-Time Religion

Doctors at PubliCare practiced medicine with wide discretion and noble commitment. But their relative autonomy also seemed related to the social distance between them and their patients and to the multidimensional nature of the problems that patients brought to PubliCare. Poor patients had neither the resources nor the cultural capital to hold doctors accountable for quality care. And it was difficult to create standardized protocols for patients with so many different kinds of medical, emotional, and social problems. One doctor told me directly that she was "afraid of the upper-class patients," since the "more-educated patients will challenge you more; they'll question you." She liked working at PubliCare because she was insulated from the sense of entitlement of, and the accountability to, more upper-class patients.

There was thus a darker side to practitioners' vocational orientation to their work. Doctors' commitments to public service could elide into medical paternalism or—for the "undeserving"—even disdain, when they felt their generosity was being exploited. As Charles Rosenberg has documented, there has long been an implicit exchange within teaching hospitals that the poor receive care while the medical student receives "clinical material" on which to practice: "The objects of charity who filled a hospital's beds could hardly refuse to cooperate in clinical teaching; it was the principal way in which they could repay society for the gratuitous care they received."[2] Wealthy, paying patients were spared these indignities. This implicit exchange had not disappeared at PubliCare. While insured patients would be admitted to the hospital by trained hospitalists, residents would admit the poor and uninsured. When the county leased PubliCare Hospital to Westside Health, the maintenance of the residency program was of the utmost importance to the local medical establishment. One condition of the lease was that Westside maintain the residency program and "continue to provide residents with the opportunity to develop technical proficiency in those gynecological surgical procedures that they may be called upon to perform." Westside would continue to provide the patient "material" on which this technical proficiency could be developed.

Rosenberg also recounts how, in the early public hospitals of the nineteenth century, professional paternalism was often coupled with disdain, as doctors regarded their patients as a "lower form of life."[3] Among doctors at PubliCare, compassion for the needs of the poor could also be coupled with a disregard for those considered undeserving. On one afternoon, for example, a patient showed up in the emergency room who had hurt his hand by cage fighting the night before. He had tattoos across his body. The doctor said aloud as we were leaving the examination room, "Sometimes you wonder what rock people have crawled out from under." A nurse administrator expressed her dismay with another ER doctor who would complain incessantly about the number of drunks who showed up at the door.

Physician autonomy at PubliCare sometimes came at the expense of best practices. One part-time doctor at PubliCare discussed how she felt that clinical freedom was "taken to an extreme" there. At other hospitals, a doctor who ordered an antibiotic for a viral infection would be told that this order was medically inconsistent. Not at PubliCare. She was "quite surprised" at how little physician oversight there seemed to be. Doctors at PubliCare Hospital were nominally accountable to a utilization board made up of a nurse manager and several physician representatives. In theory, a doctor who was deviating sharply from clinical criteria would be referred to a physician from this committee and brought into alignment. In practice, though, the board did not seem to exert much authority over the everyday decisions of physicians, at least in part because it consisted of department chairs who themselves seemed suspicious of efforts to curtail physician independence. One case manager said, "I think our length of stays are greater than they should be, and I don't think that certain physicians are being held accountable for that." A nurse manager said that the facility needed to "look at outcomes better than we ever have" and ask whether they were doing the "right thing" for people "because we drag some old people along forever."

While the hospital did exercise limited control over its regular physician staff, it was even more difficult to control the specialists who practiced there. A nurse manager discussed a ninety-three-year-old patient who had left GroupCare after they rejected his request for a heart-valve replacement, since he did not meet the organization's criteria for such a procedure. He found a cardiac surgeon to do the procedure at PubliCare but spent the next four months in the intensive care unit, developed bedsores, and went into dialysis after entering renal failure. The episode was costing "enormous amounts" of money to PubliCare, the nurse manager said, and the patient likely should not have had the procedure in the first place. As another example, while Medicare guidelines dictated that a total knee replacement warranted three days in the hospital, some of the orthopedic surgeons who practiced at PubliCare would "sit on" patients, keeping them in the hospital until they had time to operate. Patients would sometimes "sit on the third floor for weeks preoperatively, waiting for the surgery . . . [and] we're not getting paid for that." The hospital would invariably lose money on the supplies that certain specialists demanded—like the interventional cardiologist who demanded drug-eluting stents, or the orthopedist who liked to use customized knee joints. The physician discretion at PubliCare contrasted sharply with an organization like GroupCare. A case manager at PubliCare said with a laugh that at GroupCare a patient needing knee replacement surgery would just get the standard "Group-Care knee."

The extent of clinical freedom among doctors was of increasing concern to many administrators at PubliCare, given new mandates both from government and from private insurers. During the period of time I observed, Medicare had begun to implement a recovery audit contractor (RAC) program, which investigated patient records in order to recuperate Medicare overpayments to hospitals and other facilities. Case managers at PubliCare were increasingly being asked to have difficult conversation with doctors in order to set limits as to what sorts of services could be provided. During the time I observed, however, doctors' decisions were rarely questioned.

Physician freedom at PubliCare extended beyond clinical decision-making into doctors' daily interactions. One nurse in the emergency room described how each ER doctor had his or her own different style. Some would see a patient and then order a blood draw without telling the patient, assuming that it was the "nurse's job to tell them." Others would make diagnoses and discharge patients without communicating with the patients. The nurse told me she had to ask each patient, "'What did the doctor tell you?' And then you have to make sure you don't say it in a way that make you look like you don't even know what's going on." A nurse administrator in the emergency room was frustrated that the doctors were "still trying to operate in the old ways, and they are not getting up to what we need to do for 2010 and to move forward progressively." She continued:

> They're not writing down orders; they're letting the nurses practice without a license. And even though we can start the IVs . . . we need the physician to still write those orders on that blue sheet. A lot of them aren't doin' it. 'Cause you didn't have to in the old days. But this is not the old days any more. As much as I love our physicians, at the same time, they're hindering us big-time here.

Many physicians at PubliCare seemed committed to doing things as they had always been done.

Doctors at PubliCare, relatively free from the financial incentives or bureaucratic constraints that might be used to change their practice patterns, maintained their old loyalties and old habits. The medical director of the emergency room had been around for decades. Another of the old-time ER doctors had recently had a heart attack and been told by his own doctor that he could only work for four hours at time. Rather than retiring, or taking time off, the doctor negotiated with the others in the emergency room that he would work four hours in the morning, go home for seven hours, and come back to work another four: what the rest of the medical staff referred to as the "princess shift." One morning, a doctor called from home to tell the doctors on shift that he was feeling sick and could not come in that afternoon. For the next forty-five minutes, it seemed, one of the two ER doctors on duty stopped seeing patients in order to call around to find a replacement.

According to an ER doctor at HolyCare, those at PubliCare had been there so long and were so comfortable with their jobs that they had not kept up with modern medical training. He said that he had not seen a PubliCare doctor at the countywide emergency-service meetings in years. While doctors valued their independence at PubliCare, some also recognized the need for physician accountability and change. Polyakova said,

> If you don't change what you do every year then it's no good. You tried something and it didn't work, or it did work, and you do something else. I mean, that's what you have to do, no matter what field you're in. . . . My father was in the restaurant business and I worked in all his restaurants—you try something on the menu, it works, people like it. Then something gets old and tired, and you're just having it around; you've got to change it. Everything is like that.

In the absence of financial incentives, Polyakova recognized, an organization needed to "find a way to weed . . . out" the poor performers. PubliCare Hospital did not yet have such mechanisms.

Keeping the Market at Bay

If ER doctors, hospitalists, intensive care doctors, residents, and attending physicians at PubliCare all seemed to embody a vocational (if disorganized) approach to medical practice, they were forced to interact with specialists in private practice who did not share these same beliefs. In an effort to bring in more revenue, for example, PubliCare had invested heavily in its cardiology department. The cardiologists there—most of whom were from a prominent cardiology group in town—were known as being a clever, entrepreneurial, and pompous bunch. After discussing the generosity and collegiality of working at PubliCare, one social worker made an exception:

> Except for your cardiologists, 'cause they're just a bunch of idiots. . . . They [have] the greater-than-thou attitude, you know what I mean? "I'm better than everybody else," you know. And they're the moneymakers, so we have to treat them really nice.

Several of these specialists admitted patients at both PubliCare and HolyCare Hospitals and seemed interested in making money more than in anything else. As a facility with an "open staff," PubliCare allowed surgeons and other specialists to schedule procedures without any input from other doctors. During rounds one morning, for example, Polyakova visited a ninety-three-year-old with dementia who had just gone through hip surgery. When he told her that she had just woken up from surgery she said, "Oh no, that was years ago." She had no memory of the procedure ever having been scheduled. The hospitalist thought that such a surgery was a terrible waste of resources, but if the family wanted the surgery he knew that orthopedic surgeon would not have objected. The most Polyakova could do to limit unnecessary utilization was to avoid calling specialists too frequently.

Among the regular doctors at PubliCare there were countless stories of specialist avarice. A hospitalist remembered a patient who had surgery because of peripheral vascular disease in a leg. While he was recovering in the hospital, the hospitalist called a cardiologist for a consultation, but the cardiologist refused to see the patient: "He said, 'Well, [someone's] already done the procedure that I would do on his leg, and now you're asking me to clean up?'" According to the hospitalist, the cardiologist refused because the procedure had already been done and "that's where he make his money," not by providing a consultation. On other occasions, this hospitalist would call specialists for consultations, and they would answer, "There's nothing I'm going to do for him in the hospital, send him to my office after you discharge him"—another strategy for maximizing revenue. "That's totally unacceptable to me." A second hospitalist discussed the tricks by which a specialist on call would get out of doing consultations he or she did not want to do: the specialist would say the patient either was not sick enough for the specialist to feel justified in coming or was *too* sick and need to be seen by specialists at a more advanced facility. A case manager discussed how she would be cornered by certain surgeons and podiatrists on call who wanted her to find emergency insurance for their uninsured patients just so that they could get the reimbursement.

In the case of medical emergencies, though, doctors at PubliCare were usually able to convince the consultants on call to step in. The trick, then, was to avoid having to call the specialists that one despised. Polyakova said there was one gastroenterologist he always avoided and one cardiologist who—during our time together—had seemed to make it onto the same do-not-call list.

When confronted with poor patients who had conditions for which there were not specialists on call, and for which they could not find specialists willing to accept Medicaid, doctors at PubliCare would sometimes do procedures themselves. During one shift in the emergency room, the doctors exchanged stories about doing laceration repairs on people's faces when the plastic surgeons were—according to one of the doctors—"too busy doing breasts."

Doctors at PubliCare would also work to find and sustain relationships with the rare specialists willing to treat uninsured or Medicaid patients. At one point during a shift in the emergency room, a patient told one of the doctors about a gastroenterologist in town who accepted Medicaid. The doctor was impressed, and—returning to the nurses' station—told another doctor he was "willing to trade this information" with her in exchange for a direct phone number at the local clinic. Laughing, the other doctor said that the number at the clinic would be of no use, since one had to know the people at the clinic in order for them to help.

Like the social workers who agreed to refer insured patients in exchange for accepting the uninsured or underinsured, physicians would sometimes implicitly promise to send insured patients to particular specialists if they would agree to see the occasional uninsured or Medicaid patient. Without these sorts of arrangements, specialists in town might be punished for their own kindness. One doctor in the emergency room at PubliCare discussed how there had been a young orthopedic surgeon who was "extremely generous" with Medicaid patients. But he quickly got "overwhelmed, because if no one else is taking Medi-Cal, then everyone goes to you and your practice is bogged down with people who aren't paying."

In the competitive market for health care, the doctors at PubliCare—like their patients—were getting left behind. For some this seemed to be a principled choice, a courageous stand in defense of the right to health care for all. For others this seemed like an excuse to be left alone. Serving the marginal, and being marginal themselves, gave doctors the space to do things as they always had.

{ CHAPTER THREE }

Feels Like Home

On my first morning of observation at PubliCare Hospital, I entered the emergency department a few minutes before the 7 a.m. shift change. I told the clerk at the front desk that I was supposed to shadow Dr. David Harper. She guided me through a secured doorway and left me by the nursing station. There was no doctor to be found. I took a seat and waited until a nurse approached. Since Harper was running late, she told me, I should feel free to start seeing patients myself. She seemed to assume that I was a medical resident. Needless to say, the offer was rescinded when I told her I was a sociologist.

In his famous study of industrial organization, *Patterns of Industrial Bureaucracy,* Alvin Gouldner began by describing bureaucracy's absence: what he called the "indulgency pattern." This form of organization was characterized by its leniency—rules were loosely enforced, people were given second chances, and workers had a great deal of discretion in their daily activities. In sum, "supervisors temper[ed] the performance of their managerial role by taking into account obligations that would be relevant in other relationships."[1] Managers and workers treated one another like friends, like family. The indulgency pattern was undoubtedly inefficient in some respects, but it inspired trust and generated loyalty to the company among workers. This persisted until a new supervisor, who could no longer rely on these informal ties, came to the company and so sought to formalize rules and consequences.

A similar pattern of informality and collegiality characterized PubliCare, despite Westside Health's attempts to institutionalize a more formal order. In part, this seemed to result from organizational inertia—the same people had been working in the same ways for decades. But this environment also seemed to reflect the care that the hospital delivered. As one doctor explained, "You're kinda all in this pullin' up your bootstraps and rollin' up your sleeves and jumpin' in the muck." The undifferentiated "muck" of human suffering found an analogy in the undifferentiated roles of hospital staff. Just as practitioners were forced to rely on informal ties and reciprocal obligations to take care of their patients, the same ties and obligations found their way into practitioners' relationships with one another. The doctor continued, "You're in it together, and there's a camaraderie [at PubliCare]."

Feels Like Home

Adriana Martinelli was the nurse director of the emergency department at Publi-Care. She had been born and raised in a large urban area near Las Lomas. While she was still in high school, her older brother, and confidante, was killed in a car accident. She became a "lost soul" until her parents encouraged her to go to nursing school. "The way I look at it now, it [was] . . . divine intervention." She found her calling in the oncology ward, where she would hold patients' hands at night, "letting them talk and hear things and letting them express things." She would celebrate recoveries and grieve losses with patients' families. Years later she still held on to the letters of gratitude she had received.

But she was young at the time, she recognized in hindsight, and was still grieving her brother's death. She got "too attached," and stopped being able to separate her own life from those of her patients. She transitioned into emergency medicine and realized that since she was something of an "adrenaline junkie," it was a good fit. Martinelli's training had been in a Catholic hospital, but she came to PubliCare Hospital in 1985 and liked the patient population: "They were really sick, and at the same time, they appreciated so much—it wasn't an expectation to be professional to them. They appreciated it." In 1996, when Westside Health took over the hospital, her boss began asking her to work shifts that made it difficult to take care of her two children at home. She left the facility and began working as a nurse manager in a variety of capacities at other facilities in Las Lomas, but her nostalgia for PubliCare lingered. When the nursing director called her in 2009, asking her to become the director of PubliCare's emergency room, "I just started crying, 'cause it felt like I was going home. That's all it was. It was coming back home to this place."

Since she began her work as director, Martinelli had been feeling pressure to increase the department's scores on patient satisfaction surveys.[2] She wished that the scores could reflect the staff's commitment to the place:

> We don't have the money, but we have the heart. . . . We don't have what other people have, we don't have new facilities, we don't have new equipment. You know, getting our floors waxed here is a challenge. But they have the heart. And

I wish I could put that on my frickin' patient satisfaction scores. That would be a really good thing for me!

Many nurses and ancillary staff throughout the hospital felt like their ties to one another helped the hospital stand out. According to one social worker, staff members at PubliCare were "so much nicer and kinder" than those at the neighboring hospitals, where she also worked: "And when we say we're a family, there's nothing on one floor that ain't happenin' on all floors, you know? When a party is happening here, everybody comes to it." A department manager who had worked at all three hospitals said that PubliCare was unique because "everybody thinks of each other as family. We have a lot of really long-term employees. . . . People know each other. Whole families work here." A nurse in the emergency room said that when a colleague is going through something difficult, "the whole ER will show up at your house." When a colleague's son died, she remembered, "everybody showed up." At HolyCare Hospital, where this nurse also worked, "you might have some of your coworkers show up, but that would be it." When Westside Health began a round of layoffs, a social worker recalled, some staff members who were close to retirement "gave up their jobs . . . so other people [could] stay. . . . It really follows the model of 'I am my brother's keeper.'"

Those who worked at PubliCare Hospital had different explanations for the sense of camaraderie they felt there. Some thought that it was because so many workers had been there so long. A charge nurse said that since many workers had been there "twenty years or more," they "have a history together." The sense of "teamwork, autonomy, and respect" was what "keeps a lot of us here at PubliCare." Martinelli suggested that it might be because "all of us grew up together. . . . We're watching our kids all graduate together and things like that." A case manager said that "people don't really leave this place when they work here." As a result, "we have a really good, tight-knit family, and we consider everybody's job equally important here."

Others connected the spirit of the hospital to the kind of patients that they saw. One doctor said that he thought nurses liked it at PubliCare because "they feel they are doing something good here. They're not just putting in their hours, clocking in, filling in the computer, you know, they're actually doing something that no one else will do." Another doctor said, "If you talk to respiratory therapists, specialty nurses, they can go work anywhere they want, and some of them do. But you talk to people who have done it, and a lot of them say, 'Well I always return here because there's something else I get working here. I feel like I'm not just a cog in the corporate machine.'" A charge nurse theorized that work at PubliCare "takes a different breed, maybe a little lower key . . . to have the patience to deal with a lot of the indigents or whatever." This sentiment was echoed by another nurse who had been "burnt out" from working on a trauma unit: "I came back here, within working three months my blood pressure went back down, my nightmares stopped, and everything like that." Dealing with the mundane problems of the poor—"people who come in the middle of the night who don't know how to treat fevers"—felt like something of a break compared to the cases she had been seeing.

Still others believed that PubliCare's status as a teaching hospital contributed to its egalitarianism. According to one nurse manager, the residency program provided for a consistent stream of intelligent, creative young people who were able to keep relationships "collegial" instead of "patriarchal." The head of the residency program thought that it gave "a certain lifeblood to an institution that's beyond just employment. . . . People are here to take care of patients and all, but I think that the fact that we're an educational institution, that we have young people learning and teaching, that gives credence to it." Furthermore, many of the medical residents depended upon the wisdom of the nursing staff as they gained their footing in the hospital, inverting traditional power dynamics. And the institution's commitment to education sometimes meant that people went far beyond their job descriptions in the spirit of training others. For example, on the floor one day, a nurse discussed her role as a volunteer preceptor, training new paramedics so they understood the organization of the emergency room. A nurse practitioner asked her with disbelief, "You do that for free?" According to the nurse practitioner, paramedics got paid approximately $1,000 for each student they taught. She scoffed and said, "Nurses are stupid." The nurse agreed: "I was doing it out of the goodness of my heart! We *are* stupid." She added later, "We're too good-hearted."

Even if they sometimes felt their generosity abused, nurses and ancillary staff at PubliCare generally were willing to work for lower wages than people in similar positions at either HolyCare or PubliCare. As one doctor said, "Most of the nurses will tell you that they work here for less money, but they wouldn't work anywhere else." One nurse at PubliCare joked that when people called her asking for donations to charity she would say, "Well, first of all, I don't have any money, but second of all, my work is my donation to life." Another nurse went further and implied that the lower pay actually attracted nicer people: "It seems to me that [the] people [who] are willing to make a lot less than [at] GroupCare and a little bit less than [at] HolyCare are the same people who just are generally nicer people."

Several workers at PubliCare had also spent time working at HolyCare or GroupCare. At GroupCare, one charge nurse said, employees were "really well paid" and had a "very strong union." But there was something missing there: "They do their job and they just leave." At PubliCare, on the other hand, "The nurses don't just leave 'cause your shift's over" but supported one another above and beyond the requirements of the workday. There was more interdependence at PubliCare. Compared with management at PubliCare, many nurses suggested, managers at HolyCare were unsupportive. One nurse thought that HolyCare was "management centered," whereas PubliCare was "employee centered." Part of the difference, it seemed, was that many of the managers at PubliCare had begun by working on the floors. As one nurse said, "Regular nurses became management, and they still were real people and helped you out as much as possible, and you were all in it together."

Shared Responsibility

Relationships between doctors, nurses, and managers were characterized by an informal egalitarianism at PubliCare. This was in evidence in the emergency room, where nurses seemed unfazed by the presence of their physician counterparts—they would bounce rubber balls against the wall, for example, or make collages out of construction paper while doctors worked nearby. A case manager said that it was "just a vibe or a feeling when you're here, you just kind of know right away that it's not tiered; everybody's on the same level." According to a nurse, doctors and nurses looked out for one another but also held one another accountable. She recalled an incident in which an ER doctor, who had only been working for two months at PubliCare, was fired after fighting with a nurse. She continued:

> You do not talk to the nurses that way, but do you know what? We have the ultimate respect for our physicians. We don't let the patients abuse our doctors, we don't let other people abuse our doctors, we don't let people take advantage of our doctors. We support our physicians just as much as they support us, and we kind of think of each other as a family and a team.

The camaraderie between doctors and other employees was palpable. On one morning, several nurses stood around joking with one of the ER doctors. Dan, one of the nurses, had borrowed the doctor's truck for a weekend and had taken it on Route 1, a highway that winds along the California coast. Several days later, after the nurse returned the truck, its steering shaft broke. Had this happened on the highway, everyone agreed, it would have jeopardized Dan's life. The doctor looked sheepish: "It was a close call," he mumbled. I was struck not only by the casual way in which the nurses and doctors teased one another, but also by how fluidly the relationships in the emergency room seemed to extend beyond the facility. "We kibitz around here," said a case manager. "Everybody jokes around with each other."

The informal social relationship between doctors and nurses was also evident in clinical practice. As one doctor put it, nurses liked working at PubliCare because they could "act like doctors here." At both HolyCare and at GroupCare, doctors and nurses were careful to abide by legal restrictions on nurse autonomy. At PubliCare, in contrast, nurses would do a wide range of interventions on patients before doctors entered the room. A nurse manager in the emergency department said, "I know all of us here are really comfortable going ahead and doing everything, and we know our physicians will back us up." Nurses would do a lot of the ordering—setting up the IV, administering doses of morphine, and so on—and have the doctors rubber-stamp it ex post facto. A charge nurse discussed how her interactions with the physician staff felt unique in that "we are really, really a team." She said that she valued having to "stretch herself" at PubliCare, she liked the autonomy and responsibility that came along with her role: "I don't mind doing more than I technically could, as long as it's safe."

Both HolyCare Hospital and GroupCare Hospital had clear hierarchies of authority. At PubliCare, however, power felt more nebulous. Nurses and ancillary workers were each represented by labor unions, but in each case the unions were relatively weak. Even head administrators from Westside Health seemed remarkably absent from the hospital's day-to-day operations. According to one nurse, PubliCare Hospital had been losing money for so long that it was something of a pariah: "It's like [Westside] could care less. They hate us; we are the money pit." As a result, she suggested, the administration had adopted a sort of benign neglect. It did not micromanage the facility, nor did it make necessary investments in things like heating systems, meaning that "one year we didn't have heat in the middle of winter, and we had space heaters and it was forty-two degrees in the ER."

There was a vacuum of power at PubliCare that no one seemed eager to fill. Most doctors I interviewed there seemed not to feel invested in making changes in hospital policy, nor did they feel they had mechanisms through which to do it. For example, the ER group would hold monthly meetings at which only the eight partners (and none of the part-timers) were invited. This meant that many members of the department medical staff were left out of conversations about practice protocols or changes in department or hospital policy entirely. But even those who *were* partners did not seem to have much at stake in changing things. While the medical staff would sometimes make requests for pieces of equipment, they would rarely voice more controversial demands. As one said, "There's a lot of things we'd like to change, but we've been here long enough to . . . ask ourselves this question: What's the most important thing? And we always come down to patient care." It seemed that, for this doctor at least, an interest in broader hospital policy felt inconsistent with a concern for patient care. A part-time ER doctor suggested that he was "not brave enough to go spouting off about" hospital policy. A second part-timer explained her own powerlessness by saying that since she was hired by the group that had been given the hospital contract, she was a contractee of a contractee: one of the "scabs of the scabs, you know, in a certain way."

When people did try to be proactive about organizational change it was an uphill battle. On one occasion, a department manager in the emergency department had gone to the physician chair (a "stick-in-the-mud") to complain that doctors were not following protocol. The chair responded that he could not "ask [his doctors] to do another thing." She responded, "This is the law. You have to ask 'em." But as of our interview, she was still being stonewalled. Each department at PubliCare Hospital was something of a silo, she suggested: "A lot of times what happens within these walls stays within these walls." As a last resort, this nurse director had begun to appeal to hospital administrators about the doctors' intransigence—something previously unheard of—and she hinted that she might even recommend that the hospital find a different physicians' group to run the department. While the physician director of the emergency room would "never admit it," she continued, he was technically subordinate to Westside administrators.

Organizational change seemed to get mired in old habits and old loyalties. For example, during a meeting between the emergency room and Polyakova, who was chief of the hospitalist department, several ER doctors complained about one of the hospitalists who would refuse to see patients in the emergency room and would often ignore or antagonize the ER doctors who called him. Polyakova told the group that he would take care of it but said to me privately that it was a difficult situation, since the offending doctor had actually hired Polyakova many years before and so Polyakova felt some loyalty to him. These loyalties may have helped to sustain a certain kind of communitarian feel among doctors at PubliCare, but they came at the expense of a coordinated system.

Although both nurses and ancillary workers at PubliCare were unionized, workers' informal attachments across the lines of occupation and status seemed to weaken workers' solidarity. During the heyday of public sector unionism in the 1970s the union at PubliCare hospital—which at the time represented both nurses and ancillary workers—had been a model of activism and solidarity, according to some hospital old-timers. A labor representative at PubliCare said that in the old days, there would often be sixty to a hundred workers attending union meetings, filling up the meeting room to capacity. But since then, the union's power had diminished. The nurses had broken off to join the California Nurses Association (CNA), and the ancillary workers had been shuffled among different Service Employee International Union (SEIU) locals. While some people suggested that the union legacy lived on in the camaraderie that workers felt at the facility, this solidarity now seemed more closely connected to the hospital as a whole than to any type of labor organization or class identity.

Indeed, many seemed to take the benefits of unionization for granted. One nurse admitted that the union might help explain why nurses were treated so much better at PubliCare Hospital than at HolyCare (whose nurses were part of a weak independent association) but seemed not to have spent much time thinking about it before I asked. A case manager appreciated the security that the union gave her but said, "We know it's there, but it doesn't, you know—I don't really think about it." When I asked a social worker about the union, she said, "My union is a great union." But she quickly shifted emphasis: "Let's leave the union out of this, simply for the fact that is who do you work for? I work for some of the greatest managers in the world, who really do everything they can to make us happy. So when you got managers like that, you don't need a union." Others valued the union but seemed to think that it threatened to interfere with the informal relationships among staff at the facility. One nurse said that there had been some resistance to joining the CNA because things have to "go down by chain of command of who has authority. . . . There's more restrictions." She liked the current system better, where people more informally tried to "cover each other's shifts," and said that the nurses in the emergency room were "holding our ground" with the union to keep it informal.

There seemed a similar ambivalence towards the union among many ancillary workers. According to a union representative, many employees felt that—given the hospital's financial difficulties—they would undermine the health of the community by advocating on their own behalf. Moreover, a number of managers had previously been ancillary workers themselves, and many workers seemed to feel more loyal to these managers than to their union. One respiratory therapist had become a human resources director. As the union representative remembered, "[The workers all] know him, and he's just a great guy. . . . They always believed him over me, and I would get kicked out, and have the door slammed on me." Another nurse became a nursing director after having served as a leader in the nurses' union, again suggesting fluidity between union and management that made labor solidarity difficult to sustain. At PubliCare, informality blurred status distinctions but also precluded any kind of organized voice.

Enter the Entrepreneurs

The informal, egalitarian culture at PubliCare—reproduced over decades through generations of doctors and nurses—was in many ways incompatible with Westside Health's desire to turn a profit on the facility. In recent years, Westside had sought to change this culture by turning to a different set of entrepreneurial physicians who saw in PubliCare opportunities for private profit.

Sierra Medical Foundation (SMF) was a multispeciality physicians' group in Las Lomas that consisted of family practice doctors, cardiologists, and small numbers of several other specialties. Historically, this group had done most of its business with HolyCare—the only local hospital with an advanced cardiac center.

Yet the group's dependence on HolyCare had created a strategic disadvantage for the group, since HolyCare dictated the terms of its relationship with them. This issue came to a head in the mid-1990s, when SMF sought to bring onto its staff a cardiac surgeon—a move that would have greatly enhanced the organization's revenue. HolyCare had already contracted its cardiac surgery to an independent local surgeon and refused to grant privileges to a second on the staff of SMF. As a second cardiologist from SMF remembered it, "it was a pretty hard-line business stance."

Rather than sue HolyCare, which would have been financially risky, SMF reached out to Westside Health, which had recently leased PubliCare and was looking to make the hospital profitable. As one cardiologist put it, "We decided to bleed [HolyCare] a different way." As an aside, he admitted, "We're assholes!" Beginning in the late 1990s, several cardiologists from SMF—working closely with Westside Health—began building the heart center at PubliCare, which opened its doors in 2001. PubliCare constructed a new wing of the hospital in order to house the center. The center had its own entrance, its own plush furnishings, and boasted—at the time of its opening—a coronary angiography machine that could take images of the heart with higher resolution than the equipment at HolyCare.

While the move infuriated HolyCare, it was of great financial benefit to PubliCare and a wise move for SMF. According to a cardiologist from SMF, the heart center "legitimized PubliCare as a hospital," helping it to shed some of its legacy as the indigent facility. According to another SMF cardiologist, the program had become "a big boon to the hospital" and played a role in "changing the general tilt in the future of hospitals" in the area. It also benefited SMF, in at least two ways. First, since PubliCare was so financially dependent on SMF, doctors from SMF had tremendous authority in the organization. One SMF cardiologist said, "PubliCare has a history right now of being more physician-friendly [than HolyCare], simply because they needed to be, because they needed any support they could get." As of 2010, one SMF cardiologist directed PubliCare's heart catheterization lab, and several other cardiologists from SMF played leadership roles within the hospital. And since SMF doctors built the heart center at PubliCare, it was organized to these doctors' specifications. As one cardiologist put it, "I built that cath lab. It has all the things that I want, I know exactly what balloons, what stents, what wires—I mean, I know all that. It's not the same at HolyCare."

Second, SMF now occupied positions of authority in both PubliCare and HolyCare and so was able to exert leverage with both. As one SMF leader put it diplomatically, "All along we felt like . . . it's better for [us] to be somewhat independent, and if you put all your eggs in one basket, it makes you vulnerable to the unpredictable changes in medicine." PubliCare and HolyCare had each sought to make SMF a part of their respective medical foundations, but SMF had been enjoying the power of their relative independence. Another SMF leader suggested that there was power in being able to "play one hospital off the other, just like in any business."

While the informal, collegial culture of PubliCare remained remarkably resilient across most departments of the hospital, PubliCare's cardiac center exemplified how lead administrators planned to effect change—not by forcing old actors to practice in new ways, but by bringing in new actors altogether. This plan for organizational change was made even more apparent as PubliCare administrators tried to convince SMF to join Westside's medical foundation. PubliCare had promised that should SMF physicians join the foundation, they could remain distinct from the other doctors affiliated with PubliCare. SMF doctors did not want to share profits—or an identity—with the old-timers at the hospital, whom they considered laggards. One SMF cardiologist said, "You can't decide you're going to work four days a week and [think] you're gonna make a million bucks. It's not that easy. And so you need people who are willing to work, take call, be available, do the hard parts of medicine in order to make things work." The only way they would consider a formal affiliation with Westside was if they could retain a sense of distinction from the doctors who had traditionally practiced there.

The Community against the Market

If Westside's alliance with SMF represented a reformist approach to changing the culture and economics of PubliCare, in January 2007 Westside went revolutionary. Having been unable to make ends meet, Westside announced it would close PubliCare altogether. As an ER doctor at PubliCare explained, Westside had hoped they could "change [the hospital] around . . . without losing the ability to take care of patients and leaving people out in the street." But this proved more difficult than the organization had expected. Around the same time that Westside announced PubliCare's closure, however, the local press uncovered that Westside had bought a plot of land on which it planned to build a new specialist facility. The cardiologists would be safe. An ER doctor at HolyCare suspected that Westside would "build [the specialists] a catheterization laboratory, build them an orthopedic center, and become [a] specialty hospital." Meanwhile, PubliCare planned to transfer to HolyCare the health access agreement it had signed with the county, ridding itself of its obligation to the poor and underserved. HolyCare, in turn, pledged that it would expand its inpatient capacity by eighty beds, expand its urgent care services, and double the size of its emergency department in order to accommodate the new traffic.

Those who worked at PubliCare—from ancillary workers to physicians—found out about the closure in the local paper. Many felt abandoned by hospital administration. As one ancillary worker put it, "It felt like it was upper Westside management, probably the CEO, saying . . . 'This hospital isn't making money, isn't making enough money, so we're gonna close you.'" For her, this felt like abandonment: "You've got an agreement with the county, you knew what you were getting into, you knew how bad it was. You should have seen this if you really looked." Practitioners and patients were united in their outrage. An ancillary worker remembered the feeling of solidarity she had with patients, who were similarly outraged by the news: "We had two ladies that were eighty-seven and eighty-nine, and they were knee patients, and they probably knew everybody in the county, [given] the phone calls they were making that day."

Workers and community members did not take the news sitting down. During one memorable county board of supervisors meeting in February 2007, a large hall was packed with hundreds of concerned community members, almost all of whom were opposed to PubliCare's closure. Many were concerned that HolyCare did not have the capacity to handle the increased patient volume that would result from the closure. Others worried that PubliCare's closure would signal the end of the facility's family residency program, on which the county depended for a supply of local family practice doctors. Women's health advocates were concerned about HolyCare's lack of women's reproductive services, services for which many depended on PubliCare. Labor unions were concerned about layoffs and HolyCare's historical resistance to unionization. Some of the attendees who lived close to HolyCare were worried about increases in helicopter and ambulance traffic.

Over the summer of 2007, several different coalitions of health care advocates united to put a halt to what became known as the Westside-HolyCare "transaction." Over the next twelve months, these coalitions convinced the county board of supervisors to block the deal and uphold the contract that Westside had signed with the county. In the face of this public outrage and opposition, Westside relented, and in recent years had been working to fulfill its contractual obligations by opening a new, smaller, general hospital—scheduled for opening around the time this book goes to print.

But in spite of this new community investment, many at PubliCare were suspicious of Westside's motives. The announcement of PubliCare's closure in 2007 "ruined a lot of people's faith in this company," according to one nurse. A nurse administrator concluded that Westside was building the new facility mainly to change private patients' perceptions of Westside Health: "Having the brand new facilities and be[ing] clean, with pretty floors and stuff will really help . . . bring[] the insured back." It did not seem lost on anyone that a new facility in a new location might also present an obstacle to the poor and underinsured who had traditionally relied on PubliCare. One hospitalist thought that if Westside was truly committed to maintaining services to the indigent, it would have located the new facilities in downtown Las Lomas. Instead, it felt like they were getting out of Dodge. And Westside seemed to have been divesting from the old facilities in

anticipation of its transition to a new location. One nurse said that many departments that were vibrant before the planned closure—orthopedics, pediatrics, and
transitional care—had been cut back or closed since then. While practitioners
and the public had managed to preserve some degree of right to care at PubliCare,
the future of the organization—and of the public's right to care—felt insecure.

Since leasing PubliCare in 1996, Westside Health had taken the hospital out
of the public sphere, but the company found it could not take the public sphere
out of the hospital. Even the corporation's effort to close the facility became a site
of community struggle over the right to care. Today, Westside continues with its
plan to open a smaller state-of-the-art facility and replace PubliCare—as if Publi-
Care's organizational culture and commitments, so incompatible with success on
the market, were baked into the very bricks and mortar of the place.

PART TWO

HolyCare Moralizes the Market

B y the early decades of the twentieth century, the hospital had established itself more firmly as a center of medical authority and medical practice. Because of the new technology available in hospitals, and because of physicians' increasing dependence on these facilities for their own practices, the wealthy began to consider these institutions for their own inpatient (and especially surgical) care.[1] As the medical profession formalized its authority during the first decades of the twentieth century, physicians exerted increasing authority over admissions to the hospital and over the inner workings of the organization more generally.[2]

In order to attract paying patients, a new breed of "voluntary" hospital consciously worked to dispel the hospital's reputation as an impersonal, dehumanizing place in which the poor and desperate were warehoused or reduced to clinical material. If the almshouse was concerned with the provision of care as a right, the private hospital of the early twentieth century focused energy on the emotional and spiritual *meanings* of hospital care. Some early voluntary hospitals opened special wards for paying patients so as to better honor the "dignity" of these patients. For these paying patients, writes Charles Rosenberg, "private rooms offered the comfort and convenience of a hotel with the ambience of a home."[3] Paying patients were spared from the gaze of medical students, since "[p]rivacy and payment seemed naturally allied."[4]

The emergence of a market for hospital care was thus accompanied by efforts at imbuing this care with practices that reaffirmed the paying patient's humanity and *distinguished* the hospital from other sorts of business practices. Understood in this light, the Catholic hospital's centrality in the emerging market for hospital services is unsurprising. During the first half of the twentieth century, sisters throughout the United States fluidly combined vocational devotion with shrewd political and economic calculations. To be sure, sisters found deep meaning in the care they were able to provide for their patients. As Barbra Mann Wall argues, the sisters (and some brothers) who ran these hospitals "conceived of illness . . . within a spiritual framework, and they viewed themselves as spiritual agents of care."[5] Yet these same sisters, according to Sioban Nelson, turned "overwhelming social need into opportunities for the development of health care services to the American public," and established themselves as the earliest female entrepreneurs in the United States.[6] It was sisters' religious identity, sexual chastity, and relative anonymity that allowed them the institutional space to build their own organizations within a broader patriarchal society[7] freeing them up to act "like men" well before other women of their time.[8] And while many Catholic health systems could trace their origins to acts of charity and self-sacrifice, by the turn of the twentieth century religious hospitals were heavily dependent on patients who could pay.[9] Income from paying patients made up approximately three-quarters of the revenue of religious hospitals in 1904, compared with approximately half the revenue of nonsectarian hospitals.[10]

As the market for hospital care expanded through the 1930s and 1940s, the Catholic Hospital Association (CHA) played a critical role at the national level in putting forward a "voluntary ideal" of hospital care, which could protect patients from crass commercialism, on the one hand, and a dehumanizing state bureaucracy on the other. In opposing the Wagner-Murray-Dingell bill for universal health insurance in 1943, for example, the CHA argued that under the bill, patients would become "wards of the state as opposed to wards of society," that the bill would undermine the "dignity of the patient" and destroy the "Catholic attitude toward the patient."[11] Instead, along with the American Hospital Association, the CHA lobbied in favor of the Hospital Survey and Construction Act of (or Hill-Burton Act), which passed in 1946, offering grants and guaranteed loans to support hospital construction and expansion with minimal government oversight.[12]

The voluntary hospital rose to prominence alongside an ascending medical profession. As paying patients became a more important source of revenue for hospitals, hospitals in turn became more dependent on the physicians who could refer these patients.[13] In the almshouse and early voluntary hospital, the hospital had provided doctors small salaries or paid them only in room, board, and prestige; physicians were not allowed to charge for their services.[14] But by the first decade of the twentieth century, increasing numbers of voluntary hospitals allowed doctors to collect fees from patients and had created "open staff" systems, meaning that any certified physician could practice within them.[15] The voluntary hospital became a physicians' workshop. Paul Starr trenchantly observes the wider economic context of the medical profession's emergence: "In the same period as the crafts were being subordinated to large corporations, the medical profession was institutionalizing its autonomy. The doctors escaped becoming victims of capitalism and became small capitalists instead."[16]

The voluntary hospital was particularly appealing to a young medical profession because of its sensitivity to the vocational ethics of care. As the hospital emerged as a center of medical practice, some doctors had expressed concern that an impersonal organization might jeopardize the "spiritual nature of the relationship between patient and physician."[17] Indeed, the physician's power in the early twentieth century was based largely on the patient's emotional dependence on the doctor and the doctor's capacity to "cure" by suggestion.[18] There was an important resonance, then, between the aura of mystery associated with an emergent medical profession[19] and the symbols and practices prominent in Catholic and other voluntary hospitals. Rosemary Stevens writes that these hospitals were "visible expressions of broad, non-monetary, community expectations about social virtue and moral worth, to be set against the crass materialism of business. The essential nature of any profession (and its institutions), it was claimed, was to be 'socially victorious over selfish interest.'"[20] While hospital care had become a service sold on the market, this market could only exist in conjunction with professional and spiritual values irreducible to it.

There was a final link between the emerging market for hospital care and the religious or voluntary hospital, in that notions of religiosity and voluntarism helped bring about a subservient, low-wage nursing staff that facilitated the work of physicians without making demands of their own.[21] When voluntary hospitals as a group were seeking exemption from the National Labor Relations Act in the early 1930s, the voluntary hospital lobby argued "low pay was a virtue, since it attracted staff who were motivated by the 'right values.'"[22] The role of Catholic hospitals was essential to this argument because "it extended, by analogy, the dedicated service of Roman Catholic nuns to the jobs of all hospital workers."[23]

By the 1940s, Las Lomas was forced to confront the problem of the paying patient. Throughout the early decades of the twentieth century, the County Hospital (now PubliCare) provided the most state-of-the-art medical care in the area. In 1937, another hospital building was constructed on the poor-farm property, funded in large part by a grant from the Public Works Administration. This same year the University of California established a residency program at the hospital, and many of the graduates of the program stayed in the county as private practitioners, helping to secure the area's reputation as a regional hub for medical care.

As of 1940, the County Hospital—with 178 acute care beds—was the only hospital in the area to meet the certification requirements of the American College of Surgeons. The problem was that this hospital treated indigent patients almost exclusively. According to a 1940 report on the facility, prepared for the board of supervisors, the County Hospital provided an annual average of 118,883 patient-days to indigent patients compared to an average of 5,204 patient-days to those who could afford to pay. A second report in 1940, this one to the county's medical society, criticized the fact that the County Hospital, "in spite of the publicity to the contrary . . . does not accept pay patients other than those who can not pay a part of the cost." The two small private hospitals in Las Lomas combined had only fifty-two acute care beds. This second report described a "lack of facilities" at both private hospitals, made worse by the fact that the competition between them forced patients to "pay for two complete sets of overhead." When the wealthy needed more intensive care, they had to travel almost sixty miles to the nearest hospital. The report concluded:

> It is a matter of some irony when we truthfully state that the indigent patient is able to command hospitalization without cost to himself which meets the standards accredited by the American College of Surgeons, while those who have money with which to pay for the service are unable to procure that service within this county.

Similarly, the report to the board of supervisors suggested that the medically indigent were being cared for "at the expense of, and in a better manner than the middle class income group—except that their mythical pride is not pampered to any costly extent." Private physicians were also frustrated with the private hospital practice in the area: "With inadequate records, absence of clinical and laboratory facilities, barest diagnostic equipment, minimal nursing standards being characteristic of these [private] hospitals, he (the doctor) admits a deplorable situation."

The choice facing the county, then, was whether to expand the County Hospital and open its doors to paying patients or to subsidize the construction of a private facility for paying patients. The report to the board of supervisors strongly recommended that medical services in the county be centralized in a public facility: "All expensive equipment should be centralized in a health facility, so located as to allow purchase of the finest (equipment) most comprehensively and economically through the avoidance of duplication." The report continued, "If anything should be democratized, certainly the right to receive adequate medical care and facilities should be." Yet the report also recognized that the "specious propaganda of owners of private hospitals" had influenced the debate, as had physicians' narrow conception of their interests: "Our present unplanned, anarchistic, ruthlessly competitive system of medical practice requires the physician to keep an eye too much on the patients [*sic*] purse and not enough on his health, and a long-view plan."

Private interests would prevail. Physicians had been making "many . . . attempts to induce sectarian (Catholic) institutions to build and operate a hospital of accredited standards," according to the board of supervisors report. In 1946, the town's chamber of commerce found a cherry-and-walnut orchard near downtown Las Lomas on which it proposed to develop such a facility. The fundraising effort that followed, according to one local account, was "one of the most successful in [the area's] history." The town also succeeded in its pursuit of a Catholic order of nuns, the Sisters of St. Francis, to operate the hospital. As the legend goes, the mayor of the town "climbed a cherry tree in the orchard" to pick some fruit for the head of the order, "a nice hometown touch to begin a business venture." HolyCare Hospital opened its doors on January 1, 1950. It quickly became the "ultra-professional" hospital in the area, the hospital that brought the "Age of the Specialist" to Las Lomas.

The middle decades of the twentieth century—from the establishment of Blue Cross insurance and the passage of Social Security in the 1930s to the Hill-Burton Act of 1946, to labor's successful post-war negotiations for health insurance coverage, and to the establishment of Medicare and Medicaid in the 1960s—were bountiful years for the voluntary hospital and the medical profession as a whole. Throughout this period, as recounted in the detailed histories of Rosemary Stevens, Paul Starr, and others, hospitals and physicians—appealing to the twin ideals of voluntarism and professionalism—were able to secure large amounts of public funding with minimal amounts of public oversight. Demand for private hospital beds consistently exceeded supply in Las Lomas during these years.

Moralizing Markets and Marketing Morality

For many years, the Sisters of St. Francis gave HolyCare Hospital—and the St. Francis Health System as a whole—a sense of common purpose. In a recent internal report put together by a consulting firm for the system, leaders throughout the company—from physicians to managers to system executives—reported that they identified with the "mission of the Sisters" more than they did with their professional groups, with their local hospitals, or even with the health system itself. This sentiment seemed to be shared by ancillary workers as well. A unit manager at HolyCare hospital told me simply, "To me the Sisters represented the conscience of the hospital." She continued, "Whenever the hospital administration would start getting greedy and start thinking about money versus people, the sisters would kind of go, 'Wait a minute, that's not how you treat people.'"

But the Sisters of St. Francis were aging. In 2012, the average age of an American nun was seventy-four.[24] Their relationship to their facilities was thus changing. Where they once actively administered and nursed within their hospitals, they now played a more indirect role. An administrator at HolyCare recalled how one sister, in her last years at the facility, had taken it upon herself to walk the halls giving "unconditional positive regard." According to the administrator, the sister was "the visual cue of the mission and the values, and she [made] people feel affirmed and feel part of the legacy." In 2007, however, this sister and her colleague retired and left Las Lomas, meaning that the sisters no longer had any active presence at HolyCare at all.

In response to the sisters' disengagement from their facilities, the health system sought to inculcate lay leaders with the Catholic values on which the hospital was founded. A Jewish medical administrator at HolyCare recalled going on a "pilgrimage" to the European village where the Sisters of St. Francis were founded in order to "understand this heritage . . . understand what we're responsible for." He also participated in four years of training within the system to learn the history of the order and to gain an understanding of Catholic social teaching. "It has made me no less Jewish," he continued, "But I certainly understand what the responsibility is in a leadership role in this Catholic ministry."

Perhaps the religious values on which U.S. Catholic hospitals were founded were always at least in part a framework intended to attract the wealthy, paying patient. But in recent years the instrumental use of these values seemed more transparent, at least to some. One union leader argued that since patients "want to feel that they're more than just a number," there was an economic value to "having the religious brand on your hospital." The Catholic hospital's appeal to spirituality could thus be understood as only one strategy among many used by upscale hospitals to respond to patients' emotional vulnerabilities—and to win their business.

This was the contradiction at HolyCare. Of the three hospitals, HolyCare worked most explicitly to distinguish hospital care from other businesses—to imbue care with emotional and spiritual significance for patients and for employees. Many who worked within the organization were particularly sensitive to these dimensions of hospital care and took pride in the way in which the organization prioritized the "dignity" of each patient. On the other hand, HolyCare was also, in many ways, the most business-minded. Its appeal to spiritual values provided a cover of moral legitimacy to entrepreneurial administrators and doctors. These values were advertised in order to attract a wealthy clientele and were promoted internally in order to secure a disciplined and subservient workforce. Paradoxically, however, the instrumental use of these spiritual values threatened to erode their power, reducing them to little more than HR rhetoric. So the hospital worked to buttress the legitimacy of these values at the same time they sought to put them to use. Conversely, to the extent that these values *did* have some autonomy from the economic interests of hospital administrators, they provided discursive opportunities for subordinate constituencies to make claims in relationship to them.

CHAPTER FOUR

Sacred Encounters

Amanda Roberts, a chaplain at HolyCare Hospital, was a heavy-set woman in her early forties with wide eyes and an expressive face. Roberts had been a graduate student in chemistry before she decided to begin a divinity program: "I decided that instead of being in a lab, what I really wanted to do was to be out working with people . . . to make the matter of spirit, and how we are really alive and awake in this life, part of the focus of my life." During a hospital residency she quickly came to appreciate both "how much someone coming from a spiritual perspective was needed in the hospital," and "how small my own God had been." Within the hospital she could "really feel the presence of the spirit." There, she was able to help people "to live, and live after they have experienced some of the most horrifying and difficult times in their lives." She continued, "I don't make it happen. The resilience, the amazing ability of the human self to come back from the pit is not my doing, but I accompany in amazement and encouragement."

For Roberts, delving into the depths of human suffering and redemption came naturally, but she acknowledged that this was not always what her patients needed: "Because we do not know what any interaction might bring, the ability to be flexible in how we approach is the sign of a skillful chaplain. . . . If the patient wants me to be light and positive, I can do that." In the ICU, she found, many patients and families would go into emotional shock. In those situations, "for someone then to bring you a cup of water, for someone to come in and be able to pray, when you as a patient or family member feel that you can't. . . . [That] is grace."

The emotional flexibility that Roberts's job required was exhausting: "The emotional demands, the size, the amount of flexibility required to go from situation to situation, from anguish to lightheartedness, from death to birth, is such a stretching thing." She had been uncertain she would make it as a chaplain, especially at the beginning, when other people's suffering made her see "how easily it could have been myself, my family." Over the years, though, she learned to separate patients' suffering from her own fears and realized that "it's not helpful for the patient or the family or for me to feel horrified, or for me to even try to imagine what they're feeling." Her role, instead, was "to be open-hearted and to serve and to be kind, to help them remember the presence of the divine however they name it." The trick was to achieve deep emotional identification without burnout. After all, she laughed, "It would be hard . . . to be moved by a burnt-out chaplain." In her daily interactions with physicians, nurses, and ancillary staff, she tried to help them find this balance as well.

Roberts was one of six chaplains who worked at HolyCare Hospital. By comparison, GroupCare had only one chaplain on staff and PubliCare had none. The size of the chaplaincy program at HolyCare meant that it was possible for a chaplain to visit each patient within three days of that patient's arrival. Joanne Logan, the supervisor of the chaplains, who managed the hospital's Department of Mission Integration and Spiritual Care, had sought to match each chaplain with a department suitable for the chaplain's emotional disposition. The oncology ward, for example, had a chaplain who was especially skilled at creating and sustaining long-term relationships. The emergency room had a charismatic chaplain who was a bit more of a "glad-hander," perfect for brief encounters. Still, Logan admitted that there were some chaplains who were better than others. And accountability was awkward, Roberts observed, since much of what made a good chaplain was "self-awareness, our ability to be intuitive, our ability to understand what a good word might be. . . . That's so interior." The kind of emotional intimacy and authenticity that made a chaplain effective was difficult to measure and difficult to produce in any kind of standard way. Given these factors, chaplains seemed to have more independence than the rest of the hospital staff.

Nevertheless, in an effort to increase accountability, Logan had recently decided to have the chaplains shadow one another and give one another feedback on the quality of the interactions they observed. In recent months she had also asked the chaplains to take on more weekend hours. As market pressures squeezed the hospital as a whole, Logan did not think the chaplains should be insulated completely: "You want spiritual care to be special and different. At the same time you wouldn't want to be sitting around and not be busy. . . . We're all being asked to do more with less."

The chaplains were only one component of HolyCare's Department of Mission Integration and Spiritual Care. The department, with an annual budget of slightly more than $500,000, was responsible for maintaining the "emotional and spiritual well-being" of patients as well as for elevating the spiritual dimensions of the hospital as a whole.

In the face of market pressures, Roberts admitted, "it can feel as though the spirit or the heart of the place is getting dried out." The market jeopardized those parts of hospital care that, in her mind, were most central to healing. But, she continued, "That is always an issue in being in an alive institution." The challenge was to "have heart in our work, even when it feels like there's more pressure from all sides."

Logan, a Catholic in her late forties with short brown hair and glistening white teeth, occupied an office in the old convent that sat astride the hospital facility. She had begun her work at HolyCare as a nutritionist. During this time she was invited to participate in an employee program called "Mission and Mentoring," in which managers and other employees were trained by St. Francis Health System leadership in the values and traditions of the Sisters of St. Francis. When the former director of Mission Integration and Spiritual Care was promoted, Logan was approached about replacing her. And after taking the job, Logan returned to school for a master's degree in theology.

According to Logan, the "extraordinary happens in the ordinary." In addition to supervising the chaplains, she sought to find ways to highlight the "spiritual aspects of people's needs" in the hospital. For example, Logan sent out a daily e-mail reflection to all staff "to remind people to get in touch with the sacred in them, so they can be there for patients and their families." She also sought to have all staff meetings in the hospital began with short reflections that "set the context for how you want to be." This was easy to implement within her own department (the chaplains "loved reflections" so much that she sometimes had to "cut back the time" they spent on them) and more difficult in other departments. But she was "fairly certain that a majority of departments" in the hospital did it.

If those at PubliCare Hospital wrestled with the tension between hospital care as a commodity and hospital care as a right, those at HolyCare Hospital wrestled with the relationship between the market for care and the *meaning* of care. Several hospital leaders suggested that the commodification of hospital care might erode the meaning of care, undermining its social and moral foundations. Catholic values, lived out in organizational practice, could help to preserve the meaning of care in the face of a market that eroded its essence. Conversely, however, the Catholic values at HolyCare Hospital seemed to serve as an ideological edifice within which the most blatantly individualistic and economistic health care activity in Las Lomas took place. Seen in this light, Catholic values had economic *value*, since they connoted an attention to emotional, personal aspects of care for which people were willing to pay. In this way, the hospital's marketing strategy merged seamlessly with its religious identity.

State of the Art

Leaders at HolyCare Hospital took pride in the hospital's reputation for being the most comprehensive, state-of-the-art medical center in Las Lomas. In 2000, after months of intense competition between HolyCare and PubliCare Hospitals, the county health department designated HolyCare as a Level II trauma center, meaning that the most critically injured patients in the area would be sent there. A county commission comparing the two hospitals found that HolyCare had "better trauma services, better operating rooms and facilities for receiving patients arriving by helicopter and ambulance." The decision only bolstered the hospital's already high reputation. An ER doctor at PubliCare said of the designation, "It's not necessarily such a great thing from an administrative or even from a financial standpoint . . . but it's another badge they can wear and fluff their chest feathers." Those at HolyCare were still fluffing their feathers, as the comments of a head medical administrator at HolyCare suggested:

> Our niche in this marketplace as I see it is the greatest depth and breadth of services. . . . Our depth and breadth of what we offer in almost any specialty is quite large. . . . We have a large cardiac program, a large orthopedics program, oncology program, internal medicine, inpatient hospitalist.

An ER doctor at HolyCare remembered that when he arrived in the area, HolyCare was the "flagship, premier hospital of choice for people who had a choice in the region." And despite competition from both PubliCare and GroupCare, it remained the "specialty and subspecialty hospital of choice" for the area: "The sickest of the sick are referred to HolyCare," he added. This reputation was reaffirmed by those working at the other hospitals in Las Lomas. According to a nurse director at GroupCare, HolyCare was "seen as the aggressor in the community in terms of having state-of-the-art care." A charge nurse at PubliCare Hospital admitted that HolyCare was "a little more cutting-edge."

Its reputation for good medical care was likely both a cause and an effect of its image as the *wealthy* patients' facility. An ER doctor at HolyCare said that there was a lot of "old money" in town loyal to the hospital. According to a doctor at GroupCare, "the richest of people tend to go to HolyCare." A doctor at PubliCare Hospital said that wealthy people liked to go to HolyCare hospital because the facility "had music playing and artwork and nice sofas." A charge nurse at PubliCare confirmed that the many of the "paying customers will ask to go to HolyCare." And an independent family practice doctor in Las Lomas said that while she used PubliCare for herself, because "I know everybody and they're going to take care of me," most doctors in the area would rather be treated at HolyCare "because it just looks nicer."

Wealthy patients (and doctors themselves!) responded to more than merely advanced medical technology. In order to attract those wealthy patients "who could choose," administrators at HolyCare invested large amounts of money into giving HolyCare Hospital a luxurious and personal feeling. A pianist sometimes played in the lobby. The chairs in the cafeteria were made of heavy oak, compared to the cheap plastic chairs that graced the cafeterias of PubliCare and Group-Care. According to one medical transporter, the administration wanted HolyCare to feel "like a hotel" and so had painted the walls brown and carpeted many of the floors. Ornate calligraphy welcomed patients entering the hospital through the lobby, and a chapel off the lobby was bathed in colorful light that filtered in through panes of stained glass. In the central courtyard of the hospital a "healing garden" had been established. Patients could walk along the curving pathway lined with therapeutic and medicinal herbs, meditate as they navigated a small stone labyrinth, or gaze at a beautiful mosaic wall. Every morning a prayer was played over the hospital intercom.

The hospital sought explicitly to honor the spiritual side of patients' experiences, to make the experience of the hospital more personal and less sterile. And in so doing the hospital was able to attract those patients who could boost the facility's bottom line. HolyCare Hospital attracted a higher percentage of insured patients than PubliCare Hospital and was more profitable than PubliCare during every year since PubliCare turned private in 1996 (see figure 4.1).

Yet hospital leaders always discussed this economic success in terms of the organization's mission. As a medical administrator put it: "We're a very robust hospital for a community hospital, and we do all that so that we can fund our mission." According to another system executive, "The question about finances is never a goal in itself. It's as a subjugated goal to help us fund our ministry." The mission of this ministry, according to a sister also on the executive team, was "to extend the healing ministry of Jesus. And that's as old as Jesus and the gospel, and it's been a ministry of the Church throughout the history of the Church." A system executive suggested that each experience of interacting with HolyCare Hospital and others within the system provided an opportunity for a "sacred encounter, sacred meaning."

If practitioners at PubliCare emphasized care as a right, leaders at HolyCare Hospital emphasized health care as a set of social interactions pregnant with meaning. One of the system's ethicists said he became involved in health care because it was the place where "many of the deepest human experiences" took place. He referenced David Rothman's *Strangers at the Bedside*,[1] a historical and sociological account of patients' increasing alienation from the care they receive. The danger, the ethicist argued, was that certain "sociological forces . . . whether you want to call it market or technology or whatever" would "distance [practitioners] from the patient." The mission of Catholic health care was to "break

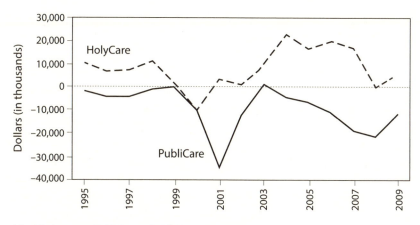

4.1. ▸ Net income at PubliCare and HolyCare, 1995–2009.
California Office of Statewide Health Planning and Development.

into that [alienation and] . . . really, really attend[] to the human person while . . . using the best of what we're continuing to develop." As one ER doctor at HolyCare put it, "The Catholic health care system first and foremost places the patient's emotional, spiritual, physical welfare at the center of the process." The *Ethical and Religious Directives for Catholic Health Care Services*, published by the United States Conference of Catholic Bishops (USCCB), stated, "Since a Catholic health care institution is a community of healing and compassion, the care offered is not limited to the treatment of disease or bodily ailment but embraces the physical, psychological, social, and spiritual dimensions of the human person."

Across all three hospitals, practitioners discussed the symbolic, ethical, and emotional dimensions to their work. But HolyCare Hospital was unique in the extent to which it intentionally worked to highlight *for patients* the symbolic and emotional dimensions to hospital care. When I asked a local religious leader why it mattered whether or not a hospital was Catholic, he responded, "You ever been scared? . . . There isn't any time in the world when religion makes more sense than when you have a problem, especially a health problem, or confronting death." An ER doctor discussed the religious icons around the facility. But more than any particular ornament, he suggested, was a "feeling" that everyone was working towards something greater than just service delivery.

Leaders at HolyCare worked explicitly to help patients understand their experiences in the facility as "sacred," yet this aspiration was difficult to put into practice. As one leader put it, "We've really struggled with this area in terms of how do you measure it? Because we want to be certain that we're faithfully carrying that out. So we've struggled a lot with the measurement of something like that." Administrators asked employees, "When did you feel respected, healed, whole by an interaction with a person? When do you think you've been able to be an agent of that for someone else?" This hospital leader continued, "I can say [to an employee], 'Have eye contact, be polite, be timely,' yes. . . . But it's really saying, 'How do I want to be all day long at work?'"

For patients, system leaders were working to take "particular moments in the patient experience"—like the birth of a child—and make them more sacred. "We're taking that moment by moment and saying, 'Where are there opportunities?' And we're asking patients to tell us about [it]: 'What does that feel like?'" These efforts sometimes seemed to prioritize the *feeling* of being cared for ahead of practical or even medical concerns. The carpets in the facility may have felt comforting, but they were quickly worn down with all the hospital traffic and easily became stained with blood and urine. In order to keep the hospital quiet at night, the hospital had set up traffic lights that would signal to employees when they were being excessively noisy. But this made moving supplies during the evening hours quite difficult, according to one worker: "There's no easy way to do it."

There was even a recent initiative to get rid of overhead "code" pages, replacing them with "code beepers" that were given to doctors. According to an ER doctor, the administration justified the decision by saying, "Everybody knows what [code blue] is now, due to TV. If you call a code blue, other patients worry." But the beepers did not work in some parts of the hospital, and physicians were sometimes unable to look at them when they were "in the midst of a procedure or something." The consequence of using beepers was that fewer practitioners were responding to codes. Meanwhile, this physician continued, the administration had decided "to play sweet musical tones every time a baby is born here," in order to highlight the positive things that were happening in the hospital. As part of another patient-satisfaction initiative, all employees of the hospital—from cafeteria workers to radiology technicians and phlebotomists—had been trained to respond to patient requests. As one technician put it, "You can respond and find out what it is they need and try to get their nurse or their aide, or whatever you can do to respond." As she put it, the initiative was intended to treat patients "like royalty as much as possible."

A system ethicist had recently been treated in another hospital run by the Sisters of St. Francis and discussed what distinguished it from other hospitals: "They made a real commitment to being friendly to everyone who walked in that door in every possible way, and you can just tell it when you go in there. It's like the difference between going into Nordstrom and going [elsewhere]. . . . You know, the staff is trained to be responsive." This ethicist was not the only one to compare HolyCare to Nordstrom. A family practice doctor who treated patients at both HolyCare and PubliCare compared the two by saying, "HolyCare always reminds me of Nordstom, 'cause . . . I walk in there and there's a piano guy in the lobby. Whereas I would think of PubliCare as kind of like Target, the bargain everything."

As these examples indicate, the "sacred encounters" that hospital leaders emphasized seemed almost indistinguishable from the sorts of customer service practices to which all hospitals—and indeed all service industries—aspire.[2] When I made this point to hospital administrators at HolyCare, however, they demurred. A system ethicist answered, "It's a bit unusual sometimes to think that way. . . . I don't want to speak for the congregation or for the sisters whose shoulders we stand upon, but they never thought about it as a business practice. It was just the way they work." The mission of the hospital had nothing to do with "good business practice" but rather emphasized "how we want to connect with [patients]." Another executive in the system said that the "underlying assumption of [mission and market] being opposed to each other is a wrong assumption." She saw the hospital's financial health as a "subtext" and preferred to use the word "stewardship" when it came to discussing money. She continued:

> Theologically, we've been given responsibility to steward the resources, so to me it's still part of the ministry. . . . We've been asked to be accountable for resources and how resources are bought and used, and that, to me, is what financial management is—it's stewardship of our resources. And that's how we refer to it even in our goals. We have a set of goals that we're working on in a three-year process, and it's a stewardship goal; it's not a finance goal. Because it's not about achieving a certain dollar amount, it's about financing the ministry.

A sister on the executive team discussed the importance of how they "framed" their discussion about the market for hospital care: "Framing it in the way we're framing it, finances are the supports to doing the ministry, finances, and everything else. . . . We've been very disciplined [with] the use of the word 'stewardship.'" The market was understood through the lens of the mission.

Ethics and the Market

Tom Peterson, a physician in his early sixties, was a pioneer of palliative care practice in Las Lomas and around the country.[3] He had trained at PubliCare Hospital during the 1970s and seen doctors "doing all sorts of things to patients with a sense that [they were] doing the right thing, when you could tell it was futile and the wrong thing." Soon after he began working as a private-practice family medicine doctor he received a call from the first hospice in Las Lomas to ask if he would serve on its advisory board. He assented, quickly rose to become medical director of the hospice, and went on to become a founding member of the American Academy of Hospice and Palliative Medicine.

Peterson spoke about the "collusion of silence" between doctors and patients surrounding death and dying. Specialists did not want to admit to their "potential for failure, if you define failure as death," while patients were often "unwilling to ask about it." Rather than delivering care in an open and honest way, doctors too often constructed an "optimistic dream about things [being] okay." For Peterson, this mutual denial undermined patients' informed consent, since patients— whether complicit or not—were not in a position to choose based on full information. "We've got to get away from that model," he said.

Peterson did most of his hospital consultations at HolyCare Hospital. While his "loyalties were with" PubliCare, he said, he did not get called very often for patients there. He thought HolyCare was more committed to "good end-of-life care" than PubliCare at least in part because of HolyCare's "Catholic tradition." And while he thought the hospital's current policies regarding end-of-life care made sense, he expressed trepidation about conservative tendencies at the top of the Catholic Church. HolyCare Hospital supported the withdrawal of feeding tubes when the patient or family requested it, but "the Vatican has looked at [that] more lately, and there's risk of interpreting the Catholic tradition a little more conservatively right now." Thankfully, this had not yet become an issue.

Peterson felt supported by the ethics department at the St. Francis Health System headquarters, which in recent years had advocated for increased investments in palliative care programs at all of the system's hospitals. But his everyday work at HolyCare felt like more of a struggle, perhaps because the palliative care program conflicted with the local hospital's economic strategy. As Peterson explained, "At the moment, this hospital's in big financial difficulty, and so . . . my sense is there's a lower-than-appropriate impetus to support palliative care." Since the hospital was paid based on how much care it delivered, the more intensive the care that was provided at HolyCare, the more money the facility (and other doctors) would make. And so while Peterson was aligned in principle with the ethics governing the organization as a whole, in practice he was left mostly on his own. He was a symbol of the hospital's ethical commitments but was unable to wield much influence organizationally.

According to one executive, St. Francis Health System was one of the first systems in the country to institute an ethics committee—an institution now commonplace in hospitals across the country, though one that varies widely in its practices.[4] A department head who served on this committee described the majority of the work of the committee as helping to determine what incapacitated people would want done "if they could speak for themselves." According to Peterson, the ethics committee at PubliCare did not meet regularly and the number of ethics consultations was much lower than at HolyCare.

As a Catholic facility, HolyCare Hospital was guided by the USCCB's *Ethical and Religious Directives*, which gave answers to ethical questions ranging from patient-doctor interactions to organizational relationships to medical decision making. According to Peterson, "We constantly have to deal with those [questions] in terms of what we offer patients." Many of the seventy-two directives were relatively abstract statements about the dignity of the person and the rights and duties that both individuals and providers had to the functional integrity of the body. But several were specific in the ways that they delineated the moral boundaries that economic and technological forces must not cross. With regard to organ donations, for example, the directives instructed that "economic advantages should not accrue to the donor" (#30). Surrogate motherhood was prohibited by a similar logic: "Because the dignity of the child and of marriage, and because of the uniqueness of the mother-child relationship, participation in contracts or arrangements for surrogate motherhood is not permitted. Moreover, the commercialization of such surrogacy denigrates the dignity of women, especially the poor" (#42). In both of these instances, the Church suggested, contractual relationships risked undermining important social values—from altruism, in the case of organ donation, to a woman's "dignity," in the case of surrogacy.

In recent years, the St. Francis Health System had expanded the focus of its ethics committees beyond clinical cases to take on matters of *organizational* ethics, with the goal—according to a report on the initiative—of achieving "a measurably improved realization . . . of the core values" of the system. One commentator aptly described such efforts as "corporate soulcraft."[5] And while this commentator applauded St. Francis's efforts at "focusing its resources internally to realize a moral life to which it has committed itself,"[6] he also pointed out the ways in which this "next generation" ethics committee risked becoming little more than a corporate compliance-assurance program.[7] Achieving "measurable improvements" in "core values" implied a top-down process that seemed inconsistent with the open-ended and inclusive participation necessary for authentic ethical inquiry.

Yet here, again, leaders in the St. Francis Health System sought to reconcile the system's corporate needs with its ethical aspirations and traditions. Leaders up and down the system described the elaborate process by which the organization sought to arrive at decisions that reconciled the market position of the hospital with the organization's ethical imperatives. One system leader distinguished St. Francis Health System from other systems by the "way we do ethical decision making. . . . We gather community concern, really try to think through things and not do it in one particular way." Another system leader outlined a formalized process of "discernment" that leaders used when confronting big decisions. Explaining this process, she said, "Otherwise you . . . fall into the market factors of making decisions." She continued:

> We decide who needs to be in the dialogue; we have all the stakeholders. . . .
> Then we have a process we go through within that dialogue that says, "Let's first
> recognize the biases that we come with, let's set those aside, let's try to explore

all the facts and get all the information, let's generate possible solutions, let's see, let's identify where there may be conflicts, . . . let's stop and reflect on that action, and then let's act."

As if to emphasize that this process of discernment did not always lead to decisions consistent with the system's short-term economic interests, several executives highlighted a recent decision to keep open the system's founding hospital in spite of its poor financial performance. Not only was the hospital symbolically important to the sisters, but the hospital was also "the only major provider in the area." As one leader put it, "Anyone else looking at that on the financial side would have exited that market because it didn't make any sense." Summarizing the discernment process more generally, he said, "We continually try to apply who we are and what we stand for to the realities of the marketplace and what's happening today to keep us consistent with who we are."

One of the hospital system's chief ethicists discussed the more quotidian concerns that the system faced in relationship to the market for care. For example, he discussed how the system responded to drug companies' influence on the prescribing habits of physicians. The goal of the system, he said, was to help make doctors aware of the influence of advertising on prescribing patterns. Interestingly, pharmaceutical company influence was understood as an *ethical* problem rather than a *regulatory* one. GroupCare, in contrast, prohibited all pharmaceutical spokespeople from meeting with its doctors in the first place. According to HolyCare, what was needed was an ethical infrastructure that would enable doctors to make the right choices on their own. When I asked a hospital director how ethical considerations constrained the hospital's business practices, she answered, "Well I'd like to think that we consider the people more." The ethics committee sought to balance what was "good for the person," the individual, and the "value of the whole" organization, she said. Yet she seemed unable to provide an example of an instance in which the committee had chosen to prioritize the good of individuals over the financial health of the organization—a decision to outsource the hospital's medical transcriptionist services, for example, was a "really hard" one, but one that the hospital made nonetheless.

The Church's most well known ethical directives, of course, concern women's access to reproductive services. Abortion and sterilization are generally prohibited at Catholic hospitals on the grounds that they are "medical practices that undermine the biological, psychological, and moral bonds on which the strength of marriage and the family depends," in the words of the USCCB's *Ethical and Religious Directives*. When PubliCare Hospital threatened to close in 2007, many in Las Lomas were concerned about losing access to women's reproductive health services.

Several practitioners at PubliCare felt that HolyCare's ethical restrictions violated patients' right to care. According to one physician administrator at Publi-Care, HolyCare's prohibition on doctors' prescribing the morning-after pill was unjust: "The conflict is in human rights, I think, being violated by a religious belief. It's a strong thing to say, but I believe that." For the same reason, several regular doctors at PubliCare Hospital who worked occasional shifts at HolyCare admitted to violating HolyCare's policy. According to one, "There were times when I did [prescribe it], actually, because I felt like they can't come and tell me not to." Another recalled being prohibited from referring patients to abortion providers but said that he "did it all the time."

An ER doctor at PubliCare grew angry when he discussed HolyCare's "ethics." HolyCare would only treat the needy, he argued, if they "fit into a pattern that [they] feel is appropriate and not sinful." Not only would they refuse reproductive health services, he recalled, but during the "crisis years" of the HIV/AIDS epidemic they would have "nothing to do with" the disease: "Every HIV patient who was picked up on the street by the paramedics came to [PubliCare] hospital, *this hospital.*" People were "dying in the ER" at PubliCare Hospital, he continued, his voice rising, "because, to them, homosexuality and IV drug use did not into their pattern of Catholic rights and morals." The doctor laughed: "Now it sounds like I'm angry. Maybe I am."

Preference for the Poor

According to many hospital leaders at HolyCare, the mission of Catholic health care extended beyond the "sacred encounter" of patient care to encompass what one leader called "a special preference for the poor and the marginalized." This charitable mission was consistent with the USCCB ethical directives, which stated that "Catholic health care should distinguish itself by service to and advocacy for those people whose social condition puts them at the margins of our society." One physician administrator said, "We do look at high-profit services because that's how we pay for low-profit services." An ER doctor said, "We've got a mission: we've got to take care of the less fortunate." When they were actively involved in hospital administration, the Sisters of St. Francis had established a program to provide mobile medical vans and dental clinics to poor communities in Las Lomas and had founded a low-income primary care clinic. In recent years, HolyCare had also set up two urgent care centers for people whose conditions were serious but did not warrant emergency room visits, and funded community programs that provided medical education to underserved populations in Las Lomas. One administrator at GroupCare admitted, "I would tend to give the Sisters of

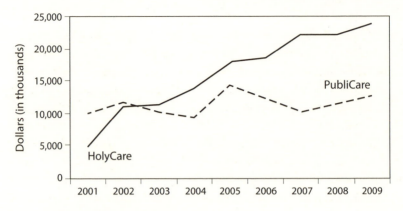

4.2. ▸ Uncompensated care, 2001–2009.
California Office of Statewide Health Planning and Development.

St. Francis the benefit of the doubt that a lot more of their activities are driven by the belief that they really are supposed to minister to the poor with some of their resources, as opposed to GroupCare and Westside Health which don't have that as a real central part to the way their leadership thinks."

The vast majority of almost any hospital's charity consists of the care that the hospital gives away to the uninsured or underinsured. Practitioners and administrators at HolyCare said that while PubliCare Hospital may have seen a higher percentage of uninsured or underinsured patients relative to its patient population, HolyCare Hospital—as the premier hospital in the area—committed a greater amount of total resources to unreimbursed care. Figure 4.2 illustrates the uncompensated care provided by PubliCare and HolyCare hospitals between 2001 and 2009 and supports the claim that HolyCare had given more uncompensated care, especially in recent years.

But the graph is also an indication of just how difficult it is to parse out reality when it comes to hospital charity care. First, "uncompensated care" combines care that was given freely alongside bad debt (as well as including an adjustment for participation in the county indigent program). Figure 4.3 compares the amount of *free* care given by the two hospitals (excluding bad debt), and suggests that PubliCare had—in the recent past—regularly given much more care away than HolyCare. And so while HolyCare could accurately claim to have granted more charity care, much of the hospital's "charity" was in fact bills on which the hospital had been unable to collect. (This is analogous to a person who was robbed calling her losses a "gift.")

Furthermore, calculations of both free care and uncompensated care are based on hospital *pricing* that varies widely between the two hospitals. Since Medicare and Medicaid pay standard amounts based on diagnostic and pro-

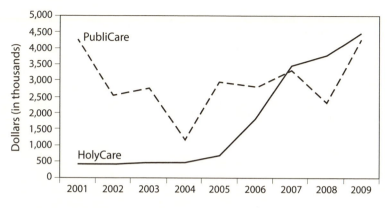

4.3. ▸ Free care, 2001–2009.
California Office of Statewide Health Planning and Development.

cedural groups, and insurers negotiate their own rates with hospitals, hospital prices are almost meaningless except as indications of what hospitals charge the uninsured. Figure 4.4 compares average pricing for common diagnostic related groups at PubliCare and HolyCare Hospitals. It suggests that HolyCare's pricing also likely inflated the amount of uncompensated care the hospital provided.

Some surmised that HolyCare's share of charity care rose unintentionally in the years after winning the county trauma designation in 2000. An ER doctor at PubliCare suggested that HolyCare had miscalculated when it fought for the trauma designation, and as a result it was seeing a higher proportion of homeless and uninsured than expected: "It turns out . . . that lots of trauma [in Las Lomas] is homeless people who fall down and hit their heads." He laughed while he explained this as "karma" catching up to HolyCare Hospital: "From those days of never wanting to see a bum or a homeless person or HIV person, when they became the trauma center" they began to be on more "equal footing" with PubliCare. The trauma center designation may have been a symbolic victory—recognition of HolyCare's status as the preeminent hospital in the county—but, this doctor implied, it was probably a financial loss.

Even the urgent care clinics that HolyCare Hospital had opened around Las Lomas had an ambiguous relationship to the poor and underserved. The clinics nominally were established as resources for those that did not have easy access to primary care doctors. One ER doctor at HolyCare said, "You can go into those urgent care centers, and you don't have to give them insurance, you don't have to tell them anything, they'll take care of you for free." But a physician administrator at HolyCare acknowledged that the clinics were also established in order to "take [a] load of patients off the ER and put them into places with lower costs." In other words, the uninsured were becoming a burden on the emergency room at

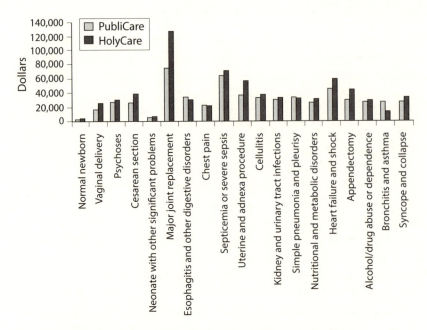

4.4. ▸ Average charge per stay by benchmark diagnostic related group (MS-DRG) at PubliCare and HolyCare, 2009.
California Office of Statewide Health Planning and Development.

HolyCare Hospital, and the urgent care centers—staffed by family practice doctors in facilities with fewer medical technologies—would take care of this population more cheaply. Moreover, this administrator said, it soon became clear to HolyCare's CFO that the urgent care centers were not paying for themselves as planned. So the hospital started publicizing the clinics as places where insured patients could go, "advertising in very high-end publication and billboards in such a way that . . . they were likely to attract a patient population that had a higher insurance rate."

According to several physicians and nurses, despite HolyCare's declarations, the environment there was actually less welcoming to the poor and vulnerable than the environment at PubliCare. One doctor recalled that at HolyCare "they don't give out meals, they're not as soft and fuzzy, they're a bit more like 'Deal with it and move on.'" A nurse who worked at both facilities said that Holy-Care refused to perform many of the small kindnesses that were part of care at PubliCare: "I haven't seen them give showers [at HolyCare]," she said. A physician administrator at PubliCare suggested that while HolyCare was seen by many as the "charitable, Catholic religious organization," he had seen its "seamy underbelly."

A local priest and old friend of the Sisters of St. Francis suggested that while the sisters previously had used the hospitals to support their mission, they now used the mission to support their hospitals. They had "developed a language and a theology to protect themselves" and their economic interests and had even modified their mission statement over the years to make it more consistent with their increasing immersion in the economics of care delivery. He saw HolyCare's work on behalf of the poor and uninsured as little more than a way for the sisters to "solve their conscience," a kind of paternalistic philanthropy that helped them rationalize their deep ties to the market for medical care.

At HolyCare Hospital, Catholicism seemed to provide the ideological framework within which hospital leaders and some physicians were able to understand an unabashed participation in the market for health care. The accumulation of money was not understood as an end in itself for those at HolyCare Hospital but rather as a means for living out Catholic values. But at HolyCare Hospital the relationship between means and ends was ambiguous. Did it participate in the market in order to forward its mission or was its mission part of its strategy for doing well in the market? Barbra Ann Wall suggests that since the first Catholic hospitals were established in the United States, "there has existed an inherent conflict between the Church's clearly enunciated spiritual values and the market realities with which they had to compete." And while this is certainly true, it is also true that HolyCare Hospital's spiritual values had served as a productive ideological shell within a health care market in which economic success is rewarded to those who appeal to noneconomic values.

And when the system's ethical commitments contrasted too sharply with its economic interests, the economic interests took precedence. For example, between 2002 and 2009, the St. Francis Health System sponsored its own Center for Healthcare Reform. A system ethicist who had helped to spearhead the center explained his involvement: "I would like for Catholic health care as a national body of shared ministry to be more aware of how much we are the captive of a large network of irrational, unjust hodgepodge of cobbled-together craziness." He continued by comparing Catholic health care to the "warden who really understands a different model of the criminal justice system but is living in the U.S. of A. in 2010 and . . . is trying to do whatever limited things are possible as well as [trying to] somehow transform that larger world of misunderstanding." The goal of the center was to envision and advocate for a "longer-term transformation of American health care" that would lead to health care being treated "for what it is, and that is a social good, and not a market good." The center put forward a vision for the role that St. Francis Health System might play in the health care world and suggested that the system might be *unable* to live out its mission without a transformation in the organization of care in the United States. But these ideas were perhaps too radical for the system as a whole. The center was closed in 2009.

Certainly, the Catholic values on which the hospital was founded had some autonomy from the market and were not merely ideological window dressing. The Sisters of St. Francis were simultaneously committed nuns *and* owners of a corporation, and the spiritual values they espoused resonated with patients and practitioners alike. We might usefully understand these values as constituting a semiautonomous field of struggle within which different constituencies fought to articulate and advance their own interests. For example, as I argue in the next chapter, doctors based at HolyCare seemed the most entrepreneurial and individualistic of any in Las Lomas. For them, these values seemed to provide a spiritual framework that legitimized their pecuniary orientation to medicine. As I explore in the subsequent chapter, the sisters had used these values to encourage hospital workers' vocational subordination. Over the course of a union-organizing effort, however, workers rearticulated these values in a way that supported their efforts to win more power within the organization.

CHAPTER FIVE

Good Business

During an early morning coffee break in the small cafeteria at PubliCare, an older emergency medicine doctor began describing the emergency room down the road at HolyCare. In order to understand it, he told me, I should read a book with a provocative title: *The Rape of Emergency Medicine*.[1] Published in 1992 by James Keaney, a disillusioned ER doctor and the founder of an alternative professional association for ER physicians, the book documents how a few entrepreneurial ER doctors had, over the course of the 1980s, established large national corporations that contracted with hospitals to manage hospital emergency rooms. These contracts yielded large sums of money for the doctors-qua-administrators[2] and offered some stability to hospitals, which no longer had to worry about staffing their emergency rooms themselves. But the contracts came at the expense of practicing ER doctors, he thought, who increasingly worked at the will of the management companies.

Emergency Medical Incorporated, one of the nation's largest contract management groups, held the contract for the emergency department at HolyCare. The company managed the scheduling, billing, and workflow of the emergency medicine physicians, who were technically "independent contractors" with the company. It also provided them with medical malpractice insurance and helped them minimize legal risk.[3] For a fee it even offered doctors personal "scribes" who, wearing polo shirts emblazoned with the Emergency Medical Incorporated logo, followed doctors around to facilitate documentation for reimbursement.

In exchange, Emergency Medical Incorporated took (or "skimmed," according to some ER doctors) approximately 30 percent of physician billing revenue. For about 10 percent more, the company also collected on late payments, since it ran its own collection agency. While no ER doctor in Las Lomas knew exactly how much profit Emergency Medical Incorporated made from its contract with HolyCare, most assumed that it was substantial. One ER doctor said, "They have fairly low administrative costs, and they have great economy of scale." Another said, "They've got this cash cow. They've got poor ER docs doing the stuff, and they're making a fortune, an aggregate fortune." This type of third-party management was strikingly different from the organization of the ERs at either PubliCare or GroupCare. At PubliCare, a group of local physicians cooperatively owned the contract with the hospital. At GroupCare there was no hospital contract per se— all doctors in the emergency room and throughout the facility were on the staff of the same large GroupCare Medical Group that was closely affiliated with the hospital.

Many of the ER doctors in Las Lomas regarded Emergency Medical Incorporated with suspicion. One doctor at GroupCare had considered working at HolyCare but worried that Emergency Medical Incorporated could "pull you out without any rhyme or reason." He was attracted to the money he imagined he could make there but thought, "I don't really trust these guys." He and others told me that a longtime ER physician at HolyCare recently was fired after he began to question the way that Emergency Medical Incorporated was managing its finances and "asked for more of an open book."[4] Another ER doctor, who had worked at HolyCare before moving to GroupCare, said that the arrangement worked all right until "the interests of the ER doc and the hospital [were] divergent." In these cases, Emergency Medical Incorporated would "do whatever the hospital said," leaving physicians without any recourse.

As one example of these divergent interests, according to a physician administrator, the hospital had begun to open up urgent care centers in low-income neighborhoods around Las Lomas, an effort that was initially intended to reduce the number of uninsured patients visiting the emergency room and so increase the hospital's (and physicians') revenues. Emergency Medical Incorporated was asked to manage these clinics, which were staffed by residents, nurses, and nurse practitioners, all of whom were paid at a significantly lower rate than ER doctors. Over time, however, as described in the previous chapter, the CFO of Holy-Care decided that the clinics were not making enough money and that the hospital should advertise the clinics so as to attract more paying patients to them. As a result, HolyCare's emergency room actually began to see a *reduction* in its number of insured patients, while Emergency Medical Incorporated was able to make a wider margin of income on insured patients who were seen in the urgent care clinics. The physician administrator explained, "All of a sudden it wasn't the hospital doing things that were against Emergency Medical Incorporated and the physicians' best interests, it was the hospital and Emergency Medical Incorporated doing it against *our* best interests." Physicians had little option but to acquiesce or leave—the latter of which they were doing in increasing numbers. According to those with whom I spoke, approximately half of the ER physician staff at HolyCare had left recently or were preparing to leave.

The insecurity that ER physicians felt at HolyCare was—according to some doctors—precisely the appeal of such a contract for the hospital. As one ER doctor at HolyCare explained, "The hospital [has] enough problems, they just want physicians who don't piss off the medical staff, don't piss off patients. . . . Because the hospital has to staff with nurses and techs and supplies and the last thing they want is to be futzing with the docs." If physicians were performing poorly, a group like Emergency Medical Incorporated could simply "get rid of them." At a place like PubliCare, this doctor implied, it was more difficult to fire a difficult doctor: "If you've got a partnership of physicians and then one of them starts acting up, it's much more difficult to kick a partner out."

Matthew McEvoy, a local physician administrator at Emergency Medical Incorporated, came to the defense of his management company as the best solution to the organization of emergency care in an increasingly market-driven health care environment. McEvoy had practiced as an ER doctor at HolyCare since the mid-1980s and still worked the occasional shift. We met at his large house in downtown Las Lomas on the day before Emergency Medical Incorporated was planning to make its initial public offering. As he remembered it, HolyCare doctors organized themselves into a corporation only as a defense against external market pressures. In the 1980s, according to McEvoy, HolyCare told its ER doctors that, due to financial constraints, the hospital would no longer handle the doctors' billing. If the ER doctors did not figure out a way to organize billing themselves, the hospital would look elsewhere to staff the department:

> It was kind of a wake-up call for us, because we were full-fledged members of the medical staff. . . . We were shocked that an administrator would take the position [that we were] expendable. So we [organized our own group], and actually it was good for us that we did it. It's a little microcosmic sort of picture of what was going on, on much broader terms throughout health care, which was it was becoming much more impersonal, much more business and economic driven.

McEvoy explained the company's expansion in defensive terms as well. After establishing themselves as a small medical group, the founders recognized that they remained "vulnerable" if they had only one contract, since *other* contract management companies (and managed care organizations) might use their market share to pressure hospital chains into using their services across an entire hospital system: "Our worry was that, as those seemingly unstoppable juggernauts rolled across the country, that they would begin . . . dominating emergency medicine." And so began a process of growth and consolidation: "We started slowly getting contracts at other hospitals in the area, and then ultimately throughout California. We turned our group into a much, much bigger group." Emergency Medical Incorporated became a juggernaut so as to avoid being overrun by other juggernauts.

McEvoy acknowledged that he became increasingly removed from the practice of emergency medicine as he learned the financial side of the organization:

> A lot of my focus is on making sure that we have good relationships everywhere, that we don't lose any of our relationships, we don't lose business, we don't lose market share. Because we're like any other organization, we have to grow. . . . And that's just a principle of business in a capitalistic society. So we do try to grow and get new business, get new contracts, and in emergency medicine, that usually means taking somebody else's business.

While McEvoy acknowledged growth as a "principle of business in a capitalistic society," he also saw the corporation's financial success as being closely tied to the quality of care the organization ultimately was able to provide. He suggested that the company's size now enabled it to offer resources with which smaller companies could never compete. From malpractice insurance to risk-management tools for physicians to programs to document patient outcomes and programs to enhance patient satisfaction, Emergency Medical Incorporated could help physicians and hospitals negotiate a "rapidly moving marketplace."

In addition to the resources that Emergency Medical Incorporated was able to provide its doctors, McEvoy emphasized the ways in which he and other physician-managers could foster the right kind of "organizational culture," both in the sense that doctors had an incentive to work hard and in the sense that doctors felt they could get their work done easily and were recognized for doing a good job. The right culture, he suggested, depended on creating the right financial incentives. Among the emergency rooms he managed, he thought that an incentive system based on relative value units (RVUs) was most effective. In this system, after a management company took its proportion of patient reimbursements, the remainder was distributed to doctors according to the number of RVUs that the doctors produced. RVUs represent a way of rationalizing the unit of care delivered and documented by a physician in the ER. Cases that demand more time or more expertise are assigned a higher number of RVUs than simpler or quicker cases. An additional, small pool of revenue could be distributed according to measures of customer satisfaction or adherence to practice protocols. This sort of system, according to McEvoy, had several advantages for physicians and for the hospital managers. For individual physicians, the advantage was that the RVU system "separate[d] the payment aspect from the work aspect," so that physicians would be paid for the work they did regardless of the insurance status of the patients they saw. For hospitals and the physicians as a group, the advantage was that RVUs were assigned based on *documentation* of services delivered. When third parties are paying the bill, "If you don't do a good job of documentation, then you basically have lost that revenue." Doctors thus had an incentive both to work hard and to document their work well, maximizing reimbursements for the hospital, the management company, and the pool of doctors as a whole. The additional pool of money could be allocated according to whatever the hospital's (or the management organization's) priorities were at any given time—whether that be customer service, adherence to practice protocols, or something else entirely.

Such an RVU system, designed to reward physician productivity and billing, used market incentives more than the systems in place in the emergency department at either PubliCare or GroupCare. At PubliCare, the physicians who jointly owned the contract split profits based on the number of shifts they worked and "subcontracted" shifts to other doctors for an hourly wage. At GroupCare, physicians were paid a yearly salary with minor financial incentives for meeting certain practice goals.

The doctors at HolyCare, however, had actually rejected this RVU system as being *too communal*. One explained his suspicion of the RVU model: "Their preferred model is to separate the physicians as far as possible from the actual money that's collected, because for every level that you're removed from the collection . . . [there are] more opportunities to take a percentage here for this or for that." Since Emergency Medical Incorporated had been founded at HolyCare, the company had "a little bit of special connection" there. This allowed HolyCare doctors to maintain a system of individual billing, meaning that they were paid based on the particular services they offered to particular patients. Indeed, throughout Holy-Care Hospital, doctors were much freer to practice medicine as the individual craftspeople they had been in the golden age of professional autonomy.

Disintegration

Paradoxically, the most explicitly spiritual hospital in Las Lomas was also the organization within which physicians were the most brazenly individualistic and entrepreneurial. But Catholic hospitals have always tended to have a hands-off approach to their physician staffs. The majority of Catholic facilities were founded in the early part of the twentieth century at a time when the medical profession had only recently established its authority. Catholic hospitals could not flourish unless physicians decided to use them. And so the sisters who founded these hospitals—entrepreneurs who had managed, through their tireless work, to win some autonomy from the men of the church—now found themselves dependent for their hospitals' survival on the men of the medical profession. When the Sisters of St. Francis founded their first hospital in Northern California, according to one historical account, they faced the skepticism of a local medical community "reluctant to bring their patients" to the hospital "for they believed the Sisters were untried and uneducated." It was only through three years of arduous work and training that the "rooms were filled and . . . ledger books indicated that the convent would be enjoying some financial security."[5]

Doctors at HolyCare continued to be more financially independent than doctors who worked at the other two hospitals in Las Lomas. Every doctor who worked at GroupCare was part of the GroupCare Medical Foundation. Since taking over ownership of PubliCare, Westside Health had also been working to expand the number of doctors there associated with the company's large Westside Medical Foundation. In each of these cases, the medical foundation, closely affiliated with (though formally distinct from) the hospital, allowed the hospital to exercise a degree of accountability and control over the doctors practicing there. Moreover, to the extent that these medical foundations attracted primary care doctors, they guaranteed the hospitals a steady supply of referrals. As one administrator associated with HolyCare said, "Every health care organization in the country wants to have a physician strategy. And the physician strategy is all about how do we retain our market share."

But HolyCare resisted the drive towards physician integration. As the hospital's chief medical officer explained, "HolyCare for the most part is an open medical staff," meaning that doctors applied for credentials individually and then could practice at the hospital at their discretion. As a result, according to one ER doctor, the situation at HolyCare was "very grim. . . . HolyCare is years behind the organizational curve." Indeed, despite its reputation as the only high-end, state-of-the-art hospital in the area, several physicians with whom I spoke suggested that HolyCare's very survival was at risk.

Paradoxically, HolyCare's vulnerability was due in large part to way it sought to cater to the high-end specialty physicians. In the 1980s, facing an expanding managed care industry, HolyCare—in association with a local HMO, Coastal Health Net (CHN)—had contracted with a group of primary care physicians to manage the care of a large group of patients. CHN would pay the primary care doctors on a capitated basis, and the primary care doctors in turn would pay the specialists for referrals. This move roiled the specialists, who were forced to depend on the primary care doctors for their pay. As an ER doctor at HolyCare put it, the specialists were "used to being in control and getting paid a lot more." CHN soon went bankrupt, moreover, and the specialists did not get paid for work they had done. As a result, according to a physician administrator at HolyCare, the specialists threatened to "blackball" HolyCare. And the hospital learned its lesson. As the ER doctor put it, "HolyCare pretty much made a commitment to its medical staff to move away from capitated programs and just focus on PPOs [preferred provider organizations] and fee-for-service" on those programs that would pay doctors for the work they did individually, in order to keep the specialists happy.

For some leaders in the medical community, HolyCare's financial difficulties were payback for the way that the organization had truckled to the interests of the highly paid specialists. According to one physician administrator, who had experience at several different health care organizations in Las Lomas, HolyCare had

> made a business decision to preserve a certain margin at the expense of a long-term view of what they really knew was the right thing to do. The right thing to do would have been to persist with developing an integrated delivery system. . . . Why was it the right thing to do? It would save lives, suffering would be assuaged, and in the end they would have been successful from a business perspective. I would guarantee it. I will also guarantee that they are now in the death throes. . . . They do not have a primary care base for referrals. And they will die.

Rather than organize large medical foundations in order to tie physicians (and their patients) to HolyCare, as Westside Health and GroupCare were doing, HolyCare continued to appeal to doctors the same way they appealed to patients: as autonomous customers. As an ER doctor at HolyCare put it, "HolyCare historically has taken a 'Come on, why don't you work with us' [attitude]." And a physician administrator at GroupCare said, "HolyCare doesn't make money unless doctors admit there, right? So doctors are . . . coddled." The physicians' lounge at HolyCare was unlike anything one could find at the other two hospitals. Lunch and dinner were catered each day by the hospital's cafeteria staff, and a Starbucks coffee machine provided free lattes and cappuccinos. While the hospital may not have offered the amenities typical of Silicon Valley, it certainly aimed to please more than the others.

A surgery scheduler at HolyCare emphasized the ways in which the hospital aimed to woo surgeons. As she put it, "It's a symbiotic relationship: the physicians can't do surgery without the hospital; the hospital can't do surgery without the physicians." She described how the hospital had "sales reps that go to the doctors' offices and say, 'Hey, look at our new toy! Don't you want to play with this?'" According to her, the hospital bought an expensive "heart laser" in order to attract cardiac surgeons. It was very rare that a doctor would use the machine, she continued, but it had great symbolic value among the cardiologists and cardiac patients. She saw her own role as developing "rapport with the doctors' offices" and trying to "make it as easy as possible to schedule surgeries" so that they would use HolyCare. When a particular surgeon's monthly utilization was down, she would call the "gal in the [surgeon's office]" to ask, "Hey, what's going on?"

Administrators at HolyCare seemed to encourage nurses and ancillary workers to treat doctors as if the doctors were clients of the hospital—which, in a sense, they were. A hospitalist, who had practiced at GroupCare before recently joining HolyCare, said, "I sat down the other day, the nurse went and got me a chart and brought it to me. I was like, 'What the heck is that?' . . . That would never happen at GroupCare." He continued, "At HolyCare, they might be a little more old-fashioned, in the way they treat the doctor with more respect."

But if this lack of integration gave certain doctors a degree of power within HolyCare, it also made it very difficult for doctors to coordinate patient care. Tom Peterson, the palliative care doctor at HolyCare, expressed frustration that the hospital was unable to develop a protocol for dealing with end-of-life care, despite the system's philosophical commitment to this sort of ethical question: "This is an open campus, open ICU, open everything. And so people aren't governed by a set of institutional rules on how to collectively go forward in the best way; everybody's operating in a silo." A critical care doctor at PubliCare, who had previously worked at HolyCare, described how "there are no dedicated ICU [intensive care unit] doctors at HolyCare," meaning that each patient in the ICU was managed by a doctor who also maintained a private office practice. According to this doctor, the lack of coordination "makes it a little difficult to get protocols going, and that's really important for care." A hospitalist at PubliCare, who also had worked at HolyCare, said there was such lack of coordination at HolyCare that each day of a patient's stay he or she would see a different hospitalist, who would do a separate history and physical, and bill separately: "Patients would routinely complain to me: 'I was in the hospital for a week, I got bills from six different hospitalists.' What's the sense of that?"

The lack of integration also meant that the hospital had a difficult time regulating physician practice. A physician administrator said that most doctors were subjected to only "soft and indirect" feedback from the hospital. Granted, if any doctors were practicing in a blatantly unethical manner, the hospital could "kick them off our staff." But within the boundaries of acceptable conduct there was still wide variation. Individual practitioners were thus often left to decide on their own to which doctors they felt comfortable referring patients. One hospitalist described how he refused to refer patients to a particular interventional cardiologist because the surgeon seemed excessively concerned with maximizing his profits: "I never use him for anything that he's going to make money on. Because I don't trust him."

You Eat What You Kill

The significance of trust (and its absence) at HolyCare was heightened by the fact that doctors there billed on an individual basis, collecting money only for the patients that they saw. When an ER doctor from GroupCare interviewed at Holy-Care, he was told that doctors there "eat what they kill." This system had several related effects on physicians' practice patterns, on the relationships among doctors, and on the relationships between doctors and their patients.

Given that they made money based on the number of patients they saw, the doctors at HolyCare had a clear incentive to see as many patients as possible. An emergency medicine doctor at HolyCare said with evident pride that ER doctors at HolyCare saw an average of 2.4 patients per hour, compared with an average of 1.2 at GroupCare. Moreover, he continued, "our admit [admission] rate is much higher, and our patients are more critical," making the faster rate even more remarkable. Interestingly, to this doctor, the fast pace suggested a stronger work ethic. Those at GroupCare would likely argue they were merely more attentive to their patients.

Across several different departments at HolyCare, doctors seemed to work more quickly and for longer periods of time than they did at the other two hospitals. A hospitalist at PubliCare, who had previously worked at HolyCare, said that at PubliCare he could go home when his shift ended—usually around 5 p.m. At HolyCare "finishing at eight or nine o'clock is routine." He described one doctor who worked the day shift at HolyCare but often stayed until midnight: "She can't get done because she's one of those methodical people who shouldn't be in that kind of practice." Yet many doctors at HolyCare actually resisted reducing their workloads. When the hospitalist above proposed hiring more staff, he faced resistance from the rest of the hospitalists who felt that additional staff would be "cutting into [their] income." An emergency medicine doctor spoke about how adding another physician would mean "an immediate dilution of physician earnings."

While some doctors seemed to relish the pace and autonomy of work at Holy-Care, several others found it overwhelming. A hospitalist who had left HolyCare summarized his experience: "You're getting called constantly, and you don't know what's going on, you're living on the edge, you're admitting multiple patients—it's brutal. I couldn't take it." The ER doctors ultimately agreed to hire an additional doctor only after "we sort of saw . . . our lives were just sheer hell, all the patients were just yelling at us all the time, and you felt frustrated because nobody was checking things that needed to be checked."

Others felt more ambivalent about the trade-offs. Fred Lombardi, a hospitalist, left HolyCare for GroupCare after his wife gave birth to their first child. At HolyCare he felt as if he could not refuse the requests of referring doctors, since his financial success depended at least in part on the informal relationships he had established with them: "I help them out, it's better for the patient ultimately, and then not only that, I mean, to be honest with you, you do that, they're going to use you. And if they use me, it pays the bills." Yet he often found himself at work from 7 or 7:30 in the morning until "seven, eight, nine, ten o'clock at night." When he got home, "my daughter [would be] asleep. . . . So I'm like, 'What kind of life is this?'" At GroupCare he had a more predictable schedule and more standardized salary. Yet having come from the fee-for-service world, Lombardi chafed at the slow pace and bureaucratic rules at GroupCare. He recently returned to Holy-Care, with a new appreciation for its flexibility: "I know I work harder during the day [at HolyCare], I know there are definitely going to be late nights. But I can work for six less days a month and actually have full days off [at the same pay]."

A system of individual billing meant that doctors were, in some sense, competing with one another for those patients likely to reimburse at a high rate, and—conversely—avoiding the uninsured. Within the Emergency Medicine and Hospitalist Departments, several physicians and nurses discussed the problem of "cherry-picking." A new hospitalist at HolyCare, unfamiliar with the individual billing system, was once assigned twelve patients only two of whom had insurance. "Did that happen by accident?" he asked rhetorically. Over time, he said, he had to "learn how to defend [himself]" against other doctors' attempts to stack the deck. A second hospitalist, who had left HolyCare to work at PubliCare, described how his colleagues at HolyCare would sometimes say, "Oh, I don't want to see that patient, I want to see this one." This hospitalist assumed that his colleagues were averse to treating a certain kind of condition: "It took me a long time to realize that they would routinely do that for patients who were uninsured. They would never see the uninsured. And I'm too stupid to realize it. I had no idea that that's what they were doing. They're better businessmen than I am."

A similar competition would sometimes arise in the emergency room. A charge nurse recalled an incident in which one doctor signed up for a critical patient only to have another doctor steal the patient: "So the one doctor who signed up first took the other doctor to the patient's bedside—Can you imagine? This is like two of my boys at home—and said, 'Okay, Mrs. Jones, which one of us did you see first?'" Occasionally, the charge nurse continued, she would have to serve as mediator, ensuring that the most lucrative patients (generally critical patients who had insurance) were evenly distributed across the physician staff. "I feel like I'm babysitting," she said.

Matthew McEvoy, the HolyCare ER doctor and administrator of Emergency Medical Incorporated, suggested that cherry-picking was not a significant problem, in large part because "you don't know the patient's insurance status when you're taking care of them." But several other ER doctors and hospitalists described the strategies that their colleagues used to distinguish the paying customers from those likely to be uninsured. For example, those patients who had no primary care doctor listed—or whose primary care doctor was listed as being located at one of the community clinics—tended to be either uninsured or on Medicaid. Latino surnames were also red flags. Patients who came in for pancreatitis were often alcoholics who had not sought treatment and so were usually uninsured. "Blunt traumas," such as the victims of car accidents and falls, were more apt to be insured than "puncture traumas," such as the victims of gun and stab wounds.

Among the ER doctors at HolyCare there was one physician in particular whom others—both physicians and nursing staff—suspected of cherry-picking. A physician administrator confirmed that this doctor saw approximately twice as many critical care patients as the staff average. A second physician administrator discussed how, given suspicions within the department, he had analyzed the data and found that this doctor actually *did* see significantly fewer uninsured patients than the others—more than two standard deviations below the mean. But when he brought the data to his superiors at Emergency Medical Incorporated they did not think it merited an intervention. So when his colleagues asked him about it, "I lied to the members of my group," and told them that the suspected doctor did not see fewer uninsured patients.

Since doctors at HolyCare did not get paid for treating the uninsured, there seemed to emerge among several doctors a disdain for the neediest patients—a disdain that contrasted sharply with the moral framework espoused by the sisters who founded the hospital. One ER doctor complained about how he lost money when he treated the uninsured, since he had to pay for malpractice "in case the person for whom I'm providing the free care decides to sue me," and had to pay "to submit a bill that I know is going to be uncollectible." This doctor tried (with, evidently, only partial success) not to think about his earnings on a case-by-case basis "because if you try to dissect the patients that you see based on their payer class you'll go nuts. It'll start to eat at you." A charge nurse in the emergency room at HolyCare described how two other ER doctors also became upset having to deal with the problems of the uninsured and underinsured. One doctor had several patient complaints against him because, according to the nurse, "He has a big issue with addiction. He feels that if you want to do that, that's fine, don't bother me with it." He would refuse to offer pain medication to people whom he suspected of drug-seeking, even when he had very little evidence to support his suspicion: "He gets himself in a lot of hot water." A second doctor "can't stand the homeless" and felt that they were "wasting his time," said the nurse. Even the department chief in the emergency room expressed frustration with the kinds of social problems with which the medical staff was forced to grapple: "We could probably employ, you know, four full-time social workers and six full-time case managers, if we sent everybody that needed some sort of help with their social situation, but we just can't get there from here. No money, no mission." Even those doctors who tried to think about caring for the poor in positive terms seemed to have to work at convincing themselves. As one hospitalist explained,

> The way I look at it is, hey, 25 percent of the people I see are uninsured—so be it. Who cares? Maybe that's a little bit of a contribution to the community and the homeless. Try to look at it with a positive spin to make yourself feel good about it, as opposed to "Oh, my god, I have 25 percent that aren't insured. How am I going to make a living? This is bullshit."

At PubliCare and GroupCare, uninsured patients could be understood as a burden borne by the organization as a whole. At HolyCare, however, where doctors' financial relationships with their patients were more direct, each uninsured patient became a target of resentment, an object of personal charity, or something in between.

Individual billing also undermined the hospital's efforts to create efficient processes for patient care. In recent years, for example, Emergency Medical Incorporated had been trying to reduce waiting times in the emergency room. In this vein, it sought to introduce a system of triage, in which a designated physician would see those less serious patients who could be discharged quickly and thus increase the number of beds available for the more serious patients. This sort of system had been implemented successfully at GroupCare. But at HolyCare it was untenable. The less-serious patients were often uninsured patients who used the emergency room as a primary care clinic, and no physician wanted to work the triage shift. One doctor explained, "It broke down, essentially from passive-aggressive behavior of the physicians." With individual billing, it was difficult to persuade physicians to act in the broader interests of the organization when these did not align precisely with the physicians' narrower economic interests.

Medicine and the Marketplace

The effects of physicians' individualism on the quality of care at HolyCare were somewhat ambiguous. Some suggested that market incentives encouraged physicians' best work. As one ER doctor put it, "It encourages you to do good work, document accurately so that you can be paid, and make patients feel happy so that they'll pay their bill, so that they feel like they've gotten value for what they've received." At the other facilities, he implied, the doctors had less incentive to work hard, document accurately, or please their patients. A hospitalist at HolyCare suggested that market incentives also facilitated a degree of collegiality and cooperation among physicians, since physicians depended upon one another for referrals.

Physician individualism at HolyCare almost certainly led to more treatment there than took place at the other two hospitals, after controlling for the severity of patient conditions and patient demographics. But the causes and consequences of this difference were difficult to disentangle. Several practitioners at HolyCare acknowledged that doctors there were incentivized to offer care even when it may not have been necessary. The chair of the emergency department admitted:

> If our billing is improved by ordering more tests on a patient and the complexity of the patient is higher, then it is an incentive at some level to order more tests. And the proof of that is that the physicians with the highest incomes are the ones that order the most tests.

A charge nurse in the emergency room described how these incentives sometimes led to inarguably unethical behavior: "One of our doctors has been known to chase patients down the hall on the way to the OR, when he hasn't seen the patient to say, 'Can you open your mouth? Oh, okay, great.' And charge for an airway assessment." Doctors at the other hospitals were also sometimes openly critical about physician practice at HolyCare. As one put it,

> HolyCare practices bad medicine. . . . They just charge out the wing-wang all kinds of ridiculous tests, mostly radiologic tests. Oh, the radiologists are high on the hierarchy? Yes, they are. And so they do all kinds of overtreatment there that's financially lucrative.

But many others, while acknowledging that the care was more intensive at HolyCare, had more intricate understandings of it. The ER department chief at GroupCare said, "We all see things with the glasses we've been handed." Without accusing those at HolyCare of practicing unethically, he nevertheless believed that "where everybody's got an incentive to take the patient with a two-second twinge of chest pain to the cath lab, then you start to think that [you're] delivering high-quality care by taking all these patients to the lab." At GroupCare, which did not have a cath lab, doctors had neither the incentives nor the resources to practice this style of medicine.

Others went further and argued that the higher levels of treatment at HolyCare might actually be indicative of better care. A nurse who worked at both GroupCare and HolyCare recognized that doctors at HolyCare sometimes "over-order things." A patient who came to HolyCare's emergency room with a bad headache would almost certainly get a CT scan to look for a subarachnoid hemorrhage from a leaking brain aneurysm, whereas the attitude towards the same patient at GroupCare would likely be, "Oh, you have a headache? Big deal!" Yet this same nurse continued, "I think that most of the doctors at HolyCare are slightly more competent or more aware of what's going on than some of the doctors [at GroupCare]. . . . If I drop dead or drop down in the parking lot [at GroupCare], somebody's going to take me to HolyCare Hospital." A hospitalist at HolyCare argued that it was better to err on the side of too much care, particularly when patients might not reliably follow up as outpatients: "Overtreatment may come into play, but I think it's trumped by the bigger oath that we took of doing what's best for the patient. I don't think you see that everywhere." He continued, "Sometimes certain . . . institutions go above and beyond. It's nice to be associated with those institutions." Implicit in his account seemed to be the idea that HolyCare doctors treated their patients more intensively because they were more committed to them.

At first glance, one might be surprised to see such individualistic, entrepreneurial doctors at HolyCare, the hospital in Las Lomas most attentive to the spiritual dimensions of care. Yet ever since the chamber of commerce first asked the Sisters of St. Francis to open a hospital in Las Lomas, HolyCare was intended to serve as the physicians' workshop. The sisters were expected to provide the spiritual aura that would help paying patients feel dignified within the institution's walls, and to subordinate themselves to the medical staff. Moreover, there was a certain elective affinity between the sisters' relationship to Catholic values and doctors' professional ethics at HolyCare. In each case, noneconomic values and commitments seemed to serve as ideologies through which actors pursued their market interests. Doctors at HolyCare often seemed to use their medical expertise as a tool for maximizing their earnings. Yet their entrepreneurship was structured within larger organizations (from the physicians' group to the hospital itself) that also profited from doctors' profiteering.

The Martyred Heart

A unit manager at HolyCare, who began working at the hospital while the sisters were still an active presence, told me, "You haven't really and truly been scolded until you've been scolded by a nun."[1] And while the sisters were no longer actively working at the hospital, which meant that I never got to experience such a scolding firsthand, I did get an impression of the rigid disciplinary regime that persisted there.

It is common knowledge among qualitative researchers that the process by which one enters the field often contains important information about the field itself. At PubliCare, my entrance was easy, if a little unstructured. Since I could pass for one of the medical residents who rotated in and out of PubliCare's emergency room, the nurses there seemed ready to let me treat patients by myself before I betrayed my complete lack of medical training. In order to spend any time at Holy-Care, on the other hand, I had to submit to blood tests and a background check. I was also required to attend a two-hour training session about the history of the Sisters of St. Francis, the expectations of the hospital volunteer, and the broader significance of the hospital's "auxiliary service." And when I had finally completed the training and spoke to the nurse manager of the emergency room about shadowing doctors, she said curtly that it was fine if I wanted just to be a "looky-loo." I should come talk to her again if I was interested in becoming a *real* volunteer.

If relationships at PubliCare were relatively egalitarian and informal, at Holy-Care they were hierarchical and codified. Paradoxically, in the name of the "patient experience," most of the people working at HolyCare seemed relatively miserable. This was true across many different strata of hospital staff members. One physician administrator at PubliCare suggested that there was a "lack of collegiality" at HolyCare. When it seemed, in 2007, that PubliCare might close, certain rotations of PubliCare's residency program shifted to HolyCare. Yet, according to the physician administrator, the residents did not feel welcome: "For the most part, [doctors] felt like [the residents] were an annoyance and an inconvenience: 'What am I getting out of this? And am I going to be liable for what the resident does?'" When he himself applied for staff privileges at HolyCare, he was struck by the amount of information they requested. Whereas the application at PubliCare was about eight pages long, at HolyCare it was over sixty: "I felt like I was applying to the Department of Homeland Security, honest to God. The paranoia that exists in that—it's like the place is being run by lawyers, not doctors." As described above, there was also tremendous conflict over the allocation of resources between the primary care physicians and the specialists at HolyCare, a conflict that—ten years later—still inflamed passions.

Relationships between nurses and doctors were also more hierarchical at HolyCare than they were at either PubliCare or GroupCare. As one nurse who worked at both PubliCare and HolyCare said, at PubliCare, "if a nurse is sitting there and the doctor comes up, [the nurse] is not going to leave their seat just because he showed up." On the other hand, at HolyCare, "that's kind of expected." Another nurse who had worked at both PubliCare and HolyCare said that the doctors at PubliCare "got our back" more than those at HolyCare. A physician administrator at GroupCare admitted that one of his doctors, who came from HolyCare, had a "little bit tougher time getting along with some of the nurses, because he was a little bit more old-fashioned—'I'm the doctor, I'm right'—which just doesn't fly at GroupCare." A charge nurse who had worked at both Group-Care and HolyCare said that there was "definitely more hostility between the doctors and nurses at HolyCare."

Nurses and ancillary workers described the experience of working at Holy-Care as one defined by fear and insecurity. Unlike at PubliCare or GroupCare, where nurses and ancillary workers were represented by national labor unions, ancillary workers at HolyCare had no union representation and nurses at Holy-Care were represented by a small (and rather ineffectual) in-house nurses' union. An obstetrician technician said that workers at HolyCare were "scared of their immediate supervisors." An ancillary worker at GroupCare, who had spent time at HolyCare, described an authoritarian structure at HolyCare that made workers "unhappy." Given the arbitrary power of management, workers were "scared of retaliation, . . . scared to say anything." A charge nurse at GroupCare, who had also worked at HolyCare, described a "top-down" culture at HolyCare: "The managers can make these decisions without any input from their staff and could care less." He continued, "If you talk to any ER people, and if they're honest with you, they'll all tell you they hate management [at HolyCare]."

Several people with whom I spoke suggested that doctors had equally grim views of HolyCare's administration. A nurse at PubliCare said that "even the doctors [at HolyCare] are kind of intimidated by management." One doctor who practiced at HolyCare remembered how the administration had decided to close the hospital's unprofitable rehabilitation unit without telling the department's medical director: "They do what they want without much communication." A nurse leader said, "Nurses and physicians right now seem to share a lot of the same opinions about our administration."

Vocational Subordination

Despite their evident frustrations, doctors at HolyCare were in a position that was structurally distinct from the positions of the nurses and ancillary staff. Doctors at HolyCare tended to treat the hospital as a workshop within which to ply their wares individually. Most doctors were not paid by the hospital directly but rather by insurance companies, by the state, or by patients themselves. When a doctor's affiliation with the hospital felt unsatisfying, it was relatively easy for him or her to work elsewhere. And while many doctors seemed to feel excluded from hospital decision-making processes, the hospital's dependence on them— particularly on the specialists—meant that HolyCare spent significant time and resources working to secure their loyalty.

For nurses and ancillary workers, however, the situation was different. These workers were understood to be responsible for carrying on the work of the sisters who founded the hospital. The legacy of the sisters' sacrifice and dedication framed the ways in which workers' subordination was justified and provided the terrain on which it was contested. Among managers at HolyCare, the sisters' legacy of service was used to elicit what I call elsewhere the "martyred heart," subordination through an appeal to vocational service. Many of the nurses and ancillary workers with whom I spoke suggested that the labor regime at HolyCare was the most exploitative of the three hospitals in Las Lomas, yet this exploitation was couched within a framework of religious values and vocational ethics. On the other hand, as a campaign to unionize HolyCare Hospital suggested, these same values became a terrain of struggle on which workers were able to challenge their powerlessness.

I was exposed to this logic of vocational service during the volunteer training I was asked to attend in order to spend time at the facility. The director of the volunteer program, a broad-shouldered, middle-aged white woman with short-cropped hair, began HolyCare's volunteer training with a short video about the history of the Sisters of St. Francis that recounted their origins in Europe and their struggles as they made their way across the United States. "This is why we exist," she said to me and the other assembled volunteers—a high-school-aged white boy, a young Latina, and three elderly white women. Two other videos followed. The second trained us how to sneeze and cough in the correct way (into one's sleeve). The third, based on a book named *The Simple Truths of Service*, told the story of a grocery bagger with Down syndrome who begins putting "thoughts of the day" in customers' bags. These notes inspire customers so much that when they return to the supermarket they deliberately stand in his line. When the video ended, the trainer turned to us and said, "We want you all to be Johnny." According to the trainer, patient satisfaction scores were on the decline in the hospital. As volunteers, we could make the difference by being particularly attentive to patients' needs. A training that began with the sacrifices of the Sisters of St. Francis ended with the inspirational grocery bagger.

When the Sisters of St. Francis were active at the hospital, according to several workers, they were models of a vocational commitment to hospital work. And while the sisters had already begun to withdraw from daily practice at the hospital by the time most of the current employees arrived, several workers recounted fondly the administrative roles that the sisters continued to play—a combination of human relations manager and spiritual adviser. One licensed vocational nurse remembered how the sisters served as an emotional resource for patients: "I could always call them and say, you know, 'This person's having a really tough time, could you come over and just talk to them?'" The support the sisters provided to the nurse herself was just as important. Recalling how difficult it had been when she had patients who passed away when she was a young nurse, she said, "[The sisters] would seek me out in the lounge and ask me, 'Are you doing okay? Do you want to talk to me? I know you had a relationship with that patient,' and 'How are you doing?'" Their concern for their employees went beyond the workplace as well. A worker in central supplies remembered that "people depended on them, and they knew that they could go to them. They actually honestly listened to you and tried to help you."

While the sisters were still active in hospital administration, workers also felt that they had a means to discuss the difficulty of their jobs and come to collective solutions. One sister would hold open meetings at which workers could talk about what was going on. A unit secretary recalled how "people would be crying about how they wanted [more time] to care for the patients. And [the sister] would follow up with everybody and try to see that the situation was rectified." These meetings would often stretch over several hours, giving space so that "everybody in the room who wanted to talk got to talk."

Under the leadership of the sisters, a rigorous disciplinary regime was softened by a sense of maternal caring. A unit manager recalled how one of her first memories at HolyCare was of being "chewed out" by one of the sisters on staff. But she was not resentful. Rather, she continued, "To me the sisters represented the conscience of the hospital," upholding standards and serving as a buffer against financial considerations. "Whenever the hospital administration would start getting greedy and start thinking about money versus people, the sisters would kind of go, 'Wait a minute, that's not how you treat people.'" Even as the sisters' presence in the hospital diminished, this unit manager seemed to think of them as guardian angels. There was a rumor going around the hospital that a sister had played a part in getting a bad manager fired long after the sisters left active administration. This sister, who was still involved in a local Catholic school, had observed the manager as a parent, "saw that her son was afraid of her," and then heard about her employees being unhappy. "I think [she] put two and two together and said, 'Yeah, this is somebody we don't want around here.'"

For several employees, the sisters' religious conviction resonated with their own values even more directly. This was especially true among some Latinos at the hospital who were also practicing Catholics. A Latina medical translator appreciated the chapel in the hospital and the visible presence of Catholic symbols and values. When her biological sister offered to help get her a better-compensated union position at a nearby facility, she declined. A kitchen worker also felt some resonance between the Catholic values of the hospital and his own values growing up: "Going to mass and church school, I mean, it really influenced me in the way I think and the way I carry myself." Soon after he began working at the hospital he realized that this work motivated him more than other kinds of service jobs he had worked before, because of the way he was able to help out those in need, "nursing them with good food."

A cynic, of course, might understand the sisters as little more than skilled HR representatives, helping workers individually navigate the difficult parts of their jobs while soothing their frustration with hospital management. But the sisters' own self-sacrifice—their clear devotion to principles beyond the bottom line—gave them tremendous legitimacy throughout the organization.

The last sisters left Las Lomas in 2007. And while managers continued to speak of self-sacrifice and vocational devotion, this rhetoric came to feel like a patina of spirituality over an increasingly businesslike core. An operating room technician said with more than a hint of irony, "Everything's push, push, push as far as making sure you charge the patient, making sure you're not stockpiling, making sure that you've got the minimum you need for the time. They always are watching you and pushing you about that, and they call it 'being a good steward.' There's no spiritualism in it at all. It's just sterile." A kitchen worker and practicing Catholic suggested the "values that they're preaching go to garbage" in management's daily practices. A radiology technician assumed that the "suits are hiding behind these values. They're espousing them all the time, and it strikes such a phony chord."

The values on which the hospital was founded had become, in managerial practice, rather blunt instruments through which to prod staff into obeisance. In order to promote the proper attitude among her staff, for example, a nurse manager within the emergency room required all nurses and ancillary workers to read a book titled *Eat That Cookie*[2] in which the author—a health care administrator—argued, "Focusing on service does not make the job more difficult. It makes it more rewarding. . . . It makes people feel proud about their work. It makes for a much more positive work environment. And that's what we need in health care."[3] In the words of one nurse, the book's argument was "basically 'be glad you have a job, and do your best every day.' And she repeats it for 125 pages."

The way in which the hospital's values were distorted for managerial ends was evident in the hospital's annual employee evaluations, during which workers were asked to discuss the ways they and their coworkers had lived out the values of the hospital. While the values publicly espoused by the hospital were "Dignity, Excellence, Service, and Justice," justice was excluded from the list in these evaluations. Each of the other values was interpreted in ways that were consistent with the hospital's managerial priorities:

Adaptability—Service

- Seeks to understand and responds to changing individual or team priorities.
- Accepts and deals with changes positively.
- Accepts direction willingly in order to adapt his/her role to organization or team change.
- Supports team and organizational leaders in change implementation.

Communication—Dignity

- Smiles and greets others. Communicates in a respectful manner.
- Listens attentively to others to understand what is being said.
- Initiates difficult or uncomfortable conversations including requests for personal feedback.
- Discusses private matters in a private area.

Continuous Improvement—Excellence

- Champions/supports efforts that boost the organization's overall efficiency and quality.
- Seeks help in understanding and incorporating . . . best practices and continuous improvement philosophy.
- Uses experience, knowledge, and data to make informed decisions.
- Adapts to changing needs by acquiring new skills, knowledge, and behaviors.

Customer/Patient Focus—Service

- Attends to individuals needing assistance by saying "I will help you find out," rather than "I don't know" or "That's not my job."
- Seeks to understand and exceed customers' service expectations by creating an environment characterized by hospitality, trust, and a spirit of community.
- Makes response to patients and others served a priority.
- Seeks to provide assistance that respects cultural health beliefs and practices.

Incorporated into an evaluative rubric, "dignity"—a foundational principle in Catholic social thought—was reduced to smiling and being respectful; "excellence" was reduced to efficiency. Universal values were reduced to match the profile of a dutiful and subordinate employee.

Supervisors ranked employees on a scale from one (below expectations) to four (exceeds expectations) in relation to these values. Several employees discussed the ways that the process seemed designed to discourage them. A radiology technician referred to the evaluations as "intellectual purgatory" and suggested that his manager deliberately gave people low marks. If "everything's going smoothly," he observed, workers get a two out of four, "and you got to walk on water to get a four, so nobody generally gets fours." Since the evaluations were not tied to worker pay, he continued, "You'd think this would be used as a morale-building exercise." Instead, it seemed, the evaluations were used as a sort of annual repentance, a way for supervisors to demonstrate how workers might live out the hospital's values more observantly. A medical translator once overheard an administrator speaking with her supervisor about not giving high evaluations to employees because it might lead employees to ask for raises. Even a charge nurse admitted: "The joke is that you never hear of anything you do good, ever. And that is true."

Nurses and ancillary workers at HolyCare were asked to take on significantly more responsibilities than their counterparts had at the other two hospitals. According to one worker with experience at both HolyCare and GroupCare, HolyCare workers did not seem to have clear roles, and the hospital "cross-train[ed] people that maybe shouldn't be cross-trained." At GroupCare, in contrast, there were more "skilled workers for appropriate classifications." A respiratory therapist at HolyCare expressed frustration that while respiratory therapists had significantly more responsibility at HolyCare than they did at GroupCare, GroupCare's therapists still made much more. An obstetrics technician who worked at both HolyCare and GroupCare noted that while she was asked to work only in the labor and delivery department at GroupCare, she was often asked to "float" to different departments at HolyCare when volume was low in labor and delivery.

Yet some workers at HolyCare appreciated the amount of responsibility they were given there. One nurse discussed how he had much more discretion at HolyCare than he did at GroupCare: "I like HolyCare a little bit better, just simply because I feel there's more autonomy there." He continued, "At HolyCare, what happens is we get somebody comes in with chest pain, we start an IV, we order an X-ray, we order the labs, we do the EKG, and all that stuff's done— usually before a doctor even comes in." This, he implied, would never happen at GroupCare, where only doctors could order such extensive testing. Similarly, a nurse who worked at both PubliCare at HolyCare observed how she was allowed to "order expensive tests [at HolyCare] that we would not be allowed to do [at PubliCare] . . . If we had a patient that we know could have a stroke, I could order in triage a CAT scan, which is a very expensive test. And it's part of their proto-cols—if someone has, you know, abdominal pain, and I'm suspecting appendi-citis, I can order [a scan]." This nurse suggested that nurses had more discretion at HolyCare than elsewhere because "they have paying customers" at HolyCare. In contrast, PubliCare saw many uninsured or underinsured patients, meaning that there was no guarantee of reimbursement for tests; and GroupCare, as a prepaid group practice organization, also had financial incentives to limit such testing.

As one labor leader in Las Lomas observed, the Catholic values at HolyCare— "the dignity of the patient," "caring for others," and so on—were "more articu-lated in Catholic hospitals." While these values were often used to rationalize the poor treatment of employees, these same values *did* seem to inspire workers to strive towards a particular quality of care. One hypothetical situation discussed by several different workers, managers, and union staff involved a worker who was taking care of a critical patient when it was time for the worker's lunch break. A charge nurse at HolyCare described how nurses from GroupCare, when they occasionally took shifts at HolyCare, demanded that they be given a lunch breaks even when critical patients were in need:

> I don't want an hour lunch, what am I going to do for an hour? But the nurses who work at GroupCare full-time and work with us as a per-diem, kind of opposite of what I do, are very into their breaks. They want their breaks. They want their this, they're entitled to that, and it's like, you know, go down and get something to eat if your patient is set and someone can watch your patient, that's great.

As a result, she continued, "they're not committed to their patients the way we are."

When I used this example with the labor leader, however, he said that since workers at GroupCare were represented by a strong union, they were given breaks by designated staff people. As a result, they were able to care for their patients without giving up lunch. A worker at GroupCare who came to HolyCare might just have different expectations:

> It's a union culture versus a nonunion culture, and to some extent workers [are] more empowered to get their breaks and [have] some sense of entitlement around things like that, because it's what they know is fair. To other workers, they don't know that it's fair, they see it as almost arrogant. "What are you doing? You leave a patient?" Yeah! Let management take them. It's almost crass, but my point is . . . let them figure it out.

This official suggested that the self-sacrifice of workers at HolyCare undermined more profound organizational change. He quoted a nurse who once told him, "We can't continually be the Band-Aid and then wonder why we keep on, these things keep on happening. We're always the people who stretch to make everything work. And that's kind of like, it's like setting ourselves up as opposed to demanding change or demanding a real fix." On the other hand, even this official acknowledged that "there are times when the management can't [take the patient] and the worker should stay." But when was self-sacrifice appropriate, and when did it only reinforce workers' subservience?

Values as a Terrain of Struggle

While spiritual and moral values were used to justify worker subordination at HolyCare, they also provided the most promising terrain on which workers could challenge this subordination. This was true for two related reasons. First, despite the ways in which management used the hospital's values to advance its own agenda, these values continued to have a significance for workers that was irreducible to the interests of management. As one labor organizer put it, "Workers really believe in [the values espoused by the hospital], they really do, but they'll say all the time, 'We're the ones who make these values real, not management.'" Second, the sisters who owned HolyCare were themselves immersed in a world of theology and values distinct from their market position—their investment in being "good Catholics" meant that they were susceptible to pressure regarding the proper enactment of Catholic values. When I asked a second union leader whether he thought the sisters were like other executives or whether they were susceptible to religious argument, he answered, "They're both." Unlike executives in other health systems, the sisters who govern Catholic hospitals are often deeply embedded in two overlapping yet distinct worlds of business and of faith.

Given the hospital system's strong financial position, workers' economic leverage against the hospital was limited. Moreover, given the sisters' values orientation, it was unclear how effective economic leverage might be against them. A union leader explained that for-profit companies "have a clear objective—they want to make as much money as possible" and would capitulate if the union caused them to lose enough money. On the other hand, he continued, Catholic systems "have an ethic," and the sisters who owned HolyCare believed that they were "good advocates" for their workers. The sisters might be ideologically opposed to unionization even if it made economic sense to settle. Moreover, using economic or political leverage against the system might only inspire the sisters to dig in their heels.

Between the fall of 2004 and the spring of 2005, worker leaders tried unsuccessfully to win a union election centered on workers' economic concerns. Within five weeks of going public, they had received the support of 68 percent of workers in the service and technical units of the facility. The union filed its petition in December 2004, and a vote was scheduled by the National Labor Relations Board for early February. In response to the union drive, hospital management conducted a standard antiunion campaign: it hired an antiunion consultant; held one-on-one meetings between workers and supervisors; conducted mandatory group meetings in which antiunion literature was distributed; gave selective wage increases; and threatened union leaders. These strategies have been shown to be quite effective in undermining union success.[4]

Yet the antiunion campaign also drew heavily on the workers' emotional commitment to the hospital. Many workers felt uncomfortable with the conflict and tension that the drive had elicited. Those who thought the union would be a way to improve the hospital now wondered if it might in fact be the adversarial force the hospital described. One oft-repeated story among union supporters was how a nun had approached a pro-union worker and told her she was "greedy" for wanting a union. While rarely so explicit, workers were consistently reminded of the vocational nature of their work and urged to mirror the sisters' own selflessness.

The rhetoric that the hospital used, one organizer explained, "made it very clear that supporting the union means you're against the hospital. Which is a big deal. . . . That resonates with people in a big way." This organizer recalled that people turned against the union faster than he ever expected:

> There's this guy I met with who was like, "I'll do whatever it takes, we gotta win this union, I'm down, you can count on me." And then the week before the election he wouldn't even talk to me. Just 'cause the campaign management had run had scared the hell out of people. That stuff is surprising the first time you see it.

In the days leading up to the election the union came to the conclusion that it could not win. Support had dropped from 68 percent to less than 50 percent in a matter of a few weeks. The union withdrew the election petition and filed unfair labor practice lawsuits with the National Labor Relations Board. Four months later, in June 2005, after the NLRB documented seven violations of federal labor law, HolyCare settled with the labor board.

Union and worker leaders recognized that the union would not be able to win in the face of a concerted antiunion campaign. As a result, they regrouped and decided to wage a public campaign for what the union called a "fair-election agreement": a set of ground rules and accountability mechanisms that would limit the hospital's antiunion campaign and create an environment in which workers could "freely" choose whether or not they wanted a union. As unions across the country have struggled against concerted management opposition and weak labor law, these sorts of longer-term campaigns—campaigns over the process leading up to the NRLB secret-ballot election—have become more common.[5]

The union also recognized that it must wage a *moral* campaign to convince the Sisters of St. Francis that antiunionism was inconsistent with Catholic values. The Catholic Church's support for labor unions harkens back to Pope Leo XIII's encyclical on labor and capital, *Rerum Novarum* ("Of new things"), published in 1891. The document argued that the labor union was the best mechanism through which to ensure the dignity of working people while protecting the private property on which the foundations of society must be based. More recently, in 1981, Pope John Paul II argued in *Laborem Exercens* ("On human work") that workers have a right "to form associations for the purpose of defending the vital interests of those employed in the various professions." In 1986, the U.S. Catholic Bishops asserted in a pastoral letter on the economy, "No one may deny the right to organize without attacking human dignity itself."

Among union organizers, the challenge was to elevate this Catholic teaching in ways that would compel the sisters to agree to negotiate election ground rules. Organizers argued that the sisters remained at the helm of the organization, at least formally, and that these sisters struggled with the tension between their values and the business of running a hospital. It was this tension that provided the union with the possibility of moral suasion. One organizer recognized that while the hospital was a business, "there are some sisters monitoring the mission, or aspiring to, who act out of that charism. And that has a softening impact, that has a pastoral dimension that is part of the culture, that is different from a for-profit hospital."

The union's challenge on the terrain of Catholic social teaching forced Holy-Care leaders to reconcile its antiunion practices with its ongoing moral commitments. Publicly, executives of the hospital system, both sisters and lay leaders, rejected that they were antiunion. Privately, the sisters worried that a union would "replace covenants with contracts" and reduce the hospital's mission to a set of rules. One ethicist worried that a union would "formalize and juridicize [*sic*] . . . things that don't need that." A nun who met with hospital leaders reported that they worried that a union would ruin the good relationship that existed between workers and managers. According to one sister on the executive leadership team, "We want people to experience the workplace . . . as a community, as teams, focused on the mission, patient care, and care for one another." A union, she implied, would make this more difficult.

In addressing the question of fair-election ground rules, system leadership disputed the idea that it represented a "powerful organization" in opposition to a "voiceless worker." As one system ethicist put it, "I came to realize through study, through research, and through the discernment that that is not the landscape of this issue. The landscape is, there is a health care organization with power, there are unions with power. And there are two voices of employees, some employees who want [a union], and employees who don't want [it]. So for me, that's the landscape." HolyCare leaders expressed concern that the voices of *anti*union workers might be silenced with fair-election ground rules. According to one sister who was also an executive, when a group of workers files for a union election, "to that group and to that position come a whole range of resources—money, training, . . . the shirts and the buttons and all of that. And those resources are not available to the people who have a different opinion." To her, the field was lopsided in *favor* of the union.

Despite their protestations, however, leaders in HolyCare were affected by the union's theological campaign. Beginning in 2007, several prominent Catholic organizations and intellectuals issued statements in support of workers' organizing efforts at HolyCare. Over the summer of 2008, the union staged a weeklong vigil outside the sisters' annual leadership retreat, garnering coverage in national religious and secular news outlets. By the fall of 2008, the system had agreed to negotiate fair-election ground rules for the HolyCare election.[6]

The theological debate not only lessened the intensity of the hospital's antiunion campaign; it also seemed to help affirm the workers' sense that they could honor the values of the hospital while advocating for themselves and their patients. Religious leaders had come to their rallies and had provided a framework within which workers could feel they were unionizing in order to *maintain* the Catholic values of the hospital. On one emblematic occasion, during a candlelight vigil in April 2008, a locally beloved Latino priest spoke powerfully about workers' rights to collective representation. During the speech, several Latina cafeteria workers who had been "too scared to come to any events," according to one organizer, walked out of the hospital to hear him on their break. In a secret-ballot election held in December 2009, workers voted narrowly in favor of unionization.

As I have argued, HolyCare hospital moralized the market for hospital care. Producing "sacred encounters" was good business. In a similar way, the organization used the spiritual and emotional dimensions to discipline its nursing and ancillary staffs, demanding sacrifice in the name of spiritual service. In each case, market interests were expressed through the spiritual meaning of hospital care.

Yet this chapter also highlights the ways in which social values retained a degree of autonomy from exchange relations. The vocational values through which managers sought to secure an obedient workforce could be turned on their head and be used to advocate against management for the resources and power necessary to provide for themselves and their patients.

PART THREE

GroupCare Tames the Market

By the early 1970s, across the United States, there were growing calls for restraint and rationalization in what had become—in the minds of many—an unwieldy and unreasonably expensive health system. Patients' rights advocates, business leaders, and political figures on both the left and the right began to mobilize against the autonomy and excess of the medical profession and the hospital industry. In 1971, the Nixon administration began advocating for grants and loan guarantees incentivizing the establishment of "health maintenance organizations," or HMOs, integrated health systems that would combine health insurance with health care provision and so provide medical organizations with incentives to manage the health of patients (or members) in a cost-efficient manner.[1] This idea actually originated in the 1930s and 1940s among industrial employers and health practitioners as a strategy for efficiently maximizing wellness across a workforce.[2] In the 1970s it gained renewed attention, and broader support, as more constituencies began to conceive of health as a technical problem that might be solved through efficient management.

Whereas the public hospital was founded in order to guarantee a limited right to care for the poor, and the voluntary hospital offered paying patients an emotional framework that helped reconcile their "dignity" with hospitalization (and to distinguish themselves *from* the poor), the HMO was founded as a medical organization meant to bring hospital care in line with ideals of standardization and cost efficiency for the middle class (and for its employers).[3] Whereas the public hospital was founded in opposition to the market, and the voluntary hospital framed the market in moral terms, the HMO sought to bring medical care into line with market norms. And whereas the public hospital was founded for the indigent, and the voluntary hospital accommodated the wealthy, the HMO began as the medical organization for the industrial working class.

Las Lomas's first HMO, the Community Health Association, was a short-lived endeavor spearheaded by a coalition of labor unions in 1959. And while the organization planned on constructing its own hospital facility, the enterprise dissolved in 1968. GroupCare arrived in Las Lomas in 1979, when it bought the twenty-three acres on which its hospital and clinics now stand. The organization began seeing patients in 1980. Since GroupCare did not initially own its own hospital, its arrival in Las Lomas was at first a boon for PubliCare Hospital, which contracted with GroupCare to provide its members with hospital services. One nurse at PubliCare remembers that period as particularly intense: "To go through three code blues on an eight-hour shift was just another day, because there were so many patients here." A GroupCare doctor remembers how PubliCare was "way buoyed up by GroupCare patients" during that time.

Among many observers, the growth of managed care has been understood as a key indicator of the market transformation of American medicine. Yet it is, on its face, somewhat paradoxical that we consider managed care and the marketization of health care as being so intimately related. Outside of health care, the bureaucratic connotations of "management" seem antithetical to a "market" made up of autonomous buyers and sellers. Indeed, early managed-care organizations (like GroupCare) were impugned not for being excessively market driven but rather for being *socialistic*. A longtime GroupCare physician remembered that GroupCare's early philosophy in Las Lomas was that it could create a system staffed only by family practitioners "who would be able to do everything." The physicians were all paid the same amount, he recalled, and as late as the 1980s they were "considered commies" by the established medical community. As he put it, "We were the radical fringe of our truly reactionary profession."

While many different forms of managed care emerged in the 1980s, what was common to them all—and distinct from the past—was their focus on cost efficiency. Integrated systems that combined insurance with service provision, like Group-Care, were able to achieve these efficiencies with less conflict than those HMO insurance plans that contracted with various service providers. Threatened by the competition from GroupCare, the County Medical Association established its own not-for-profit health maintenance organization in 1980. Like GroupCare and other HMOs, this plan would offer a range of services for a prepaid fee. In turn, the organization would negotiate reduced rates with providers like hospitals and physicians' groups. But unlike GroupCare, the medical association's plan had limited strategies for allocating health resources and and continued to pay medical providers on a fee-for-service (as opposed to capitated) basis.

GroupCare continued to make inroads into the county. In 1990 the organization opened its own hospital facility, which meant that PubliCare Hospital lost the business it had been getting from GroupCare members. PubliCare Hospital was now in deep financial distress, leading ultimately to the board of supervisors's decision in 1996 to lease the hospital to Westside Health Corporation. That same year, the HMO initiated by the County Medical Association began a period of financial difficulty that would lead to its dissolution in 2002. Members of that organization were then compelled to join GroupCare or one of several national insurance companies that competed for business in the county. The medical association plan would be replaced by for-profit insurers.

As GroupCare grew in Las Lomas and throughout the state, the wider medical community remained wary. Several GroupCare doctors recalled that their colleagues at other health systems teased them for joining the "big-box store" of health care. A family medicine doctor at GroupCare paraphrased the critics: "You guys are coming in here and you're going to just give standard care and poor service and undercut us, because you're so big and you can give it cheaply." Some referred to GroupCare as the "Darth Vader" of health care in the area. An emergency medicine doctor recalled how she was the only person in her class at medical school to work at GroupCare because "people definitely looked at that as a second-rate place to work." A hospitalist said that GroupCare was considered the "bottom rung of health care"; a nurse administrator said it was thought of as the "meat market of health care."

Rational Care

In recent years, that reputation started to change. As a physician administrator put it, whereas the outside medical community once was "openly hostile" to GroupCare, now "it's kind of resignation. . . . There's a lot of recognition that we actually have the best system for delivering care." When the County Medical Association's HMO went out of business in 2002, GroupCare received an influx of new members, many of whom were assigned to GroupCare involuntarily. A GroupCare administrator recalled running into a friend, who was one of these new conscripts, at a Christmas party. According to the administrator, his friend "cried for two days" after finding out she would be going to GroupCare, that "awful place." But her experience at GroupCare had been transformative: "I'd never been taken care of this well in the other plan," she told him. This administrator continued, "I started hearing a similar story over and over." Even a long-time family medicine doctor in town, one of a dwindling number of primary care doctors still in private practice, admitted that GroupCare had "done a really good job at looking toward meeting patients' needs and trying to take better care of the patients."

A rheumatologist at GroupCare said, with tongue in cheek, "First we were hated and despised. Now we're hated and feared. That's better." Increasing numbers of private-practice doctors were signing up with the organization. The family medicine doctor still in private practice was shocked when the people he assumed "would *never* leave private practice" left for GroupCare. "One in particular, whose dad was a family doctor, and he took over that practice. It had been going forever. . . . It just didn't seem in character." Moreover, according to the GroupCare rheumatologist, whereas doctors used to join GroupCare "because they believed in prepaid medicine," they were now joining because "it's the only game in town." He continued, "There really aren't any viable alternatives in private [practice]."

Meanwhile, in the early 2000s, it seemed that PubliCare and HolyCare were engaged in a medical "arms buildup" for the shrinking pool of insured patients that remained. HolyCare established a neonatal intensive care unit in order to take business away from PubliCare; in turn, PubliCare established a heart center to take business away from HolyCare. As a physician administrator at Group-Care put it, PubliCare and HolyCare were "circling the wagons and shooting each other. . . . You just kind of shake your head, you know? I mean, it's a mess out there. It's really a mess."

Given the different organizational arrangements at PubliCare, HolyCare, and GroupCare, it must be emphasized that a comparison of the three is necessarily somewhat imbalanced. Despite the efforts of Westside Health and the St. Francis Health System to integrate their hospitals with primary care and specialty clinics, PubliCare and HolyCare remained stand-alone facilities. In contrast, Group-Care's hospital facility sat directly astride its clinics and was deeply integrated with the GroupCare Health System as a whole. Where PubliCare and HolyCare hospitals saw patients with many different sorts of insurance, GroupCare hospital primarily saw its own members (more on this below). My analysis of GroupCare is thus necessarily an analysis of the GroupCare *system*. At PubliCare and Holy-Care hospitals there were no such systems to analyze. And this is precisely the point.

CHAPTER SEVEN

Flourishing

Ted Booth was a palliative care physician in his early fifties at GroupCare, thin with dark curly hair and thick-rimmed glasses. After attending medical school, he arrived in Las Lomas to attend the family practice residency program affiliated with PubliCare. He finished his residency in the mid-1980s and joined the family practice clinic at GroupCare. Booth began practicing medicine just as HIV/AIDS was starting to appear in the county. When GroupCare patients began developing symptoms, he saw how there was "no coordinated care at all, and very little support within the organization." So he and a few other family practice doctors "took on the issue of taking care of HIV patients." As he recalled, he "ended up taking care of a lot of young men who went on to die." He said, "It was a real formative experience."

Booth had worked off and on at GroupCare for the past twenty-five years, first in the family practice department and then taking care of GroupCare members who were living in local assisted-living facilities. In 2005, GroupCare started investing resources in a hospital-based palliative care service at the Las Lomas facility, for which Booth served as the only physician, seeing patients every afternoon. In 2007 the organization formalized the service with a full-time nurse and full-time social worker. Booth also got the assistance of another physician.

On the first consultation of one particular afternoon, during which I was observing, Booth and the palliative care nurse met with the two grown children of an eighty-seven-year-old woman who was only partially coherent. Before we even arrived at the small conference room where we were to meet, the son said to the nurse, "I've been through a lot of these things, but it's different when it's your own mother." Over the course of a short conference Booth explained how the hospice care program would let their mother "die with dignity." Whereas there was often "a lot of tension" within the hospital, the local hospice house was more peaceful. The two children seemed to have been crying, but they also seemed resigned to their mother's death. Booth asked whether the mother had any religious beliefs or practices. And while both children answered "no," the son said that it would still be helpful to have a chaplain visit the hospice house and offer a prayer for the mother.

The second consultation of the afternoon was less straightforward. A middle-aged man was unconscious, having gone into acute liver failure, but he had previously stated that he wanted to be resuscitated under any circumstances. Booth and the palliative care nurse met with the man's cousin as well as the man's thirty-year-old daughter, who had taken on primary responsibility for her father's health. Also in the room were a woman from the local hospice program and a second social worker. Booth began by asking the daughter to describe the father. She said that he was a party animal, that he did a lot of drugs, but that he was a "great father." Yet she soon admitted that he had left the family when she was twelve or thirteen and only reunited with her when she began to do drugs with him. In recent months she had sobered up, though, and had taken her father into the small apartment she shared with her boyfriend and child.

Outside the conference room, and out of the daughter's earshot, one of the support staffers remarked how hard this situation must be for the daughter. Booth agreed, but cautioned that they should not imply that the father's death might make the daughter's life easier. Instead, he suggested, they must make an argument in terms of the father's best interests. They had to consider how the daughter would feel six months from then about the father's death, and they did not want her to feel guilty about having made the decision for her own sake. Nevertheless, Booth himself admitted that he felt the father was being abusive to the daughter just by forcing her to make such a decision. Within the conference room, Booth explained their medical options. They could "still do things," he said, but it would involve tying the father down and administering laxatives in order to reduce his rising ammonia levels. Booth framed the choice as being one between comfort and prolonged suffering for limited gain. After the consultation, outside of the family's earshot, the palliative care nurse suggested to Booth that the daughter would "be compliant," meaning she would allow the father to die.

Booth and his colleagues received much more institutional support for palliative care at GroupCare than Peterson, the palliative care doctor at HolyCare, received from the St. Francis Health System. Still, it was not easy for Booth to institutionalize the palliative care program. Even some of the hospital-based physicians with whom he worked closely were "very sensitive about me interfering with their primary care patients," he observed. Despite being surrounded by illness and death, Booth said, many doctors and nurses do not like to think much about it. It is "not just a consumer culture of denial, you know, it's providers." On several occasions, doctors at GroupCare had referred to Booth as an "angel of death."

Booth observed that many of the physicians working in the hospital seemed "locked into a . . . more technical, curative mindset." On one recent occasion, he had asked a hospitalist about a dying patient's quality of life. The hospitalist replied, "Well, to be honest with you, I was just really focused on her urinary tract infection." Booth suggested that this orientation among his colleagues was at least in part a product of the pace at which they worked: "They are running so quickly from morning till night, taking care of their group of patients." The palliative care team, on the other hand, often spent over an hour with a patient:

> We have this huge luxury that the three or four of us can sit in the room with a patient and a family for a whole hour or more, and they really see us going in there, turning our pagers off and just say[ing], "What are the issues?" And many times, you know, there's a lot of venting, and we have a style that allows them to many times say the things that they need to say, and then [we] are able to gently steer things back.

The palliative care team had the space and time for difficult, emotional conversations that were nearly impossible in other circumstances. In those sessions I observed, the conversations often felt intimate and open-ended. After working through the patient's medical history, Booth or one of his colleagues would step back and ask the patient or the patient's family something like, "So what do you think is going on?" Out of the uncomfortable silences that followed would sometimes emerge a new clarity: "Now they're freed up to begin to think, 'What do I want to do with my time?'" The crisis in a patient's life became an "opportunity" for the palliative care team to "talk more about what their options and alternatives are."

Other doctors' reluctance to talk about death and dying also seemed to be a psychological defense, given the proximity of death in hospital work. Booth recalled how one of the social workers on his team, who had transferred from hospice care, was used to working with patients who already "understood the trajectory of their illness." There was something different about *delivering* the news that a patient was dying. The social worker found it especially exhausting to accompany people daily as they came to terms "with the fact that they were dying." Booth explained, "You can watch the pain that we cause. . . . It's part of the job description. So there is a certain sadistic, cruel quality to it." The palliative care team began to have conversations as a team about how to cope with the emotional difficulties of the work.

Given doctors' resistance to thinking about death, Booth said, if the palliative care program merely waited for referrals, they would not see any patients.

Instead, the program identified patients admitted for conditions like congestive heart failure, chronic lung disease, declining renal function, or cancer. The palliative care doctors then worked to "convince the hospitalists and [specialists] that we are not there to push the patients in one direction or another; we're simply trying to open a conversation." With patients, in turn, the work was often merely to "help people with planning," to create documents that would help name people to speak on their behalf and to get a sense of "what's important to [patients] in terms of cure versus the things that are most important to them in their lives." This often then led to discussions about "preferred intensity of care." Slowly but surely, Booth and his colleagues were working to "change the medical culture" around death and dying within the GroupCare system—both for providers and for patients. As Booth explained, "If we can steer more of those patients to what they really want and provide the services, the resources, and the infrastructure to make it be a good experience, then it's a win-win."

Booth and his colleagues on the palliative care team were supported both by national literature on the importance of end-of-life treatment and by evidence from across the GroupCare System that investments in palliative care teams *paid off.* The team model was initiated at a facility in Salt Lake City, where the team showed correlations with increased patient-satisfaction scores, shorter hospitalizations, more referrals to hospice centers, and fewer emergency room visits at the end of life—all of which suggested it was worth the investment. In a related move, the Las Lomas facility had also recently hired a clinical social worker to run clinics for new advanced-cancer patients. Patients would have six sessions of interviews and consultations intended to "talk about disease trajectory, care-planning choices, . . . making legal and financial plans for the future, emotional support, and things like that." Among GroupCare's oncologists, those in Northern California were reported to have a higher percentage of patients die in the hospital than those in Southern California. The clinical social work sessions were intended to help bring those numbers down.

Neither PubliCare nor HolyCare had any financial incentive to invest in the development of these sorts of end-of-life programs. Yet at GroupCare, a system based on prepaid group practice, the system made more money the less it spent on end-of-life treatment. Ted Booth admitted that the "palliative care service at GroupCare wouldn't exist if we were not that interested in 'appropriate utilization'"—a phrase that, in this instance, he seemed to use as a euphemism for cost control. With that said, Booth had to be careful lest he—or GroupCare as a whole—be perceived as advocates for the "death panels" that haunted Obama's health care reform campaign.[1]

Booth's role at GroupCare embodied a paradox of this large, bureaucratic health system. On the one hand, Booth and his colleagues created a space for intimacy, honesty, and personal connection that has become exceedingly rare in the U.S. medical system, as financial pressures have risen for hospitals and practitioners. On the other hand, GroupCare considered the palliative care program to be consistent with its goal of "appropriate utilization" and—according to Booth and others—likely would not have invested such resources in the program had it not been seen as economically efficient. Booth's deep empathy for his patients arguably made patients more willing to forgo life-extending treatment. As explored throughout this chapter and the chapters following, the staff at GroupCare tended to believe that through evidence-based medicine, technical savvy, and systems integration, it could make the mission of health care and the market for health care consistent with and supportive of one another.

In some important ways, GroupCare seemed to have succeeded in taming the market for hospital care and aligning the health of its membership with the economic interests of the organization and the practitioners within it. In so doing, however, the organization elided two different goals: that of allocating resources in order to maximize the health of their prepaid membership *as a whole* and that of maximizing the health of each individual member. In their language and practices, many at GroupCare spoke of the former as if it were the latter. One physician administrator asserted, "Rational care is not rationing care." And yet GroupCare inevitably rationed care, and it did so much more deliberately than either of the other two hospitals in Las Lomas. Such collective choices, or collective trade-offs, are at conflict with a competitive marketplace premised on individual choice. GroupCare was the only health care system in town willing to confront such collective choices in its organizational decision making. But it was, perhaps necessarily, unwilling to openly embrace doing so.

The GroupCare System

Over ten years, GroupCare invested approximately four billion dollars implementing an extensive electronic medical record (EMR) infrastructure across its multistate health system, generating what one system executive called "the largest electronic medical record in the world." The intention, according to this executive, was both to make patient information more consistent and reliable and to develop a common language across previously disparate and disconnected practices. Because each site had previously been so different, "it was relatively difficult to transplant stuff from one site to another." He continued, "You can't reengineer a system until you have a system to reengineer. So you first have to engineer a system." The EMR system was not intended to standardize practice at first so much as it was to make *differences* in practice understandable, so that everyone would have "the same dataflow and the same process and starts from the same set of underlying interactions with the patient and database." This similar structure would allow the system to analyze and make use of existing variation: "We can take a variation that happens in Detroit and move it to Nebraska, because when it lands in Nebraska, it lands into the same basic [framework]." Five years ago, the executive continued, "we had 125 [different] billing systems," making financial comparisons across the different facilities next to impossible. Now there was a standard system that allowed comparisons to be drawn. For this executive, and many people at GroupCare, processes of bureaucratization were not necessarily inconsistent with innovation. The standardization of the organization's information infrastructure allowed good ideas to percolate upwards and spread from one facility to another. While the organization had always had "many very creative things going on" in previous years, he said, it was "relatively hard to transplant stuff from one site to another."

If the EMR made possible a new level of standardization, it also allowed for a more thorough monitoring of and interaction with each patient's individuality—both longitudinally, as it tracked each member's care over time, and horizontally, as it tracked each member's care relative to that of other members. When I observed doctors at PubliCare Hospital or HolyCare Hospital, the doctor would often rely on the patient to provide an account of his or her medical history. At GroupCare, in contrast, doctors would study the electronic record before joining a patient at the bedside.

Several practitioners discussed the usefulness of having patients' medical information easily on hand. Physicians and nurses could log on to computers from anywhere in the hospital to access patient records and could even use bedside computers to go over X-rays with patients in their rooms. The electronic records helped physicians analyze patient records quickly and helped prevent them from duplicating tests or treatments unnecessarily. One hospitalist described how, if he was considering ordering an echocardiogram on a patient, he could easily discover if the patient had recently had the test. Another ER physician discussed how he could quickly discover whether a patient had been coming to the emergency room regularly without seeing his or her primary care physician, or if a person had been asking for too many narcotics. An electronic trail of all of the patient's visits—from lab tests, to X-rays, to EKGs, to prescriptions—were all a click away. Since doctors prescribed medications on the system, the computer was also able to test for dangerous and unusual drug interactions; and the system would draw doctors' attention to unusual test results that might otherwise go unnoticed.

The wealth of new information also allowed physicians and GroupCare researchers to compare patients with one another in new ways. According to one specialist, the system "allowed every physician everywhere in the entire system to have every bit of information everybody else has." A physician administrator in family medicine explained how the new system allowed him to use the database and "take out one aspect of" care. For example, he continued, he could easily generate a list of his diabetics, analyze how well his doctors were managing their diabetic patients, and "find out whether or not we're accomplishing what we want in terms of goals." Moreover, the system would allow him to analyze, in real time, whether a particular level of diabetes control resulted in an improved outcome—for example, whether there was a lower rate of heart attacks among these patients. The advent of the EMR opened up the possibility of practice and research occurring concurrently. The same system allowed each physician to see his or her own outcomes more clearly. According to one family medicine doctor, "The fact that I have ways of knowing how I'm doing in general, controlling my diabetes, controlling my hypertension, controlling other chronic medical problems, is valuable to me. And I then can use that data in a way that would be constructive to patients."

Over the last several years, GroupCare had also been using its technological infrastructure in new and innovative ways. For example, members could schedule appointments and check lab results online through member accounts, and they increasingly were able to get in touch with their primary care physicians through e-mail. According to one family practice doctor, these technologies allowed patients to avoid having to "make a visit just to get a question answered or get a medication that you know you need." Furthermore, GroupCare recently introduced a consultation system that allowed primary care physicians to consult with specialists over the phone during primary care appointments. As one family practice doctor explained, "For many of these referrals you can call up and get an answer right there." If a specialist did not think he or she needed to see a patient before scheduling a surgery, for example, the surgery could be scheduled immediately. There was a rumor that once physicians mastered phone consults, the system was going to introduce video consults. In some of the GroupCare facilities that had already implemented this consultation system fully, one executive said, there was a 15 percent reduction in referrals. These types of innovations helped to shorten waiting lists, according to one family practice doctor, so "you have immediate access, which is what patients want."

Some physicians at GroupCare recognized that there were trade-offs to this degree of standardization. One family practice doctor suggested that the "personal touch" was sometimes lost. Still, he continued, "Here I have the ability to call up their X-ray [on the computer] and see the fractured ankle, call the podiatrist on the phone. . . . he looks at the ankle X-ray too, on the computer, and talks to the patient, does the interview over the phone, says, 'You're gonna need a splint, and I'll see you in a couple weeks for the fracture,' and it's all done. And you could never do that in private practice." Another family practice doctor recognized that while GroupCare was not a "boutique practice," he was able to offer many more resources to his patients: "I've got a health educator down the hall, I've got a behavioral therapist right next to me. I can get somebody on the phone and talk with a specialist. I had none of that in private practice."

More commonly, however, those working at GroupCare did not recognize these trade-offs at all. One executive discussed how he disagreed with the characterization of "standardization as being cookie-cutter—we treat everybody exactly the same." Rather, he suggested, standardization actually gave doctors "more time to talk to the patients and be with the patients" since they spent less time deciding on a medical course of action. While some people might describe patient-doctor e-mails as "so impersonal," he suggested, "Even if you have these really quick interchanges, . . . you're really building a relationship, even if it's on e-mail." Overall, a physician administrator suggested that these technologies could reconcile medical and financial concerns—that is, to make the mission of health care consistent with the market:

> From a medical care model, it makes sense. It also aligns itself with the business. And so, as long as we can always keep in our heads, you know, 'Does this make sense medically?' Then, if the winds are changing, [we can] say, 'Okay, the winds are changing, how do we adapt to those changing winds but still keep us on that care path?' And I think that we'll be okay.

As a result of its extensive bureaucracy, he said, GroupCare was able to "align" the mission of care with the market for it.

Flourishing

GroupCare's motto, "Flourish," was ubiquitous around the Las Lomas facility as well as on advertisements for the system that proliferated on television and radio. Ads for most hospitals and health plans included doctors or patients singing the praises of the treatment they have received. In contrast, as I began my research at GroupCare, a highway billboard en route to the facility displayed only the silhouette of a young woman dancing beside the "Flourish." And within the medical campus, the motto was unavoidable. On my early visits to the facility, for example, in the middle of an expansion of the main hospital, construction signs around the parking lot read, "We are growing to help you FLOURISH. Thank you for your patience during our construction." But while it may have become something of a mantra, the idea of flourishing also embodied the organization's commitment to the well-being of its members in general—not merely to treatment of acute medical problems. This commitment also made sense from the perspective of the organization's bottom line. Given that the organization was based on a prepaid group practice model—in which members paid a set amount regardless of how much care they received—the more that members were flourishing, the more net revenue the system was able to bring in.

More than many other health systems, then, GroupCare invested resources in preventative health care—in keeping members out of the hospital in the first place. For example, the system tracked what percentage of members had their blood pressure and lipids checked during the year, then created incentives among doctors and staff to increase these numbers. GroupCare also created elaborate programs to help people manage conditions like childhood asthma or diabetes, and programs to address the social determinants of health like mental health and diet. During the H1N1 influenza scare of 2009–2010, GroupCare was one of the first health systems to acquire and distribute vaccines. According to one physician administrator,

> When somebody joins GroupCare, we assume they're going to be members for life. So we want them to have all their preventative screening. We want them to have a good weight and low cholesterol and all those things that are going to make them healthy for the long run. Whereas the for-profits, you know, they know that a lot of those members will have switched to somebody else next year.

In recent years the system also experimented with ways of giving members incentives to manage their own health more rigorously. A GroupCare executive recalled that such steps "used to be illegal" because the state was "afraid you'd be discriminating against people who were genetically overweight or something." But GroupCare gradually introduced new programs: "If you fill in a health history and then do a couple healthy things, . . . you can go to the GroupCare store and buy running shoes or something." Outside the Las Lomas facility, GroupCare held a weekly farmers' market, one of thirty that were organized around the entire system. Members also received discounts for joining weight-loss programs.

As another example, the system has put energy into rethinking members' relationship to primary care providers. Consistent with a patient-centered medical home (PCMH) model endorsed by many contemporary health policy scholars,[2] GroupCare emphasized the importance of primary care physicians, who would manage the care provision of particular panels of patients—not as a gatekeeper so much as a "contractor," to use a metaphor of Atul Gawande's, responsible for understanding the patient's health in an integrated and holistic fashion.[3] Not only did this model of care prevent multiple specialists from doing needless procedures or working at cross-purposes, it was argued, but it also reduced staffing costs by increasing the scope of practice of primary care providers and increasing the ratio of primary care doctors to specialists. This model also allowed family practice doctors to expand their own knowledge about some specialties.

According to many doctors and administrators within the GroupCare System, all of these programs were simultaneously good for patients and made good economic sense. There was "alignment" between the organization's economic incentives and patients' well-being. These physicians and system leaders drew a stark contrast between the incentives that existed at GroupCare and those that existed in the "real world." According to a GroupCare executive, health care "is just like every other business in that the people who sell whatever it is they're selling do whatever it is they need to do to get the money. And so, if you can make more money by doing lots of scans, lots of scans happen." He and others cited countless examples of overtreatment in the fee-for-service world. At GroupCare, the implication was, the incentives were aligned so as to maintain members' health without costly and ineffective treatments. An emergency room physician put the point more bluntly as he compared working in GroupCare to working elsewhere: "[For] an emergency physician [elsewhere], it's much easier to admit people. . . . So, in some ways, I think their job is easier, because their incentives are aligned to utilize resources and to admit people to the hospital and then call in consultants. That's where their incentives are aligned." At GroupCare he had to use more discretion. Another physician administrator argued that only at GroupCare could members be assured that they were getting the "best care possible" because the "incentives are aligned."

Leaders at GroupCare spoke about a "culture of continuous improvement." Organizationally, however, continuous improvement was sometimes indistinguishable from the process of streamlining—doing more with the same amount of resources. One physician administrator discussed how, in anticipation of lower revenues after health care reform is implemented fully, the organization's goal was to increase productivity by 20 percent. He rattled off examples of how the organization was doing this—shortening the length of time between CT scans so that the radiology department could conduct more scans per day; increasing throughput in surgery so that orthopedics could do four joint replacement surgeries per day instead of two; doing more cataract surgeries every day and more epidural steroid injections. Six months ago, he said, the blood infusion center "was in total chaos," scheduling people in what looked like a "hairdresser's appointment book." Now the department's scheduling has been computerized and made "more scientific" while increasing throughput.

While some of these efficiencies came about through enhanced technology, many of them entailed increased pressure on the people responsible for implementing them. A charge nurse in the emergency department discussed one initiative to increase the speed with which patients were admitted to the hospital from the emergency room: a goal of the previous month was to admit 50 percent of patients within fifteen minutes of occupying a bed in the emergency room. He described how a supervisor would time him "with a stopwatch," calling him "constantly." The nursing director of the critical care department discussed how she was budgeted for "six patients per day," explaining that the system worked "like a checking account"—if she consistently treated seven or eight patients a day she would be harassed by the "finance people" about going over budget. For her, there seemed a disconnection between the financial side of the organization and the clinical side:

> Our finance person now understands, but the first twenty times [he] came to me and said, "Why are you over your budget?" And I was, like, "Okay, so how about this? If your grandmother is going to—you want her to be admitted to the unit, and I say 'I'm sorry, but I can't afford to admit your grandmother to the unit.'... How would you feel?... You'd feel that your grandmother's getting terrible care, right? Right?"

At its worst, then, "continuous improvement" seemed little more than a euphemism for speedups and cutbacks.

As a result of this same commitment to efficiency, GroupCare promoted some programming that—at least at first glance—seemed to treat patients as interchangeable parts. For example, a physician administrator discussed how the organization was using group appointments to discuss chemotherapy with recently diagnosed cancer patients, since each individual consultation "ties up the chair" that could be used for treatment. A specialist remembered being "aghast" when he learned that the system was conducting group therapy for depression in place of individual treatment. In each of these cases, however, practitioners suggested that the benefits of the programs turned out to be medical as well as financial. The specialist was surprised to learn that "the statistics . . . say that [the group therapy for depression] actually works pretty darn well. . . . There are things that we didn't predict. . . . I think there's something about the group process that helps people." The implication was that the system's constant search for more efficient ways of doing things could lead to some surprising and counterintuitive outcomes. The market, again, was consistent with the mission. Nevertheless, this specialist also recognized the limits of these sorts of efficiencies:

> We're already getting terrific pressure at our most efficient nursing facility to cut down length of stay, because it's so long. And we look at the patients who are driving length of stays. When a patient gets admitted to a nursing facility for six weeks of intravenous therapy for their bone infection, [it's] very hard to change that.

While this specialist was surprised at the positive effects of group therapy, he also suggested that GroupCare had already picked the low-hanging fruit, and he seemed to worry that the drive for efficiency might eventually lead to erosion in the quality of care.

At GroupCare, medical discretion had been taken out of the hands of practitioners much more so than at the other hospitals in Las Lomas. As a result, members were better served when they learned to navigate the bureaucracy—for example, those who asked explicitly for particular procedures or particular drugs during primary care visits, those who knew how to speak on the phone with the advice nurse in order that she or he might schedule a same-day appointment, and those who knew which clinics and specialty departments needed a primary care referral and which ones members could call without a referral. One nurse with experience at all three hospitals in Las Lomas suggested that at PubliCare and HolyCare Hospitals patients needed to know the "players," whereas at GroupCare patients needed to know "how the play works." While patients at the other hospitals could advocate for themselves by having personal connections to the staff, he continued, at GroupCare "it's kind of a system thing, . . . knowing where things are at and how it's played out." And whereas the scale and scope of the bureaucracy was "hard for customers a lot of times," there were "some customers who know the system really well, and they know exactly what to ask for and where to go and how to get things."

Rational Care

John Scott was the chair of the emergency room department at GroupCare. A short and muscular Iron Man competitor, he had a no-nonsense affect with his patients and colleagues alike and was widely respected as both a physician and an administrator. Recently, Scott had seen an elderly woman in the emergency room with a high white blood cell count and diagnosed her as having diverticulitis. He was unsure about whether to admit the patient, who made it clear that she "did not want to be admitted to the hospital." So, in coordination with a gastroenterologist, Scott sent her home. Two days later, the laboratory found that her blood cultures were growing bacteria. The hospital called her back and she returned to the hospital, although she "still did not want to come in." Within a day or so she went into septic shock, and Scott did not know how she was doing at the moment. He said openly, "She may die."

In retrospect, he admitted, "If you're going to look at that, you might say, 'Well, did our incentives push us to get her home instead of bring her into the hospital?'" In a fee-for-service environment, Scott pointed out, an ER doctor would likely have thought, "Oh yeah, little old lady, high white count, boom, bed, no problem." On the other hand, the patient might have died of sepsis even if she had stayed in the hospital. And hospital admission brought with it all sorts of other risks. What might be viewed as the "wrong" decision in this particular case may well have been the right decision in aggregate. Scott believed that the "balance of evidence" pointed to the course of action he took:

Our incentives are aligned the right way. . . . Certainly for controlling costs, which—we can't just spend money we don't have. I mean, if we get to a point where 50 percent of income is spent on health care, we're going to fail as a society. So sooner or later we're going to have to change the way we align things. And I believe strongly that we're on the right side, but still sometimes it makes my job harder.

But Scott's account was somewhat contradictory. In one breath, Scott suggested that his course of action was more medically sound than any other—that the risks of returning home were less than the risks of remaining in the hospital. In another, Scott suggested that this course of action *also* took into consideration the need to allocate scarce medical resources across the membership—that part of the process of "alignment" inevitably included "controlling costs." Granted, in this case, the twin goals of quality and efficiency may indeed have been aligned. But there was little acknowledgment—here or anywhere within the organization—that these goals could not always be as easily conflated.

Several physicians and nurses alluded to the ways in which GroupCare weighed financial costs against medical benefits. For example, one ER physician discussed how the emergency room at the Las Lomas facility did not have its own MRI machine: "When you really look at it carefully, there are very, very few indications for an emergency MRI, and it's extremely expensive." He and his colleagues agreed, "You . . . have to make some economic decisions." Given that there were "very few reasons that you would ever need it" in the emergency room, they decided to rely on the radiology department for the "one time a year" when it was necessary—which meant that they would not have access to the machine at night. "It's probably okay," he concluded.

A family practice physician administrator discussed how the facility did not "quite have the capacity" for conducting the colonoscopies needed by its membership. But, he continued, comparing the colonoscopy with a sigmoidoscopy or stool sample, there was "no survival benefit" to doing a colonoscopy every ten years versus doing a stool test every year or a sigmoidoscopy every five years. He admitted, "the perception of the public is that we're withholding care because we emphasize the other two first." But he countered that "any patient can ask for a colonoscopy . . . hear the discussion why the other ones might be just as good and less invasive or painful. And if they opt for a colonoscopy, we sign them up." The same physician administrator discussed how GroupCare used generic drugs instead of their brand-name equivalents. One patient recently told him that he "only wanted Valtrex for his cold sores," and he had to argue with the patient that the generic would "do the same job for pennies on the dollar." The patient ultimately capitulated. In all of these ways, physicians reaffirmed that quality medical care was consistent with cost efficiency.

GroupCare also saved significant money by relying on a "tertiary care system," meaning that different GroupCare campuses specialized in different conditions—for example, one city for neurosurgery, another for critical pediatrics, another for complicated cardiac patients, and another for rehabilitation. According to one charge nurse, "GroupCare knows it can't give everything to everybody immediately." But while this was often more a matter of convenience than of care, it occasionally had serious consequences. Since the GroupCare facility in Las Lomas did not have a catheterization laboratory for its heart attack patients, for example, cardiologists gave these patients thrombolytic drugs instead of performing an angioplasty and then transferred them to San Francisco. One cardiologist estimated that this system probably led to one death per year, but he implied that the cost savings made it justifiable.

There were other, more subtle ways that the system saved money as well. For example, family practice doctors could not order certain MRIs or ultrasounds without the approval of a specialist. The cardiology department at GroupCare began to review every echocardiogram order as soon as it was requested so that the doctors requesting the test would read the EKGs and look at blood tests before ordering the more expensive echocardiogram. This red tape was justified as a way of ensuring that expensive diagnostic procedures were not being used as "handicaps." GroupCare also pushed to discharge patients from the hospital as soon as safely possible. Indeed, for nearly every common diagnosis or procedure seen across the three hospitals in Las Lomas, lengths of stay at GroupCare were the shortest (see figure 7.1).

Among health practitioners in and around GroupCare, discussions about the "rationing" of care tended to be characterized by extremes. One group of practitioners—most of whom were not currently employed at GroupCare—tended to see undertreatment at GroupCare as a problem even more dangerous than the overtreatment in the fee-for-service world. If the GroupCare executive cited above was correct, and "people who sell . . . do whatever it is they need to do to get the money," then GroupCare had a clear incentive to withhold treatment even in cases in which it was necessary. One of the more disillusioned physicians at GroupCare, for example, was skeptical about whether GroupCare was "designed with such a noble mission as to make sure that the patients . . . *flourish.*" He suggested that economic calculations pushed the system to ration treatment in ways to make money: "I think if you don't do a bilateral shoulder MRI it will save us four or five hundred dollars that's going to go in somebody's pocket up the pyramid there. . . . No matter how you try to get away from the dollar, from the capitalistic side, you can't. I mean, it's a symptom of our society." According to him, GroupCare merely flipped the incentives of the fee-for-service world on their head, leaving the underlying market logic unchanged. An ER physician at HolyCare, who had previously worked for GroupCare, began yelling at me in the

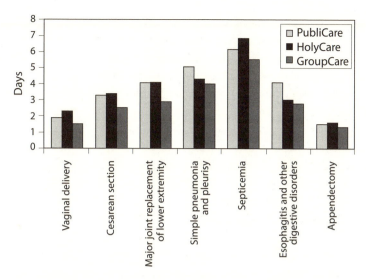

7.1. ▸ Average length of stay by common diagnostic related group (MS-DRG) at
PubliCare, HolyCare, and GroupCare, 2009.
California Office of Statewide Health Planning and Development.

middle of HolyCare's emergency room when I praised GroupCare's pediatrics
program: "They almost killed my son!" He said that GroupCare was an "insurance
company masquerading as a hospital system." He stopped working at GroupCare,
he said, because he could no longer "put his head on his pillow"; he could not live
with himself for working there.

On the other extreme, several leaders in the GroupCare System denied that
any sort of trade-offs occurred at all. One executive said that there was "no need
for trade-offs," given the amount of money currently spent on U.S. health care.
Given the inefficiencies in the fee-for-service world, he implied, GroupCare was
able to provide patients with all the care they needed while still managing to sustain high net revenues and keeping insurance prices lower than the competition.
GroupCare had "more than enough money to do just about anything we need to
do."

The truth was likely to be between these extremes. Without question, there
is rampant overtreatment in the fee-for-service medical world—treatments that
drive medical bills up while doing nothing for patients or even harming them.
Nevertheless, at GroupCare this belief tended to take on the quality of an ideology, masking decisions about resource allocation that necessarily exist within
such an integrated system. For example, one department chief even bought for
all his physicians copies of Sharon Brownlee's *Overtreated: Why Too Much Medicine Is Making Us Sicker and Poorer*, which argues—using powerful statistics
and vignettes—that up to 30 percent of health spending in the United States is

wasteful.[4] The legitimacy of Brownlee's argument is not the point; rather, what seemed significant was the chief's unambiguous endorsement of the notion that less is more. While there is plenty of evidence to suggest that particular tests and procedures often do more harm than good, even this evidence is often ambiguous, as in the case of the recent controversy over PSA testing for prostate cancer.[5] Confronted with enduring medical uncertainty and limited resources, Group-Care has chosen to practice conservatively. And while, in aggregate, this strategy may have benefited patients as well as the organization's bottom line, the organization was never transparent about this strategy *as* a strategy.

GroupCare's Community

Unlike either PubliCare Hospital or HolyCare Hospital, GroupCare had a defined group of members who received their care within the system. This organizational structure was a legacy of the industrial insurance program out of which the modern-day GroupCare emerged, a history in which large industrial employers bought insurance for their employees through GroupCare. One hospitalist remembered how the system was developed for the "blue-collar workers, the shipyard, the union guys." It was "affordable" and "no frills." When she started working at GroupCare in the late 1970s, the doctors in the organization were still regarded as "commie-pinkos," and the system was still regarded as providing "socialized medicine."

While GroupCare's membership has grown more affluent over the years, it is still widely regarded as the working person's hospital system. As one specialist explained, some current members have been members since the system's inception: "I have a number of patients who have told me that they'd been members since '48 . . . since the shipyards." Comparing GroupCare with PubliCare Hospital, one family practice doctor said, "There's more down and outs there than there are down and outs here." Yet the "richest of people tend to be at HolyCare, patient-wise." He said that GroupCare used to be "more middle class," whereas now the "upper middle class would be here too."

Many doctors described how different the patients at GroupCare were, compared with other practice environments. One specialist, who had trained at PubliCare Hospital before joining GroupCare, was used to taking care of "poor people, marginalized people" who treated the medical system as "one of the few areas where they could seek out some entitlement." He remembered at PubliCare Hospital "struggling with patients about them wanting time off work," having to push back against patients when they wanted more time off than their medical conditions indicated. At GroupCare, in contrast, he would have to encourage patients to take any time off at all: "I'd say, 'I think you need to take the rest of the week off,' and they'd go, 'Oh, no, doc. I got a job. I gotta get back to work!'" Another family practice doctor said that since most GroupCare members worked, "they really would prefer to be working and so they aren't going to be coming in to see us all the time." An ER doctor put the point even more straightforwardly:

> This isn't what I would call the real world. It's not. I mean, basically, I'm taking care of people. . . . They're motivated, they have prescription medical coverage, they have insurance, they have sort of a better place in life, because they have certain things. . . . So if you go through your career thinking that everybody's a GroupCare member and you just kind of bebop along, 'cause everyone has insurance, then you're really forgetting the reality of the world we live in.

The archetypal GroupCare member was understood to be hardworking and motivated to take care of his or her own health. This was in stark contrast to practitioners' perceptions of the poor and marginalized who depended on the medical system as a social safety net. One charge nurse at PubliCare Hospital, who had worked at GroupCare as well, said that at GroupCare "the people you take care of are like your mom and pop. I mean, they're polite people, appreciative people, patient people." GroupCare took care of people "like us."

GroupCare's integrated system led some people outside the system to accuse it of not doing its part within the broader community—particularly as Group-Care's market share came to include the plurality of insured patients in the area. One physician administrator said that when he became a leader in the organization, "we were clearly considered . . . the carpet-baggers . . . that were there to suck everything out of the community and not give anything back." A family practice doctor anticipated a similar criticism when he said, "It's not like we live somewhere else and just come in here and grab all your money and then go home. I see patients in the stores." That being said, many practitioners at Group-Care acknowledged that they did not see as many uninsured patients as those at the other hospitals. While GroupCare's emergency room—like all emergency rooms in the United States—is technically open to anyone in need of help, many patients "think of GroupCare as members-only," according to an ER doctor, and so they "go to other hospitals." Another ER doctor suggested that people think, "'Well, I don't have GroupCare, I'm not going to GroupCare,'" and that this "insulated" the system from most uninsured patients. He continued, "I think that is used against us." Granted, GroupCare did not go out of its way to advertise the fact that its emergency room was open to the public. At both PubliCare Hospital and HolyCare Hospital, the emergency rooms were easily visible and accessible from the adjacent streets. At GroupCare, in contrast, the emergency room was at the back of the hospital and not immediately discernible to passersby. During one community meeting, in the spring of 2007, a leader from HolyCare Hospital suggested—tongue in cheek—that some of the financial pressures on the community's other hospitals could be alleviated if GroupCare put up a sign directing emergency patients to its doors.

But if GroupCare did not want a flood of uninsured patients at its doors, it *did* want to be seen as a "pillar of the community," as one physician administrator put it: "If we're not a community player, it's going to limit our future success. We can go so far, but if you're a community player, you can go up to the next level." Other GroupCare employees suggested that the organization had been under pressure from local politicians and advocacy groups to do more locally to warrant its tax-exempt status. A first step for the organization was to become more integrated into ongoing charitable endeavors. As one public relations specialist said,

> Everything's relationships—everything! So if you're not out there on the boards, if you're not active at dinners and events, and you're not working with the chamber, you're not working with different groups, they don't know who you are. . . . But if you're sitting across from this guy twice a month at a board meeting and he says, "Yeah, that doc's a pretty smart guy, he's pretty cool too, he's a bike rider just like I am," you start building relationships and credibility and trust, and that's what we really started to do.

In order to improve GroupCare's local reputation, one physician administrator insisted that each medical department have a business plan that included being "involved in the community some way . . . drives for this and drives for that, and food drive, and school supply drive." The organization began to purchase tables at chamber of commerce events, Heart Association events, and other charitable fundraisers. Many system leaders also took on leadership roles in local nonprofits—a couple of physician administrators became doctors for local high school teams; several doctors even began to volunteer at some of the health clinics for indigent patients.

One specialist discussed how local institutions, from the local newspaper to the local medical association, had historically been hostile to GroupCare. This changed, however, when these same institutions ran into financial trouble—one of the main sponsors of an important charity event run by the newspaper went bankrupt, and a foundation withdrew funding from the local medical association. GroupCare "jumped at the chance" to step in. It began to contribute to the newspaper's annual charity; and it began to pay dues for each of its doctors to join the local medical association, with the result that GroupCare doctors came to make up the majority of dues-paying members. As one specialist put it, "That tends to shift the dialogue within the medical association pretty quickly."

In one sense, GroupCare might be understood to have found an efficient way of enhancing its reputation as a community asset—building goodwill without having to take care of the neediest and most expensive patients. But the organization also had a broader vision for its public involvement. Just as leaders at GroupCare seemed to understand the market and mission of health care to be reconcilable through technological innovation and rational administration, it saw its role in the community as being a rationalizing force. The organization shared its information technology infrastructure with a local network of indigent primary care clinics. One leader explained, "Okay, so we're not providing a lot of direct care to a lot of the uninsured that the clinics see—that's their job and they do it well—but we provide infrastructure.... We provide for improving their electronic technology." Moreover, the organization shared the care protocols it was developing in order to help the clinics "do things more efficiently." An emergency doctor asserted, "We've given literally millions of dollars to improve [the clinics'] quality." As another, less ambitious example of the same commitment, a leader at GroupCare transformed the database for the local medical association in order to make it more streamlined: "They're still using the database that I wrote.... They just hit a button and it faxes people their dues and all that stuff."

More generally, leaders and practitioners seemed to suggest that GroupCare's role in the community was to serve as a model for health care in the county and even the country—a model that would combine market efficiencies and health care quality. In coordination with GroupCare leaders, the local Medi-Cal program was beginning to restructure itself in line with GroupCare's prepaid group practice model. GroupCare would not *care* for the indigent so much as it would model for them, would provide the organizational and technological templates in order that others might take care of these patients more efficiently.

Among the three hospitals in Las Lomas, GroupCare worked most intentionally to resolve uncertainty and anarchy in the market for hospital care. Because it was a prepaid group practice, the organization had the incentive to prevent health problems before they began. Through detailed electronic medical records, the organization could track the health trajectories of individual members, allowing the organization to intervene before health problems became acute, to avoid medical errors over the course of treatment, and to practice according to protocols developed in light of the latest medical science. Using these same records as data, the organization's large research arm could develop *new* medical knowledge concurrent with its ongoing practice. And because all of the providers were integrated within the same organization, GroupCare was able to tweak practitioners' incentives to as to bring them into alignment with the organization's broader project: the optimal population health of its membership.

But if GroupCare was in some ways the picture of "scientific medicine," a bureaucracy that strove to extract the guesswork and profiteering from the provision of hospital care, the organization also illustrates the limits of this science in the context of a health care market. For the line between rational care and rationing care is not as clear as the leaders of GroupCare would have us believe. A rational weighing of costs and benefits to any test or procedure, which includes the opportunity costs of spending resources on the particular intervention as opposed to something else, necessarily leads to choices *not* to intervene in certain cases in which expensive intervention might lead to marginally better outcomes. Evidence-based medicine cannot answer ethical questions about those treatments that *are* marginally effective but are also very expensive or may lessen patients' quality of life.[6] And there are certainly times in which individual patients' relationship to medicine is understandably *irrational*: sometimes a patient does not want those tests that seem reasonable given the symptoms but wants *any* test that has *any* chance of yielding results, or the patient *wants* the expensive treatment that has an infinitesimal chance of curing a serious illness.

In the fee-for-service market, these ethical questions become financial ones—those who have good insurance can undertake the most expensive experimental treatments and explore that "ragged edge"[7] beyond which medical science has not yet reached; while others without insurance die of easily preventable or treatable causes. GroupCare avoided these ethical questions entirely. Yet lurking in the background of the GroupCare system, inevitably, were monetary values on life itself—costs that implicitly motivated decisions about resource allocation within the organization.

The systemization of patient data described above played an important role in this process—helping to transform the GroupCare member from a "case" or "consumer" to a set of *components* or variables that could be understood at different levels of analysis. The goal of the GroupCare system might be understood to be allocating its resources most efficiently across the system as a whole—in other words, working to maximize the value of every dollar it spends. To the extent that patients could be reduced to sets of independent variables (disease histories, demographic characteristics, patient preferences, courses of treatment, prescriptions) and dependent variables (outcomes of treatments or drugs), then models might be developed in order to predict the benefits of using resources in particular ways and to help prioritize spending over a population of patients. But along the way, judgments were made—judgments *had to be made*—about what costs were too high to pay.

In places with national health systems, such as England, this sort of rationing is done more transparently. The National Health Service typically offers only treatments the costs of which are expected to be less than $31,000 to $47,000 per expected year of life gained, adjusted for quality.[8] Yet at GroupCare, it seemed, a similar logic could not be made explicit for fear of driving its members to providers and insurers who set no such limits. Paradoxically, then, GroupCare's process of rationalization seemed to depend on a degree of deceit.

CHAPTER EIGHT

Disciplined Doctors

Ron Schmidt, a senior medical administrator at GroupCare, was a tall, loping man in his fifties.[1] Before attending medical school, Schmidt had worked as an electrical engineer at a large defense firm, and then as a medical researcher. As he rose through the ranks at GroupCare, from physician to department chief to senior administration, he sought to apply his engineering background to the organization of care: "I started reading about Toyota and the lean production methodology," he said. But he soon realized that other physicians were not as responsive to the language of efficiency as he was: "You say, 'Well, we're going to use these Toyota principles,' and the response, especially from physicians, is, 'They make cars. They don't take care of patients.'" How, then, to rationalize the organization's physician staff? Schmidt came to appreciate that you "have to take the concepts and ideas and sort of repackage them in ways that are more palatable for medical professionals."

Just as GroupCare worked to convince patients that each member's well-being was consistent with the optimization of the membership's health, so it sought to convince physicians that their submission to the organization's disciplinary authority was in the interests both of patients and of physicians themselves and that an efficient, rationalized delivery of medical care was synonymous with health care quality. Doctors were encouraged to treat individuals while at the same time keeping an eye on the interests of the membership in the aggregate.

Every doctor at GroupCare was salaried. GroupCare justified physician salaries by pointing to the misalignment of incentives in the fee-for-service world, a world in which doctors were paid according to the number of tests they ordered or procedures they performed. Nearly every doctor I interviewed at GroupCare cited examples *outside* of the organization in which doctors did damage to patients by conducting needless tests or conducting unnecessary procedures. At GroupCare, they noted, the incentives that did exist were unrelated to utilization. One department chief said, "We pay people more for good outcomes. But we don't pay people more or less for utilization. We draw the line there." A medical executive explained, "We draw a firewall between any personal financial gain and utilization. It's just not even on the table."

But if a salaried physician staff solved the problem of overtesting and overtreatment, it presented GroupCare with a challenge familiar to other employers: how to turn purchased labor time into labor power; or, said more simply, how to get doctors to work hard. This challenge was made even more difficult by the uncertainty inherent in medical work and the degree to which medical work depended upon doctors' professional expertise. As one anesthesiologist at GroupCare pointed out, how could the organization possibly determine the "right amount of time" for an epidural or any other procedure? How could the health system distinguish between a doctor's deliberative style and a doctor's shirking? How could physicians be asked to speed up their work or administer fewer tests without risking patient safety and patient outcomes? Furthermore, if doctors *were* successfully encouraged to become more productive, might they do so at the expense of alienating patients, nurses, and one another?

This chapter begins by describing physicians' understandings of their work at GroupCare. It then analyzes two technologies through which GroupCare sought to bring doctors into line with the prerogatives of the organization as a whole: the electronic medical record (EMR) and the patient satisfaction survey (PSS).

Professional Autonomy Is Overrated

On large posters that hung throughout GroupCare's Las Lomas facility, doctors, administrators, nurses, and ancillary staff were pictured in the middle of their exercise routines. Some were standing with their tennis racquets, some were riding their bikes, and some were taking part in triathalons. These pictures were part of the health system's ongoing "Flourish" campaign, aimed at inspiring patients to "partner" with the system by taking care of themselves. GroupCare was structured in such a way that doctors were able to model this lifestyle: they could balance work with other aspects of their life without feeling that they were neglecting their patients or their professional lives. According to one ER doctor, working at GroupCare was "like a job, like a normal job." At one point, she thought, other doctors might have "look[ed] down at GroupCare doctors, like, 'Oh, you just punch a clock.'" But she, and others, realized that "we're all out there fulfilling our lives and having good lives and healthy lifestyles." She concluded, "There's nothing wrong with it, and we're a model for our patients." These doctors not only told their patients to be healthy—they were able to be healthy themselves!

Doctors sometimes joined GroupCare with a work-life balance in mind. According to one assistant department chief, doctors who "wanted a family" were inclined to join GroupCare—especially female doctors who wanted to "manage their schedules better." Other doctors chose GroupCare for the stability of employment it offered more than for its limited hours. One hospitalist recounted that while GroupCare paid less than some of the other hospitals, "it was more secure." Moreover, GroupCare "had a better long-term retirement plan, health care benefits, and my family was covered as well, so I didn't have to worry about that." There were rumors that an ER doctor had moved from HolyCare to GroupCare because of his own ongoing health condition. GroupCare offered much better benefits than he was able to get through his work at HolyCare.

Many doctors at GroupCare recognized that there were trade-offs in working on salary within a large bureaucracy. One family practice doctor, who arrived at GroupCare from out of state, was more acutely aware of its limits: "I think . . . the issue that most of the new docs have who start here is the complete lack of control. You don't really think about yourself as being a control freak until you have none." A hospitalist who had transferred from HolyCare in order to balance work and family grew frustrated with the slower pace of work at GroupCare: "I don't like having down time," he explained, but doctors in his department were not allowed to take on additional patients "even if you wanted to. And if you did want to, you're not going to get paid for it. Because that would take an act of Congress or God or something." His wife started to call him a "county worker," and he came to feel like he was "in jail" at GroupCare. Eventually he left the organization in order to return to HolyCare.

But these stories were exceptions. Indeed, many doctors at GroupCare rejected the idea that they were less autonomous than their counterparts in private practice, particularly in light of the insecurity in the broader fee-for-service environment. According to one family practice doctor, "You lose some of your control, but you have a lot more control in many ways, because you're less buffeted by the insurance companies and by the trade guilds and by what hospital is doing what, and by your lack of access to specialty care, by the uninsured patients, by just the social turmoil that's currently happening now throughout the country." An emergency room doctor remarked, "People talk about the good old days. . . . They're nostalgic. But medicine got much more complex, insurers, the government. . . . So even then [those in private practice] are *so* not in charge of their own lives anymore." When I asked this doctor whether she felt she had autonomy at GroupCare, she answered wryly, "Yes. To walk out at five o'clock and go take my run! Have a bike ride!"

For the medical sociologist Eliot Freidson, doctors' formal positions inside or outside of organizational hierarchies were less important than "the characteristics of the employment position itself."[2] When doctors were employees, he argued, they may not have the "power to allocate the total resources of the organization," but they maintained at least some discretion over "the work they do and . . . how to do it."[3] Along these lines, many doctors at GroupCare seemed to feel like they had the best of both worlds: medical discretion without financial risk or long hours.

But the same factors that allowed for doctors' freedom also changed the doctors' relationship to their work in profound if subtle ways. Their relationship to the product of their labor—their patients—was increasingly mediated by the organization for which they worked. Doctors' labor power and specialized knowledge became something the organization could put to use at its discretion. The chair of the emergency department discussed how the GroupCare structure allowed the organization to allocate physicians' time in the most efficient ways without doctors worrying about compensation. For example, GroupCare was easily able to set up a physician-in-triage room (or "PIT") within the emergency room, so that those patients without serious problems were able to get cared for and turned around quickly. No matter what physicians were doing in the ER, there was "no mal-alignment of incentives there," whereas fee-for-service environments trying to implement similar structures struggled with resistance from doctors who were worried they would not get compensated in the PIT (as seen in chapter 5). Similarly, at the end of a shift in the emergency room, the chief explained, "when my shift is over, if I have a patient who's still waiting for a CT scan, then I can just sign him out to my colleague." In the fee-for-service environment, "When you pick up a patient, you see them through to the end, and that may mean staying two, three, four hours beyond the end of your shift, because why would a colleague take that patient when they're not going to get paid for it?" Since physicians' salaries were not connected to individual patients at GroupCare, physicians were less closely bound to them.

GroupCare also had a more rigid division of labor among its physicians than could be found at PubliCare or HolyCare. Again, this made doctors' lives easier in many ways. For example, the facility staffed "laborists," or obstetricians who were at the facility twenty-four/seven in order to deliver babies, so that regular obstetricians did not have to be on call to come to the hospital at night. Likewise, family practice doctors, who in private practice might have done everything from conducting circumcisions to casting fractures to doing sigmoidoscopies, at GroupCare had narrower scopes of practice and almost never visited their patients in the hospital. For family practice doctors transitioning to GroupCare, this could be something of a challenge. One said, "I want to keep kids in my practice. When the mom has an abnormal pap smear, I want to do the diagnostic testing. When the grandfather needs a sigmoidoscopy, I want to do it. I want to deliver babies, you know. I want to do that stuff." When he approached his department chief about treating a wider range of conditions among his own patients, however, the chief responded, "Well, I'll put you in a different suite where they do colposcopies. . . . But there'll be colposcopies on people you've never met. You'd be like a referral guy." This doctor, however, wanted to see his own patients, not "line up these women, have them drop [their] pants so you do the test on them."

Each of GroupCare's organizational structures had its benefits—the PIT, at least theoretically, would provide more efficient care for patients; doctors' capacity to sign over patients would prevent them from becoming overworked; narrow scopes of treatment would allow for specialization and efficiencies of scale. But each of these structures also made doctors' contributions less clear to the doctors themselves by limiting the extent to which they were able to identify patients as their own. Specialization is nothing new to medicine, but at GroupCare doctors' labor was even more abstracted from its "product" than elsewhere in American medicine.

This process of abstraction seemed closely connected, at GroupCare, to processes of organizational change. To the extent that physician labor was disconnected from particular patients and treated as something to be applied at the discretion of the organization as a whole, *changing* the organization of this work became easier. Younger doctors at GroupCare seemed to accept this ongoing change as part of the nature of medical work. According to one young ER doctor, "Medical knowledge itself is changing all the time. So [GroupCare] is more evidence-based now, so as soon as the evidence comes you have to put it into practice." This doctor suggested that older doctors would say, "Well, I've been doing this forever and it's always worked, right?" As a result, he observed, "There's a lot of pretty bitter fifty-something-year-old doctors. . . . . I don't know what to do about that." But most doctors learned to roll with the punches, to become flexible resources in an environment of continuous change.

Disciplining the Doctor

If some doctors were dragged kicking and screaming into the GroupCare bureaucracy, most seemed enthusiastic if not downright messianic about it. Most of the time, the organization managed to make doctors feel that their professional identities and commitments were consistent with—and in fact enabled by—the organization's technological and bureaucratic infrastructure. Administrators successfully elicited consent from the medical staff, I posit, through the use of disciplinary technologies like the electronic medical record (EMR) and patient satisfaction survey (PSS).

Both the EMR and the PSS are widely regarded as technologies that improve the quality of health care in the United States,[4] yet at GroupCare both came to shape physician thought and practice in less obvious ways as well. Not only did the EMR require that doctors spend more time behind consoles, but the computer language with which they interacted also helped structure the way they thought about the cases they saw. When the computer language was connected to diagnosis-specific protocols, physicians either had to comply with the protocols or justify why they were overriding them. The PSS meant that doctors had to pay more attention to the nonmedical dimension of their interactions with patients and reconcile the paternalism of the professional role with the subservience of customer service. Perhaps most important, both technologies allowed for the aggregation of data and the analysis of variation. Data generated from the EMR allowed physician administrators to analyze variation in practice across physicians as well as the relationships between physician practices and patient outcomes. Data generated from the PSS allowed administrators to evaluate the relative popularity of different physicians and to coach doctors about how to deliver a satisfying patient experience.

Through their disciplinary effects, each technology also served the economic interests of the managed care organization as a whole. At GroupCare, the EMR system was closely related to the development of practice protocols and to the implementation of "evidence-based medicine" that together obscured the rationing of resources that took place in the system.[5] By allowing detailed comparisons among physicians of utilization rates and patient outcomes, the system encouraged conformity to the mean—which, in practice, meant that those who did more tests and more procedures felt pressure to do less. The PSS encouraged physicians to think of themselves as service providers and thus to privilege customer service, occasionally at the expense of good medicine. Moreover, like consumer reports throughout the service sector, the PSS functioned as a strategy for managerial control, helping to address the problem of workplace motivation at an organization in which physicians had little financial incentive to keep patients coming back.[6]

Through their relationship to technologies like the EMR and PSS, doctors saw their professional interests as relatively consistent with the interests of a market-oriented administrative elite, although not unambiguously so. The medical standards against which physicians were measured through EMRs were widely regarded as legitimate among GroupCare's medical staff. And so their efforts at self-discipline in relationship to the EMR felt consistent with their professional values. In contrast, many physicians were skeptical of the medical value of the PSS.

Yet despite these suspicions, the PSS has effects on physician practice through the competition that it set up within the medical staff.

The Electronic Medical Record

As discussed in the previous chapter, technologies like the EMR helped to create a coherent information system across disparate GroupCare facilities and regions. At the same time that these technologies allowed the system to monitor its members more easily and more seamlessly, they also created an organizational framework through which practitioners and administrators could compare practices and results across doctors, departments, facilities, and regions.

The implementation of the electronic system was not without its rough edges, as physicians adjusted to the new infrastructure and new expectations. Several doctors said that the system had made them into "secretaries" and were frustrated by the length of time the data entry was taking. One ER doctor complained, "You can see a patient in thirty seconds for something simple . . . and then [you spend] ten minutes charting—you're sitting in front of the computer charting a lot." But in the same breath, many of these same physicians argued that the benefits compensated for the inconvenience. After suggesting that he's "a secretary now," the same ER doctor said, "But I find [the EMR system] to be actually a lot bigger benefit than a detriment." An older hospitalist explained that while on the one hand the EMR system was "intrusive," on the other, "if you're not getting any feedback, you're not going to know how you're doing." And an anesthesiologist said that while there was always the danger of imposing "technology between personal relationships," nevertheless the EMR meant that doctors had "access to information, instantaneously and in an organized fashion. So . . . it really encourages better care." Not to mention that fewer paper charts got lost.

That most physicians found the system more helpful than obstructive was a testament not only to the value of the product but also to the *process* by which EMRs were introduced at GroupCare. From its inception, physicians had played a part in the system's development. They had been offered leadership roles in pilot studies within the system and had been participants in meetings during which administrators and practitioners evaluated the system's progress. In part, this degree of physician involvement was a strategic move on behalf of the health system's administration. As important as the physicians' expertise was their investment in the system's success. According to one system executive, physicians' involvement ensured that "when the system got there, there were already pre-sold, pre-educated, pre-prepared folks." This same executive juxtaposed the success of the GroupCare system with the relative failure of a similar system within Great Britain's National Heath System: "Their system doesn't work yet, in part because they didn't do any of the upfront collaborative stuff. . . . The doctors [there] are refusing to input data."[7] Doctors felt they were a part of the design of the EMR at Group-Care, and so they were willing and sometimes enthusiastic participants.

CHANGING PRACTICE BY MEASURING IT

The implementation of the EMR system was intended initially to create a common language across physicians and across facilities, yet the imposition of this language affected physicians' thinking as well. One hospitalist discussed the ways that her use of the EMR changed the process by which she made diagnoses. Before the advent of the EMR, she remembered, she wrote down a patient's "set of symptoms and [her own] impression," ordered tests, and then used the results of these tests to begin to narrow down the universe of possible diagnoses. The EMR, on the other hand, made her arrive at a "diagnosis first" and then gave her "some order sets based on that." As a result, she felt, she and her colleagues were giving patients the wrong diagnosis more often. For example, a patient who arrives at the emergency room with shortness of breath will "usually get diagnosed with pneumonia or heart attack—some definite diagnosis. . . . But of the thirty things that can cause you to be short of breath, [doctors may] pick the wrong diagnosis." Because the EMR forced doctors to be "exact" early in their clinical evaluations, she felt, it "gets people thinking wrong." It worked well for "the person who comes in with a broken foot," she concluded, but not for the "complicated, hard-to-figure-out cases."

Whether the EMR influenced doctors' diagnoses or not, it certainly allowed them to observe one another's patterns of practice more closely. One hospitalist said, "because of the electronics . . . they're much more connected and know more what each other is doing, but also it's become much more one big group, held to the same sorts of standards." As a result of the new technology, GroupCare sought new ways to ascertain "best practice" and to encourage doctors to follow it. An underlying assumption, of course, was that doctors—left to their own devices—would not practice in accordance with the best science, and that once this scientific knowledge was communicated doctors would change their practice accordingly. According to one department chief, the "outliers" in the department, who tended to over- or underutilize certain resources, "do it out of lack of information." Either they were "just out of residency and they really don't know," or they have been in practice a long time and do things because "it was how they always did it." An ER doctor agreed, saying, "In medicine, people have done foolish things for eons just because that's the way they were trained."

GroupCare sought to create a culture among physicians in which best practices were found, circulated, and encouraged—helping new doctors learn appropriate patterns of practice, and helping old doctors break traditional habits. I outline three related processes by which physicians at GroupCare were brought into alignment, or disciplined, through the EMR system: *protocols*, *peer review*, and *peer pressure*.

PROTOCOLS

Most practice protocols at GroupCare were developed at a regional—or multi-site—level. According to one physician who ran the hospital's efforts to improve quality, practitioners were drawn "collectively from all the medical centers and they centrally come up with what's the best care plan for this particular issue." Each protocol was circulated among all physicians, "so people can critique it," and then it "becomes part of order sets that are electronically part of our medical record now." A hospitalist described how these regional committees "weigh the studies" out there and "give them a value" as they go about recommending protocol.

Sometimes, of course, the committees got it wrong. The hospitalist described a time when a committee decided that patients on IV in the intensive care unit should be given a particular amount of insulin in order to control patients' sugars. The decision was made based on a majority vote, although "a lot of people disagreed with it." A few months later, however, "some articles came out that said controlling the sugar too much is really bad." As a result, the people that had disagreed said, " 'Nyeh nyeh, told you so!' And so then they ha[d] to change it."

The development of protocols assumes that it is possible to define best practices despite high degrees of medical uncertainty.[8] According to some doctors, medical knowledge changes so quickly that evidence-based medicine is something of a lost cause. One family medicine doctor argued:

> I believe that there is no right answer. . . . You get someone who does a study, and they do all the rigorous statistical analyses, they have controls and doubles blinds and all that stuff and come up with a result. And they publish it. And it becomes gospel for a short amount of time. Then about four or five other studies come out and some of them are a little bit different. . . . You know, I mean, it is a moving target.

Most protocols, he implied, were based on questionable science—science that would likely be modified over time. An ER doctor with a more positive view of evidence-based medicine nevertheless acknowledged the lack of good data about many aspects of his own practice:

> There can be many times where . . . you've got just as much saying do it and just as much saying don't do it, and then you do have to just say, "Well, I know what the science is, I'm going to decide." . . . But I think that you accept that there's a lot of grey and very rarely just one way to do it.

Given this inevitable grey area, some physicians recognized that nonmedical concerns might seep into the development of practice standards. A family medicine doctor, for example, argued, "You can always find a research study to prove what you want to prove," implying that political or financial concerns frequently entered into the way that science was deployed within GroupCare. He continued, "After a while, you just kind of get jaded about pretty much any study. There are certainly some that have been huge. But there's a lot of crap out there too." Similarly, a hospitalist described the often-invisible influence of drug companies on medical journal articles. While this politicized research is often in the name of *more* treatment rather than less,[9] some physicians demonstrated skepticism towards any standardized set of practices.

This is not to say that existing protocols at GroupCare privileged economic considerations over medical ones; rather, the inevitable gray areas of medical science left open the possibility for economic considerations to infringe on the development of these protocols. Through the development of practice protocols, the structure of medical knowledge became more susceptible to outside intervention at an organizational level. Nevertheless, despite the fact that there were—according to one hospitalist—"group decisions about things for which there may not be good data," and despite the fact that these protocols removed some physician discretion at the bedside, most physicians saw them as useful, especially since the protocols were framed as recommendations rather than mandates.

PEER REVIEW

Compliance with GroupCare's protocols were encouraged through a process of peer review. According to one hospitalist, protocols did not "stop you from doing what you want, but you have to go through extra hurdles to do it." He continued, "So yeah, you're never ever told no, as long as you've got a good rationale, as long as you can talk to the person who's in charge of that resource and say, 'Here's my rationale.'"

A family medicine doctor agreed: "I get to practice medicine the way I think is right, but I don't just make it up, because if I were to make up something weird and goofy, I have other colleagues around me that would be saying, 'Hmm, what made you think this would be a good idea?'"

For one family medicine doctor with experience in fee-for-service practice, however, this interpersonal accountability felt like interference: "Then they start laying the statistics at you. And that's when it just starts to get frustrating, because this is one of your colleagues in there fuckin' with the talent." Another family medicine doctor suggested that it was the older doctors in the department who were most resistant to this kind of accountability. Contemporary medical schools and residencies, he reasoned, were "turning out graduates that are more [accustomed to] going into medical groups . . . and following guidelines." Given the fast pace at which some protocols changed at GroupCare, one ER doctor suggested, "I think the old-time family doc would say, 'Well, I've been doing this forever and it's always worked, right?'" For younger doctors, and those familiar with the Group-Care system, peer accountability became a normal part of everyday practice.

PEER PRESSURE

The most common mechanism by which doctors at GroupCare were disciplined with regard to utilization was also the most subtle. Physicians were shown where they stood on various metrics in relation to other doctors. As one department director explained:

> We're very successful here with standardizing the care. . . . And we do it not so much by forcing people but by bombarding people with the evidence—with their own practices, with where they fit on a curve. Are you ordering fifty carotid ultrasounds when your colleague next to you is ordering two, and the outcomes are identical? Why are you doing that?

One specialist recalled, "Every month now, I get a listing in the family medicine service about which doctors are the most successful in [making sure] their heart disease patients are on the four key drugs, for example." At first, the department chief listed only the top 10 percent of doctors, but he gradually expanded this list to include everyone, even "the outliers at the bottom." According to this specialist, these public forms of accountability "created tremendous pressure" among those who were measured.

Several doctors in the family medicine and emergency departments discussed how the public exhibition of physician statistics changed physician behavior because of doctors' own inherent competitiveness. One ER physician described how doctors "get feedback on utilization. You don't want to be on either end of the scale." One of her colleagues "was ordering way more tests than anyone else" and "made this really big effort to cut back" in the most recent period. Another emergency room doctor recounted a time, soon after arriving at GroupCare from residency, when he was the outlier, having ordered more CT scans than anyone else in the department. As he remembered it, he was a new doctor and "didn't want to miss anything." But by being made aware of his own practices, he became "more conscientious," and began ordering fewer.

While there were some financial incentives tied to doctors' metrics, these incentives were "much more symbolic," according to one ER doctor. Another suggested that the bonus "really doesn't matter, except . . . psychologically." Within the emergency department, for example, the amount of doctors' salaries that depended on these quality metrics was less than $1,000, a figure that was slightly less in the hospital-based medicine department, and slightly more in the family medicine department. Throughout the hospital, these bonuses made up a small fraction of doctors' salaries. Nevertheless, the process of measurement was itself quite effective at standardizing practice. According to the chief of the family medicine department, there was always variation in practice, but while "you still get the bell-shaped curve . . . it gets smaller and smaller." Over time, doctors' practices were becoming more and more alike.

Yet the line between accountability and public embarrassment was sometimes a thin one. As a result, the hospital-based medicine department had yet to institute any public disclosure of outcomes. The chief of the department recognized, "You want to keep some degree of privacy, but on the other hand, you know, you want transparency too, and privacy and transparency are inherently contradictory concepts." For this chief, going over statistics with doctors individually was—at least at the time of our interview—as transparent as he was willing to be. And there were certainly some doctors within the other two departments who grumbled about the public disclosure. Around the emergency room, doctors jokingly called the presentations the "wall of shame."

Across the GroupCare system, the observation of variation in physician performance inevitably raised questions about the extent to which such variation was acceptable. One specialist discussed how some ophthalmologists at GroupCare could "very comfortably" conduct twelve cataract surgeries in a day, whereas others in the same department were only able to do four. Would it not be more cost efficient to hire only those who could do surgeries more quickly? "I think it's something that eventually will need to be looked at in a model like GroupCare," this specialist continued, "But I don't know if they're ever going to be able to 'poke that skunk' because . . . you don't want to incentivize sloppy practice, either." A similar question might be asked of those who ordered more diagnostic tests without better medical outcomes, of those ER doctors who saw fewer patients per shift, or of those family practice doctors who were unable to help their patients manage their chronic conditions. During my research, the aggregation of EMR data was used to make variation more visible and implicitly to encourage doctors to move towards the mean. This was discipline, not coercion. But these measurements certainly could be used to isolate and exclude outliers more forcefully. A hospitalist at GroupCare suggested that some of his colleagues have been fired from GroupCare—or at least encouraged to leave—for ordering too many tests.

A CULTURE OF CONSTRAINT

Through protocols, peer reviews, and peer pressure, physicians at GroupCare were encouraged to think systemically about health care delivery: weighing the costs and benefits of different courses of action in order to maximize the health of the system's membership in the aggregate. One high-level physician administrator explicitly discussed this as a tension between the needs of the system's members as a whole and the needs of each individual member. Among most physicians interviewed, however, resource allocation (or rationing) was acknowledged only obliquely. One department chief said,

> Now, if you're a boutique doctor that sees three patients a day and can look up everything and spend an hour and a half with each patient, fine—you might give better care to those three patients you see. But if you've got three million members across [the state], you need to be able to do things in a systematic way that guarantees that you're doing things the right way.

This chief implied that a highly individualized approach to care might lead to better outcomes, but that the size of the system necessitated standardized procedures.

A hospitalist acknowledged that "we're conscious of costs" because "it's our patients' dollars we're spending." Nevertheless, he asserted that no decision is ever "just about the time and the money." He described a hypothetical situation in which a physician has to make a decision about whether to undertake an expensive procedure that would likely only lead to a marginally longer life. For him, the particular situation made all the difference: "Is it a young patient, who's twenty-four years old and could really use an extra month or six months of life? Or is it an eight-five year old person who's demented and in a nursing home who doesn't really need an extra three weeks?" Yet the implication of his argument seemed to change as he made it. Initially, he seemed to be making an argument about resource allocation—how the money would be better spent on the twenty-four-year-old. But he soon transitioned, suggesting that the eighty-five-year-old would not *want* a marginally longer life: "Or, if you sit down with a patient and the family, and they say it's not worth it to us to do this, I want comfort rather than three more weeks of this kind of suffering."

Revealingly, among the doctors I interviewed at GroupCare, there was never a time in which scientific medicine was discussed as something leading to *more* care; it was always brought up in the context of *reducing* utilization. This suggests that evidence-based medicine, at least in the context of GroupCare, was in part a way for talking about reducing health care utilization. Granted, rationing care—understood as allocating scarce resources across a population—must take place within any health care system. In the fee-for-service world, this rationing is masked underneath a rhetoric of individual preferences: those financially unable to pay for care "choose" not to. The rationing that took place at GroupCare, however, was masked by the language of scientific medicine and quality care, as if the optimization of each individual's health was consistent with the optimization of the health of the membership as a whole.

The Patient Satisfaction Survey

The patient satisfaction survey was a simpler technology than the electronic medical record and in some ways was more transparent in its effects. Each year, GroupCare mailed to a sample of its patients a survey about either an experience with their family medicine doctor or an experience they had in the hospital. The results of these surveys were aggregated, given to practitioners, and factored into end-of-the-year bonuses.[10]

Like the EMR, the PSS reinforced doctors' evolving understanding of their professional roles, though in a different way. While the EMR documented medical inputs and patient health outcomes, the PSS was meant to measure patients' affective experiences of care. And while the EMR was legitimated through an appeal to "evidence-based medicine," the PSS was legitimated through an appeal to "patient-centered medicine." Since the 1960s, medical attention has shifted from the body of the patient to the wider social and psychological context within which he or she lives, and the medical profession has started to appreciate the importance of patient care *over time*. The doctor is thus no longer merely the carrier of an abstract body of medical knowledge but is also an interpreter of the social and psychological dimensions of the patient. Moreover, the doctor's interventions are regarded as as occurring over time. Thus patient compliance, patient satisfaction, and the doctor-patient *relationship* are understood to have medical importance.[11] Patients, in this framework, are "co-producers" of health, who can act "as effective partners with providers in the care process," according to one health care scholar.[12] One hospitalist discussed the PSS in the context of patient-centered medicine: "It's that whole push in America that it's not the doctor saying, 'Here's what you do.' That there's some discussion. And all of us have been slow to say that how the patient feels about it counts for something."

In this patient-centered model, the doctor—who previously was the detached observer—becomes the patient's partner: "Doctor and patient were now two personalities circling around each other engaged in a process of mutual constitution," as David Armstrong puts it.[13] One public relations specialist at GroupCare put the point more bluntly:

> Quality very often in health care is the perception of service. The perception of quality is what kind of service you get. . . . If you operate on my knee, [I don't know] how good a job you did, as long as it works. And even if it doesn't work, you got a million excuses for the reason it didn't. . . . So you don't really know much about that, you just know how people treat you, and how they listen, and if they understand what you're telling them. If they treat you for what you *think* you need, as well as what you need, or explain it to you. . . . Part of health is perception.

Given patients' lack of medical knowledge, this professional suggested, their perception of the quality of service they received is often their only metric for evaluating the care they were given.

As a result, across the medical profession, but even more explicitly at GroupCare, the doctor's interpersonal skills—his or her capacity to understand the patient's broader social context, to put a patient at ease, to earn the patient's trust, to win the patient's compliance—have increasingly been subject to analysis and improvement. Since the doctor's own pathologies might manifest themselves in the doctor-patient interaction, these behaviors and attitudes need to be diagnosed and remedied.[14] One ER doctor had recently been going through a divorce and noticed a downward trend in his PSS scores: "Those scores go up and down with things happening in your personal life. . . . Whenever people go through problems, their scores go down. It's easy to see." For those who consistently scored poorly on the PSS, GroupCare offered training in bedside manner. Another ER doctor said, "If [the scores are] really low, there's all these classes that people can take. [These classes teach doctors to] empathize and smile and greet people and look them in the eye. Which are all important skills."

A focus on patients' emotional well-being, of course, occasionally risked reducing the doctor-patient relationship to one of customer service. One department chief was making changes in his department based on lessons he had learned as a waiter:

> I thought it was really important to greet people when they sit down, get them their drinks, try and get their orders in to get them some food. And then they're happy and they're eating and they've had their dessert, and I don't have to worry about dropping the check, because they're happy and eating, and I'm just going to worry about these other people coming in. Suddenly I have people [i.e., the first group] who are waiting forty-five minutes to go. Those are unhappy people. So I never close the deal, and I kill my tip. So I've learned that over time.

His department had been focusing on the beginning of patients' visits, on having patients registered, tested, and seen by doctors quickly, only to make them wait forty-five minutes for their discharge paperwork. This made sense from a medical perspective, but "screwed up the whole experience" from the patient's perspective. Another specialist said that entire EMR system, for which GroupCare spent billions of dollars, was "*probably* going to lead to better patient care, but [would] *certainly* lead to higher satisfaction." In his mind, the new system contained "bells and whistles," "things that are impressive to patients, like, you'll send them off to get a chest x-ray and you'll bring them back to the room, and you'll literally be able to show them their chest x-ray on the [screen], . . . because it's all digital now, you know?" In this case, the doctor implied, the technology was aimed as much at patient satisfaction as at health care quality.

But patient satisfaction was itself seen as a legitimate medical goal among many of the medical administrators I interviewed. One department chief suggested that doctors have historically "ignored the customer service aspect of medicine." He explained, "It's not just ass-kissing. . . . We forget that patients walk out of here, and they're going to choose to do what we ask them to do or not." Patient satisfaction, he suggested, was related to health outcomes because patients are more likely to comply with doctors' orders if they have positive experiences with them: "If we don't engage them as people and as customers, then they're not going to believe in us when we tell them, 'You've got to take your baby aspirin every day, or you need to stop smoking.'" This was becoming *more* true as a result of patients' changing attitudes towards doctors, he suggested. Previously, there had been a "very paternalistic relationship between doctor and patient," but now "they've been reading about their problem on the Internet, and they probably know more about it than you do. . . . Or certainly they have a list of the possibilities. . . . They need to believe that you're engaged in the whole process before they'll engage in it." A nurse administrator emphasized that "[your] mental health . . . contributes to your [overall] health." She continued, "So, if I'm in the hospital, and I'm particularly disenchanted, and I hate the food, and I'm upset about my diet, and I think the people are rude, all of that feeds into my ability to get well quicker." Finally, an ER doctor put the point somewhat more coarsely: "Medicine's a service job, right? It is. It took me a long time to realize that. You come in with a demand, I'm providing you a service, and I have to make you happy." Reluctantly, this doctor seemed to acknowledge the legitimacy of satisfaction as a medical goal.

AMBIGUOUS ACCEPTANCE

If physicians almost universally recognized the value of EMRs to their profession, however, their feelings about the PSS were more ambivalent. Doctors' criticisms of the PSS fell along three lines: first, sample size and sample error in the administration of the PSS made it unreliable; second, the PSS was invalid, since it was not a good measure of the quality of the doctor; and third, the PSS actually skewed care towards practices that would enhance "satisfaction" at the expense of quality care.

Several physicians suggested that the PSS was unreliable. An ER doctor said that many physicians wondered, "How good is that data when you measure only six or twelve surveys?" Another observed that "[in] any given quarter your numbers can drastically be different for some reason—sample size more than anything else." Nevertheless, several doctors also recognized that there were consistent patterns over time. One emergency room doctor said, "Consistently some people's [scores] are high." Another said, "People do complain about [the surveys], that they're biased, and they're not perfect. But the flip side of that is there are definitely trends. There are people who have consistently low [scores]—they have a little more trouble getting along with people." Overall, while there were some grumblings among doctors about the unreliability of the PSS, most acknowledged that the surveys did capture something about a doctor's interactions with patients.

A more damning critique was that the PSS was invalid. A family medicine doctor decried, "They give lip service to wanting to connect with patients, but [satisfaction] scores are popularity contests. You know, it depends on how jovial you are and, you know, if you sit and hold their hand." An emergency doctor agreed that the PSS was not related to a doctor's clinical judgment: "If you're brilliant and you make the right diagnosis, doesn't mean people are going to like you and think you're a good doctor. . . . It doesn't have much of a correlation—it has a little correlation but not much." He continued that the scores have "nothing to do with how good a doctor you are—it's a personality test."

A second ER doctor was even more scathing: "I think this whole membership satisfaction thing is a bunch of nonsense. So if the patient likes what I had to offer, fine. If not, I'll usually try and figure out if it's somebody who I think is, you know, a solid citizen. I'll try and figure it out. If it's just a drug addict, then I really don't care." This doctor distinguished between patients whose opinion he respected and those he felt were unreliable. In general, he continued, "The average Joe . . . doesn't recognize when they're getting good or bad quality. They just know whether they like their doctor. It's unbelievable the number of times I look at some [doctors] and go, 'I don't know what that guy was thinking—that's just the worst medicine,' but the patient loves them, because they're nice to 'em and they listen, or whatever it is that the patient needs to have to feel good." These doctors tended to downplay the extent to which patients' regard for the physician was related to the care they received.

Finally, a few physicians worried that focusing on the PSS encouraged doctors to *compromise* health care quality for the sake of high scores. For example, several suggested that pain medications were overprescribed at GroupCare because of doctors' concerns about their scores. According to an ER doctor, "Probably more Vicodin prescriptions get written because of [the PSS], you know?" According to a family medicine doctor, "As long as you give them their Vicodin, they're happy and they'll rank you high." A second ER doctor suggested that because of the PSS, GroupCare has "a massive, massive proportion of people that are addicted to meds." Using the example of a thirty-year-old-woman with back pain, he continued, "Now she's addicted to drugs, because every time she comes in, the doctor says, 'Oh, here you go. . . . You'll feel better,' instead of doing the right thing, which is either figure out what's causing it, or if there's no answer, get her into the chronic pain people." Of course, this same doctor acknowledged that similar rules applied in the fee-for-service world, where "the [patient] wanted more, you wanted them to want more, 'cause you can bill more." But at GroupCare, he said, "You want to do what's right medically." And the PSS scores "get in the way of doing the right thing. Because most of the time, people are complaining and dropping your scores because they didn't get something they wanted."

Yet other doctors suggested that PSS scores were not related to doctors' utilization patterns, calling into question concerns about overprescription. One hospitalist said, "Our highest-scoring doctor is a pediatrician, and I've shared some patients with her, and I don't see her over-ordering. So I don't think—'cause we would have pretty good data about that—that to get a good score you need to order lots of tests." In fact, one family medicine doctor suggested that high patient satisfaction might allow him to convince patients *not* to overutilize resources: "When you establish you relationship with a patient—you know, after I've known somebody after a year or so, they know I take good care of them." This level of trust, he implied, would allow him to push back on a patient's desire for care he did not think was necessary.

THE GAME

Just as doctors were compared with one another by their utilization rates, so they were compared by their PSS scores. These scores would factor into each physician's bonus at the end of the year, but—like the incentives surrounding utilization rates—the amount of money was less important than its symbolism. According to one department chief, "It's symbolic, and everyone has this desire to get as much of the incentive payment as possible. There's a very human feeling there. You know, you don't want that payment, however small it is, to be cut."

If discussions about practitioners' utilization rates were couched within the context of scientific medicine, and variation was examined as a puzzle as much as it was as a problem, the display of PSS scores was more obviously competitive. And so despite the different degrees to which doctors viewed the PSS as legitimate, most felt inspired to work on increasing their scores in relationship to one another. One ER doctor said, "Everyone going into medicine . . . [is] very competitive," so they do not like to be below the curve. Another ER doctor acknowledged he tried "to maximize [the PSS score], and it's just purely because of the number, because we're competitive people." A department chief said, "By nature, physicians are competitive people, and so we can put up people's statistics and say, 'Hey, congratulations Dr. A, you're at the top of the list, and . . . hey, Dr. J, how come you're . . . behind?'" Even those doctors who did not feel invested in their own PSS scores tried to avoid having scores that were too low. One ER doctor said, "You don't want to be the guy at the bottom." Another ER doctor said that while he did not personally care about his scores, "in the last few months, the gal that's at the bottom feels bad about it. So I think it does have a little bit of a shame effect."

The PSS scores were shared widely, both across departments in the same facility and within the same department across facilities. The chief of the emergency department bragged, "I have . . . five doctors in the top 10 percent of the region in terms of patient satisfaction. . . . So, you know we're doing something right here." But this transparency also led to some hurt feelings and confusion. One ER doctor recalled how the administration recently "released a lot of data about all the docs in the medical center—like a mass e-mail . . . about [PSS] scores—and docs were like 'What are you doing? Why are you doing this? Within your department, okay, but all the docs?'" This degree of transparency felt like an invasion of privacy. A specialist, who had not yet been subjected to this level of scrutiny, suggested that among those doctors who were ranked, it "creates tremendous pressure." A family medicine doctor confirmed, "They publish the [PSS] scores. . . . Your name is there, your rank, or where you are on this list of the [PSS] score." He felt that the decision to publish PSS scores was evidence that physicians "don't know how to manage people." He felt the medical administrators within GroupCare used the PSS comparisons to "just kind of pit [doctors] against each other." He continued, "We're not going to actually sit down and chastise you, we're just going to embarrass the living shit out of you, you know?"

THE MARKET MOTIVE

Despite their misgivings, several doctors suggested that the PSS was especially important given that doctors were on salary within GroupCare. While insulation from the market allowed doctors to practice without paying attention to utilization rates, according to one department chief, the same insulation meant that "it is a little bit harder to get people motivated" than in the fee-for-service world. Several others echoed this idea, suggesting that doctors in the fee-for-service world were more motivated to keep their patients happy, given their financial incentives. According to one family medicine doctor at GroupCare, "In the private practice setting it's the consummate capitalistic environment, where patients vote with their feet. They like you, they stay; if they don't like you there's a guy next door, who'd be more than happy to take your insurance." When one ER doctor moved to GroupCare from the fee-for-service environment, she remembered, "It was shocking to me when I had the first kind of experiences with the doctors who didn't want to do their job."

Variation and the Limits of Discipline

There was some variation by department in terms of the types of information that the EMR system and PSS surveys were able to capture. Among different departments, these technologies had different degrees of intensity, in that they could capture more or less detailed information, and were regarded with different degrees of legitimacy among the medical staff. Different departments, moreover, had different social arrangements within which these technologies were deployed and understood. In some departments, doctors were isolated from one another, while in other departments they worked alongside one another. As a result, different departments had different sorts of disciplinary regimes, and physicians within each had different strategies for negotiating them.

Within the family medicine department, each doctor was linked to a particular panel of patients, so each doctor could be evaluated in terms of his or her patients' health. The department chief easily collected data by physician on patients' "blood pressure, cholesterol, lipids, cervical cancer screening, mammography," among other indicators. Similarly, since family medicine doctors were responsible for particular patients over time, their PSS scores were assumed to reflect something valid about the ongoing relationships they had managed to establish. Compared with other departments, then, the family medicine department was subject to scrutiny that was seen as both more intense and more valid. Moreover, physicians in the family medicine department typically worked in relative isolation from one another, returning to private offices (or shared with one other doctor) after seeing patients.

Within this department, then, doctors were under close surveillance but did not interact closely with one another. While this combination did not bother many family medicine doctors (especially the high-performing ones), it had the potential to foster deep estrangement. One family medicine doctor said, "Definitely there's some isolation, there are some people that get belligerent. . . . This system has gobbled up and spit out some very good people." Several family medicine doctors even began attending group therapy together in order to deal with the pressure of working under such surveillance: "We actually have a group that meets every other week with a psychologist sitting at the end of the table down there. . . . And we're all reasonably tight, because we're sharing heartfelt things."

Within the emergency department, however, the scrutiny was less intense and the indicators were seen as less legitimate. The chief of the emergency department admitted that family medicine's utilization metrics are "much more robust" than his own department's. He went on to describe some quality-related metrics the department had begun to use, such as whether doctors were following protocol for pneumonia patients or whether heart-attack patients were given aspirin and nitroglycerine within thirty minutes. But he also described *process*-related metrics, such as whether doctors "follow up on patients either by phone or by e-mail" and whether they "do some training." Furthermore, the PSS surveys in the emergency department were based on single ER visits and so were not treated with the same seriousness as the PSS measures in the family medicine department. As one ER doctor put it, "There definitely are a lot of unhappy people" in the emergency room. Emergency room patients are often very sick, and they often have to wait for a long time to get treated and discharged. Emergency room doctors thus took their PSS scores with large grains of salt.

The social organization of work in the emergency room also helped to mitigate any feelings of estrangement. Emergency doctors worked closely with one another all the time. While family practice doctors often saw patients without coming into contact with one another, the ER doctors were constantly seeing patients alongside, and seeking advice from, each other. One ER doctor described the group meetings by saying, "People squawk about [the metrics] and say funny comments—we're a pretty silly, funny group." Describing how he chose to work at GroupCare in the first place, the chief suggested that GroupCare's emergency department had always been especially collegial when compared with other emergency rooms: "It's really nice to have someone to bounce ideas off of and say, 'What would you do with this person? What do you think of this x-ray?' . . . It seemed like a relatively comfortable, safe environment to practice in."

Within the emergency room, then, the effects of the EMR and PSS depended on the doctors' collective interpretation of the results generated. Oftentimes the doctors in the emergency department seemed to hold one another accountable for hard work and good results, intensifying the competition among doctors in some ways but also providing a social framework in which this competition did not feel alienating. Occasionally, however, doctors seemed collectively to challenge the technologies. For example, one doctor had earned especially high PSS scores and was teased by his colleagues: "It has garnished me the reputation among a couple of the docs within my group as being a hugger—a warm and fuzzy hugger. . . . 'Well, no, I'm just not old and crusty like you.' I don't say that." With high levels of social cohesion, the ER doctors supported one another in striving for good marks but were also able collectively to challenge the significance of these marks.

Compared to family medicine and emergency medecine, hospital-based medicine had the most difficulty tying particular metrics to particular doctors, since most patients in the department saw multiple doctors while admitted in the hospital. That being said, there were some metrics that were "either attached to the admitting doctor or . . . attached to the discharge doctor." For example, the measure of whether a doctor provided aspirin beta-blocker on admission for a heart attack was linked to the admitting doctor, and the discharge orders were linked to the discharge doctor. Nevertheless, within the hospital-based medicine department it was harder to hold one doctor accountable for the patient's health as a whole. According to one hospitalist, "if you're measuring something about that patient, like how long they were in the hospital, . . . it may involve five of us, so we can't pin it to a doctor." As a result, there were some benchmarks that the whole department was held to, but "we can't peel out each individual person, so we just take a conglomerate of the department."

Likewise, since many doctors were often responsible for the same patient, patient satisfaction scores were generated regarding the doctor who had the longest period of responsibility for the patient. The chief of the department admitted, "The attribution is very spotty, still." As a result, he continued, "You're not looking for minute differences." Rather, the PSS scores are a way of finding the doctor "that's consistently . . . in the lower end."

As a whole, within the hospital-based medicine department, clinical measurement was relatively lax. Doctors also worked independently of one another. Therefore, those who were dissatisfied with the organization seemed able to shirk without being noticed. One doctor discussed how another doctor would finish seeing his patients quickly and then "go lay in the call room and watch TV and lock the door" when he was done. The doctor relating the story would himself often finish seeing his patients a few hours after he arrived and "just sit around." Perhaps because of the lack of monitoring mechanisms, it was difficult to prevent—or even observe—this obvious inefficiency within the department.

Constructing Collegiality

Of great concern to many of the doctors I interviewed were less the physicians' relationships to patients so much as the doctors' relationships with one another. Just as some doctors suggested that the fee-for-service market provided incentives for doctors to treat patients well, they also believed that the market had a civilizing impact on specialists' collegiality with referring doctors. According to one hospitalist, specialists in the fee-for-service world, who depended on doctor referrals, often bent over backwards for the referring doctors. But at GroupCare, "It almost allows you, once you're a partner, to treat certain people in a negative way." Indeed, many of the doctors interviewed in this study mentioned how difficult it was to motivate specialists to go out of their way for patients, given the lack of market incentives *and* their autonomy from PSS scores. One hospitalist observed:

> So, yeah, the willingness of a GI doctor to come into the emergency room in the middle of the night and endoscope somebody, to risk-stratify them—do they need to be in the hospital or don't they? There's one of them on call for any given week, and they're pretty well extended out, and they're not willing to do

that sort of thing, which would help us immensely and help the patients, too. But in terms of this culture here, they're not willing to do that.

An emergency medicine doctor expressed a similar sentiment:

> And particularly in the middle of the night, when human nature says I want to stay in my bed, if they stay in their bed, they're going to get paid the same, whether they get up or not. It's a lot harder, as an emergency physician, to get [specialists] to do things that need to be done [at GroupCare].

A second hospital-based medicine doctor recounted how one of his colleagues was driven to tears when she called for a surgical consultation on a patient and was rebuffed by the surgeon, who complained, "Why are you calling me?"

Over the course of this study, GroupCare has begun to implement peer-review surveys among physicians in order to monitor those practitioners whom patients were less able to assess. Under this new system, according to a hospitalist, doctors would be able to evaluate any other doctor in the facility about whether the person "go[es] the extra mile"—whether the person was "civil, responsive, easy to deal with, available." Since the implementation of the new peer surveys, this hospitalist observed, one of the more notoriously rude orthopedic surgeons "doesn't argue quite as strenuously anymore, you know, and so it's kind of nice." And a physician administrator in a specialty department suggested that while these evaluations were not particularly useful for identifying difficult colleagues, since "if you ask the department who is the problem, . . . people would know," they did help to document bad behavior so "something can be done" about it.

GroupCare worked to reduce the uncertainty inherent in medical practice by optimizing the health of the organization's membership as a whole. As a part of this project, the organization sought to limit individual physician discretion and to produce among physicians predictable medical (and emotional) responses to particular patient problems. Leaders in the organization came to recognize, however, that consent worked better than coercion and that—through a combination of advanced technology and old-fashioned social incentives—doctors could be disciplined *through* (rather than in opposition to) their professional identities. As doctors interacted with the "language" of EMRs—shaping the system, entering information, and being measured and compared on the basis of these data—they came to think more statistically and systematically about the work that they did. They came to focus not only on particular cases but on the universe of cases. Almost invisibly, then, they came to take on responsibility for the allocation of scarce resources across the patient population, *becoming* the administrators whom, in the previous generation of health maintenance organizations, they had fought against. And as doctors became invested in their patient satisfaction scores, they came to regard themselves—at least in part—as service workers instead of as medical professionals.

Through different technologies and with different degrees of success in different departments, the interests of physicians at GroupCare were coordinated so as to be in the financial interests of the organization as a whole. Doctors were not proletarianized so much as they were *incorporated* into the interests of a large corporate enterprise out of their control.

CHAPTER NINE

Partnership

Andrew Quan was a thirty-something ER doctor at GroupCare. He had begun college as an engineering major, but when he volunteered in an emergency room he got a taste for the excitement of emergency medicine and never looked back. He switched his major, went to medical school, and joined GroupCare directly after finishing residency. Yet he soon grew frustrated by how little GroupCare seemed to "cater to doctors." At other hospitals in the area, doctors could park their cars right by the hospital entrance: "That's important to [doctors] . . . to get to their jobs and get things done." At GroupCare, they had to use the same garage as the other staff. Other hospitals had luxurious doctors' lounges, "stocked with food for breakfast, lunch, and sometimes dinner," whereas GroupCare doctors had to use the cafeteria along with everyone else. In Quan's account, the straw that "broke the camel's back" came on a Christmas. The nurses were having a holiday party, and one of them came over to ask whether he wanted to contribute some money for the event. Then she interrupted herself and joked, "Well, actually, don't worry about it. I'm getting paid more than you are anyway." While this nurse was probably exaggerating, nurses and ancillary staff at GroupCare *were* paid significantly more than they were at the other hospitals in Las Lomas. Quan left the hospital soon after this exchange, although he would return a few years later.

GroupCare's commitment to reducing uncertainty in medical care was expressed not only in the way that it managed its doctors but also in the relationships it worked to establish among different constituencies within the organization. Throughout GroupCare, the language of partnership abounded—patients "partnered" with the organization, doctors "partnered" with one another, and nurses and ancillary workers "partnered" with doctors and managers. The logic—at least as discussed by administrators—was that the mitigation of status distinctions allowed the organization to evolve into a "culture of continuous improvement." By harnessing the creativity, energy, and enthusiasm of everyone in the organization it could continue to deliver the highest-quality care at a competitive price. According to one charge nurse, GroupCare administrators "want employee participation and new ideas. They're really into that. They're really into evidence-based medicine and putting it into—you know, making it happen. They'll try anything that's progressive." At PubliCare, status distinctions blurred amidst the "muck" of human suffering; at GroupCare, in contrast, status distinctions were mitigated more formally in order to facilitate the efficient production of care.

Yet there were tensions in this vision of partnership. On the one hand, the organization sought to reward and foster participation among all levels of employees. On the other hand, in order to conduct experiments successfully, and in order to institutionalize successful experiments across multiple departments, Group-Care Health required an extensive bureaucracy. The same vision of inclusiveness and partnership thus meant that *all constituencies*, from doctors to managers to workers, were subordinate to bureaucratic authority. Moreover, as "efficient" solutions were institutionalized, there became less room to innovate; bureaucratic rules supplanted charismatic creativity.

Furthermore, the existence of an extensive bureaucracy meant that bureaucratic elites gained authority at the expense of everyone else. And while bureaucratic rules and chains of command were more formalized here than elsewhere, these rules and staff structures were supported by bureaucratic shortcuts and informal networks of authority. Practical knowledge—knowledge of how to navigate GroupCare's bureaucracy—seemed as important as one's formal position or technical skill.

Doctors as Partners

The headquarters of the GroupCare Health Foundation, one of the largest physicians' groups in the country, was situated in a skyscraper not more than an hour's drive from Las Lomas. In order to reach the executive suite, one needed security clearance. The executive I met, Roger Gleeson, had a spacious corner office and a ready supply of Diet Coke, a can of which he was still nursing in the late afternoon. Though he had been a surgeon for approximately thirty years, he only participated in the occasional surgery after moving into administration. Since he led a twenty-billion-dollar organization and taught classes at a prestigious business school, he said, he did not have time for being a doctor. It was one of the "big sacrifices" he made going into management.

The GroupCare Health Foundation was the physicians' branch of GroupCare Health. The foundation was a for-profit organization, legally distinct though practically inseparable from GroupCare as a whole. After trial periods of approximately three years, doctors at GroupCare Health were offered "partner" status by their departments. Formally, partner status meant that doctors were able to vote on admitting other doctors to partnership status and to vote on the group's CEO and the local facility's physician in chief; it also meant that doctors received a financial stake in the corporation. Beyond these elections, however, "the rest of the process, the administrative process, is not so open," according to one hospitalist. Even the leadership elections were "much more like a politburo," according to another specialist. Nevertheless, partnership status did help doctors feel invested in the well-being of the organization. It also served as a kind of tenure—according to one young ER doctor, "Once you're partner, you can fall back and do the minimum." An older hospitalist (and partner herself) agreed: "You just can't get rid of them, you know. They can screw up royally after that." A third hospitalist said that getting rid of a negligent partner was a "long, arduous process" involving several stages of documentation, meetings with administrators, and arbitration—and could take as long as two years. A final ER doctor, discussing his decision to come to GroupCare, acknowledged, "Nobody's asking me about big decisions with the hospital, but nobody's gonna can me without cause."

The partner model at GroupCare was designed in such a way that nearly all physician administrators also maintained clinical practices. According to one physician administrator, this meant that administrators "have the credibility of seeing patients . . . and suffering under the same [procedures]" that they impose. Among some physicians, though, physician administrators were regarded as administrators wearing a veil of medical legitimacy. Once people become concerned with "the system in general . . . and optimiz[ing] the system . . . they become not a physician anymore. They're an administrator, which is almost like swearing, you know."

If most doctors at the organization were partners, there was still a wide range informal authority among different doctors in the organization. Informal authority was loosely correlated with doctors' administrative responsibilities, but also distinct from formal position. Describing one of his colleagues, a family practice doctor said, "You can collect titles, put them on the shelf. . . . Titles don't mean much. *He's* actually got sway." Explaining how power worked within the organization as a whole, he continued, "There [is] a subgroup of people who—I guess the analogy would be [they] ran for student council. . . . That's just what they want to do; they want to be at the microphone during assemblies, . . . and they want to be popular. And those people, when they get an idea, they can make changes." While some people were "in," this family doctor did not consider himself "in that inner circle." He had recently written an e-mail to Gleeson about what he considered unnecessary roadblocks to ordering certain tests; Gleeson then copied the CMO of the local facility, the department chief, and others in his response; and the doctor got a call from a colleague asking what he was doing writing to Gleeson in the first place. The implication from this family practice doctor was that only certain doctors were supposed to have access to Gleeson.

Others also acknowledged the unstated differences in power held by different members of the physician staff. One older hospitalist explained that despite the rhetoric of partnership, "the process is driven by a handful of people, and major decisions are made by a handful of people and then presented to the group, and the group generally ratifies those decisions. But do you have input in terms of the way the decision was made? No, you don't." Given the informal hierarchies among the medical staff, a younger hospitalist who had left GroupCare observed that "you have to walk on eggshells a lot more" at GroupCare than at HolyCare. "You find out who has power, and you kiss their butt." There was one decision in particular that had rankled this hospitalist. The critical care department at Group-Care—or ICU—was typically "closed," meaning that internal medicine doctors were not permitted to practice within it. Yet one physician administrator in the critical care department with "a lot of power" had advocated for a system in which hospitalists would staff the critical care department between 5 p.m. and 7 a.m. For the hospitalist, it seemed as though the critical care doctor used her power in order to advance the interests of her department—not the interests of patients. The hospitalist was frustrated that the "more power you have, the more you could change things or direct things so your quality of life is better." In this case, the head of the hospitalist department himself was "afraid of her. He does anything he can to make her happy, because she has too much power. And you want to be on her good side. If you're not on her good side, then you're done with." Even though the department chief was a well-respected partner, "if he rocked the boat with her, she could make [the department's] lives more miserable."

Several nurse administrators echoed these sentiments. One suggested that there were "people in positions of power [at GroupCare] that utilize that power in a way that degrades the system." She thought that there were boundaries between work and private life that were systematically violated within the organization: "Nurses have these relationships with physicians, physicians have those relationships with each other, nurses have those relationships with each other." She was surprised to learn that one of the head doctors at the facility had gone traveling with the director of the quality department—what she considered a conflict of interest. "The director of quality shouldn't have a goddamn thing to do with the head physician." For her, the "incestuous" nature of the organization undermined people's ability to "take care of the things you need to take care of, because there's friendship involved."

But if these informal allegiances and hierarchies made the GroupCare bureaucracy an imperfectly efficient one, in some respects, they also seemed to have developed as a necessary complement to the impersonal and rationalistic elements of the organizational structure. One longstanding hospitalist explained that because doctors were on salary at GroupCare, their "responsiveness and willingness to participate is more personal than it is professional." He himself relied on these informal relationships as he advocated for his patients: "For instance, there are certain surgeons that I know I can get to see a patient right away and do what needs to be done. And some that aren't quite so responsive. And you have to play your cards right in terms of who's on call at any given time." This, he argued, was a "part of practicing medicine in an integrated system." Somewhat paradoxically, this same hospitalist implied that the increasing standardization and rationalization actually generated a type of inefficiency, since he no longer "had time to establish a relationship over a long period of time" with each new doctor. The "small group camaraderie" that helped to lubricate the wheels of the bureaucracy was wearing thin.

Organizational theory has long suggested that those within an organization able to solve its "central problem" are able to exert influence over the organization's direction.[1] At GroupCare, power tended to be held by those who were central to the processes of rationalization and systemization deemed critical to Group-Care's success. For example, the charge nurse in GroupCare's emergency room was given more authority than his or her counterparts at the other two hospitals. John Hoddess, one of these charge nurses, said proudly, "Whoever's in charge is the most critical position in the whole department. You're telling the doctors what to do because it's all about the flow." He liked the job because he was able "to make thousands of decisions every shift" and was able to intervene in crisis situations and "be the hero." He also felt "responsible for everything that goes on in the shift." Yet despite this pressure, John felt as though the organization backed up his authority. For example, in most emergency rooms, the charge nurse was the "only person that's thinking about who's in the waiting room, and [whether there is] someone dying in the waiting room." But GroupCare administrators had recently been "all about flow" and had begun an initiative to get patients admitted to the hospital (and out of the emergency room) within sixty minutes. This pressure—and other quality-improvement initiatives like this one—"really helped out" by giving him the power to do his job well. While his job had always involved managing the department as a whole, the administration's prioritization of these processes gave him organizational backing.

On occasion, however, these organizational priorities meant that there were mismatches between people's status in medical hierarchies and their power within the department. One ER doctor, for example, remarked that "when nurses get promoted to charge nurse position, . . . the relationships get more difficult."

People whom she "got along with well when they were regular floor nurses" she now found "really annoying." According to this doctor, it was "a hard position to pull off without alienating people." Yet it seemed that this doctor was also frustrated with the authority that the charge nurse wielded over her and other doctors at GroupCare: doctors were not used to taking commands from nurses.

THE LIMITS TO RATIONALIZATION

As explored in the previous two chapters, doctors and administrators at Group-Care were committed to an idea that, through evidence-based medicine and the right financial incentives, they could reduce the uncertainty and malcoordination that plagued so much of medical practice. But several doctors and nurse administrators suggested that standardization at GroupCare has taken on a life of its own, becoming an end in itself rather than a means to consistent and scientific care. One hospitalist argued that standardization initially began "for stuff . . . which there is science" to support. Yet, she continued, the administration of the hospital "seems to have . . . been riding on that success . . . to push for more things that involve micromanaging." For example, Gleeson recently mandated that hospitalists work seven days in a row. Yet this hospitalist's group had "some people that like working five days in a row" and she herself "like[d] working ten days in a row." Her response was, "What study shows that seven days is better than six days, is better than ten?"

In the emergency room, several physicians complained that administrators had made it impossible for ER doctors to send less-serious cases to the outpatient clinics—a practice that many relied upon in order to open up beds for more-serious patients. According to one physician administrator, Gleeson was "not an emergency physician, he doesn't work up here, he doesn't know our situation. He's a good [leader] . . . but he's jamming something down our throat that's pretty far down the line for him." A second ER physician suggested that the policy decision may have been made in response to an adverse event at a separate facility, in which someone was triaged to the outpatient clinics and then died. But if this was the case, it was not made public to the ER doctors at GroupCare, who were unable to change a policy that felt far removed from scientific medicine *or* efficient care.

One nurse administrator thought that these sorts of decisions were evidence of bureaucratic corruption: "It doesn't matter how much evidence-based practice you have if the people who oversee that and ensure that it's handled appropriately are corrupt." More likely, it seems, was that processes of centralization, first made in the name of organizational efficiency and quality, had led to standardization beyond the point that many physicians thought was positively related to outcomes.

Partnering with Labor

Just as physicians at GroupCare were "partners" with one another, so labor at GroupCare was "partnered" with management. At GroupCare Health, the union was part of the infrastructure—figuratively and literally. In the middle of the facility's sprawling campus, off a hallway between primary care clinics, the labor-management partnership had a small office space. Inside, I met Julia Wells, a labor contract specialist for the union. Wells was a short, stocky, charismatic Filipina in her late thirties. In the late 1990s, she worked as a phone operator for a cable company, a job she hated. When the company sold itself off to a bigger company, she took the severance package and started her own cleaning business. The business was going well, but Wells was still working long days. So when two clients encouraged her to apply for a job at GroupCare, she said she'd consider it—despite her desire to "be my own boss." As a phone operator at GroupCare, Wells started "making the most money I've ever made." In the seventeen years she had been with her husband, it was the first time she was making more than he was, a point of some pride. And while she began as a noncontractual employee, working part-time, she gradually increased her hours and joined GroupCare's full-time staff: "When I got that first check from GroupCare, I ripped up my resume. I knew that they were not taking me away unless they were dragging me out by security, kicking and screaming." GroupCare is well known for paying its employees—from nurses on down—well above the rates of the two other hospitals in town.

Wells had grown up in a union family—she remembered riding her bicycle on the picket line with her father outside his manufacturing plant while her mother and some of the other wives made sandwiches for the strikers. And as she began working at GroupCare she became increasingly involved in the union, first as a union steward, then as chief steward at the hospital, and then as contract specialist—a full-time position paid by GroupCare with responsibility for handling workers' grievances with supervisors as well as supervisors' problems with workers. By the time I met her, Wells represented roughly 1,200 union members at GroupCare facilities all over the county. She loved it: "I like to talk a lot, . . . and I think that I'm a people person, so when I walk down the hallway everybody knows me. . . . I make time to talk to each of the members, because they're important to me."

The labor-management partnership at GroupCare Health was unique in the health care industry. Since GroupCare was founded as a health plan for a largely unionized workforce in the 1940s, the organization had always been sympathetic to labor unions. Not only did union pressure help inspire the *creation* of the health system, but the health system had always counted a large number of union members as patients. According to one union leader, GroupCare "was more accepting of unions from its inception." A physician administrator agreed, saying, "We're committed to unions. We came from a union environment." And even those who were less enthusiastic about the partnership acknowledged the union's lasting influence in the facility. According to one hospital-based physician, "We will never split up from the unions because that's how it started." One worker-leader recalled how John Sweeney, then the head of the AFL-CIO, threatened to withdraw union members from the GroupCare system during some contentious negotiations. According to her, Sweeney said, "Don't forget where you came from, where your roots are, who supports you—it's the unions."

In addition to the system's working-class heritage, two other factors helped make the union at GroupCare Health especially strong. First, unlike the other two hospitals in town, GroupCare Health was an integrated health system consisting of several primary and specialty clinics in addition to its hospital. While ancillary workers make up less than half of employees in most hospitals, they made up the majority of employees in the GroupCare Health clinics. As a whole, then, GroupCare was much more reliant on its ancillary workers than other hospitals. Second, GroupCare's integrated, prepaid group model made it hugely profitable, compared with other health care providers in California. According to one physician director, despite the high wages that GroupCare provides, it could easily pay more.

The labor-management contract at GroupCare covered nearly every aspect of workers' lives at the organization, from worker evaluations to processes of interest-based conflict resolution. In keeping with her role, Wells seemed always to keep a physical copy of it close at hand. She had thumbed through the thick purple book so thoroughly it looked like it had been through the wash, although by the time I met her she seemed to have committed most of it to memory. In meetings she often told her stewards to read the contract carefully enough so that it looked as worn as hers. And at the end of our first meeting, with an air of gravitas, she gave me a copy of the contract that had been owned by one of her favorite union representatives. She had been saving it as a sort of keepsake.

In some ways the contract at GroupCare was like a union contract in any other industry. In contrast to the vague and value-laden evaluations at HolyCare Hospital, the contract required that worker evaluations at GroupCare be broken down into detailed elements tailored to specific job positions. Within each category (e.g., "Job Knowledge," "Patient Interaction," "Communication and Documentation," "Emergency Response") were sets of particular practices on which a manager evaluated a particular employee (e.g., "Effectively communicates with co-workers and members," "Clearly writes/edits, documents, and transcribes information," "Completes documentation on time," "Uses correct terminology, style, and format.") Perhaps most important, there was an elaborate process of demerits and warnings that managers had to follow in order to discipline or fire employees. One worker leader who had previously worked at a Sisters of St. Francis hospital felt that he had been "brainwashed" into not wanting the union there. When he came to GroupCare it was a revelation: "Because you actually have some representation. They couldn't just kick you out the door just because they didn't like you or whatever. They actually had to have grounds to do it and everything."

Job security, wages, and due process are the bread and butter of union representation. The GroupCare contract was much more expansive, guiding many different dimensions of work at the organization. For example, the cornerstone of the labor-management partnership was the department teams. These teams, made up of representatives from all partnering members of the work unit (physicians, managers, and selected workers part of the partnership), were responsible for making decisions about "core operational and environmental issues" using a set of labor-management partnership principles and practices, such as interest-based problem solving and consensus decision making. Another facility-wide team provided coaching for the members of these department teams. As one of several color fliers put out by the labor-management partnership explained, the department teams were intended "to increase involvement and result in improved performance." One labor leader believed that the department team "empowers workers a lot. . . . It's not just following directives; it's really thinking critically about what they can do to help and be more productive. And I shouldn't even say productive; they think creatively about what they can do to help the department."

The premise of the partnership was that productivity and involvement, efficiency and commitment, went hand in hand. More generally, the partnership embodied the idea—widespread throughout the organization—that bureaucratic innovation could tame the hazards of the market and bring stability to health care delivery; that with the right organizational structure, the interests of each part of the organization, and of each individual, could be aligned with the interests of the organization as a whole.

As one department head put it, the labor-management partnership was also "brilliant strategy." He explained that after a "horrible strike" in 1986, managers of the system and union leaders realized "We all want the same thing." He continued, "The labor unions can get the malcontents to work better than we can. . . . [They can] get their own in line." Moreover, he said, "It also works a lot better to do things in partnership and to . . . work out problems on the front lines together." The partnership ensured that workers did not feel like "'the man's' telling them what to do all the time. You know, they're 'the man.' They're making a difference in their own workplace, and they're valued and listened to." Since labor shared responsibility for the functioning of the department, "if they have someone who's not doing their job, it impacts all of their members, too. And it's frustrating to them." He continued, "In terms of discipline it's better, in terms of functioning on a module it's better." One ER doctor, who was less impressed with the partnership overall, nevertheless recognized that while the nurses at HolyCare and PubliCare Hospitals consistently went on strike, "We don't have that." So, he concluded, "the [partnership] obviously has its benefits."

Many worker leaders and union staff also understood that GroupCare's commitment to the partnership was at least in part a managerial strategy—as was "labor peace" for industrial manufacturing in the post–World War II era.[2] A union leader admitted that there was only labor peace at GroupCare Health "to the extent that they can make money." Yet many of the executives at GroupCare Health, he said, also had "an appreciation . . . that there's value to the workers having a union and there's value to the political power that the union may bring to help GroupCare Health in other areas . . . that there's value to workers having a voice."

A GroupCare executive who had been intimately involved in the development and implementation of the department team program expanded on this point. He argued that the department teams would not work as a managerial strategy if they were understood by either labor or management as being "an artificial setting . . . where we sit around and push jargon at each other." At those sites in which the partnership "was politically correct ideology, the process sort of failed. And the places where the supervisors weren't good at listening, the process failed." But in many settings, he continued, the process worked: "When the first teams were done, many of them had real successes and care was better, service was better, work-through was better. And that was celebrated, shared, publicized."

One key to a successful department team, this executive suggested, was building a sense of teamwork and group identity to bridge different employees' formal positions in the organization's hierarchy. In many cases the idea of "patient care" was able to be this unifying ideology. Since all constituencies had a common interest in the patient, he explained, "if you focus on the patient and then the team sits down and talks about how do we collectively work on making the patient fare better, you get a level of buy-in." Of course, this "sense of [group] identity" also relied on savvy leaders. The organization thus committed significant resources to "training the supervisors to be good team leaders." The partnership did not mean that supervisors "stopped [being] accountable," but rather they had "accountability for managing [workers] differently than they would have otherwise. And all the team members have an accountability to provide input and make the team better."

When the department team process was successful, this executive asserted, it led to both better outcomes for patients and higher satisfaction for workers. This was particularly noticeable, he suggested, when a team could measure its improvements quantitatively over time. "People love to be on teams," he said. "When you do it well, it's really fun. . . . You get to watch the scores go up, and you get to see things get better. And people like to win, and people like to get better." Over time, teams would come to compete not only with themselves but also with other departments in the facility or in other facilities around the state and country. Organization-wide, the aspiration was to create a "fabric of teams" that would begin to cooperate and compete along the same indicators of success. If one department, for example, was able to bring the "infection rate from fifteen down to ten down to five, all the places at ten want to know how the people at five got there." Not only would teams help to bridge the interests of labor and management in the organization, but they would also invest employees at all levels in games related to patient care. One department chief at GroupCare, who had recently taken over as the head of the regional chiefs, discussed the excitement of "the metrics that [these departments] should be following." Since there were now twenty departments within the same region, "if one facility has really good metrics on door-to-doctor or lab turnaround, . . . we can share that practice."

April, a worker leader in the family medicine department, discussed how the labor-management partnership led to the installation of floor mats around the department to reduce musculoskeletal injuries. Wells described an initiative to "turn off all the lights" when not in use: "Labor's going to help turn off all the lights, that's going to help save GroupCare money. . . . And we work that out and we track that, and then at the end it becomes a monetary value. That's the partnership, right? Because really ultimately it's saving that money, saves me, saves the employer, benefits the patient."

As important as these organizational initiatives were the daily adjustments that the hospital staff members were able to make in response to the unexpected. The labor-management partnership tried to make sure that these adjustments were made as inclusively as possible. Wells said, "You know, Susie called out sick today, so how are we going to get through the day? How are we going to serve those patients, and how is that going to work? . . . You're constantly working out those little problems." Wells went on to describe how much of her work involved "teaching the members to have those conversations with the manager," thereby helping them to *feel* like partners. The day before our interview, a group of workers discussed with Wells and their manager how they felt like the manager was "intimidating" and "bullying" them into making changes in their schedule. Wells told the manager that she could "go contract on him" and make him formally negotiate the changes since they involved changes in working conditions. But she coached him to "use some of the tools that we know: interest-based problem-solving, consensus decision-making, and let's get them to buy into it and let them decide."

COMMON INTERESTS AND THEIR LIMITS

On one occasion I was able to attend a department meeting to observe the labor-management partnership in action. Almost twenty doctors, managers, and workers attended the meeting, which began with a discussion about an ongoing training to improve the relationship between medical assistants and physicians. According to one doctor, the assistants did not yet see empathy as part of their role, did not see themselves as part of the "healing arts."

The conversation then shifted to a question of how to handle doctors who, having not been on the day's schedule, want to "open" their schedule. Several doctors thought that doctors should be able to work when they want to. A few nurse managers responded that managers should be able to say "No," especially if they did not have adequate staff to open up a doctor's schedule. At this point a female doctor, who had been knitting for the duration of the meeting, looked up and said that the staff needed to "suck it up and do it." Another doctor opined that the group should approach the problem "from a positive aspect," having an attitude that is "yes, let's do it." One manager responded that the staff "can only suck up so much," while another argued that the staff would be more willing to go along with scheduling changes if they felt "a part of the process." At this point the physician director of the department intervened, saying, "I'm glad to see where this is going," and that the department should be focused on "putting patients first."

As the conversation continued, it became clear that the group would be unable to make it through the ambitious agenda that the director had planned. While the group began a lengthy discussion about how to handle appointments for members who call at night and want to be seen the next day, the director intervened: "[The physician in chief] wants us to be more action oriented and less consensus building." The meeting ended with acknowledgments. A doctor began to acknowledge a medical assistant for "never saying no," then stopped himself and reframed: "For being empathetic." The department director added, "For kindness and generosity." The meeting them came to a close.

This meeting, while admittedly a somewhat arbitrary snapshot of Group-Care's organizational life, illustrated both the possibilities and constraints of the partnership model. On the one hand, the fact that so many different constituencies could come together and discuss the work of the department was itself remarkable. At times there seemed to be room for creative problem solving and a productive back-and-forth of experiences and perspectives. Yet it also was a stark reminder of how power does not disappear from processes of "consensus building." The few workers at the meeting remained quiet throughout, while doctors tended to dominate the conversation. Moreover, the need for "action" seemed to assure that those who had positional power in the department—the physician director and his staff—ultimately would make the tough decisions.

Indeed, despite the common interests to which the labor-management partnership appealed, labor and management simultaneously recognized the limits of this commonality. Wells did not mince words in the way she described workers' motivations for becoming involved in the union. Most active union leaders had either "been wronged [by management] and [are] pissed off" about it, she explained, or they had seen one of their coworkers "done wrong" and want to "advocate for" them. After seeing her manager intimidate workers and "pitting employees against each other," Wells decided to get involved in order to "advocate[] for the weak in the department." She also felt personally targeted when she had plans to go on vacation and "was told I had to come in." Her involvement in the union, at least initially, was motivated by a desire to assert control over her work—and to push back against an unfair and arbitrary management.

One union representative made a similar point more generally: "There's absolutely a class difference between those who own the means of production and those who don't." Yet he saw the partnership as an opportunity to "question the sovereignty of capital." For him, the partnership was an example of "taking over the shop, not in real economic terms . . . but just in terms of there's no real reason why [I] as a person who's producing the wealth shouldn't be able to really take part in the . . . decisions that are going to affect my life." Interestingly, this leader framed participation in the labor-management partnership as an instantiation of radical politics, rather than as a concession made by hospital administrators.

One worker leader expressed a tension in the partnership that many seemed to feel when she explained how GroupCare executives approached her, "talking about, 'What if we could just sit down at the table and talk about things.' And we're going, 'Yeah, that would be good. But a lot of the problems are your managers. Are you going to talk about that?'" If the partnership was part of GroupCare's economic strategy, several workers wondered, was power sharing merely a strategy for making exploitation more palatable?

According to the workers I interviewed, the partnership worked best for those aspects of work that did not involve a zero-sum game. Tom Kochan and his colleagues found something similar when they studied a similar interest-based bargaining process behind a 2005 Kaiser-Permanente contract.[3] In their study, a partnership model worked more easily on the noneconomic aspects of the contract and less well on the economic aspects of it.[4] For those technical problems that could be solved by bringing people's experiences and perspectives together, an investment in partnership made good sense. Yet for "power problems," or problems related to the allocation of resources among staff, the partnership seemed to work less well. Wells herself admitted, "We don't hire, we don't fire. So at that point, that's where that line is drawn, and we say, 'Managers manage; I don't have the ability to tell you how to manage.'" Jake Cunningham, a union representative, remembered feeling "slightly frustrated" on occasion because "sometimes management would use the labor-management partnership to blow smoke up our ass." Susanna Vaughan, a worker leader and a mentor of Wells's, was worried about the partnership for this reason when she first heard about it: "I thought it was a bunch of bullshit. In bed with management? What kind of crap is this?"

The idea of a labor partnership was even more difficult to swallow for many members of the physician staff and hospital administration. According to one physician administrator, the "lack of autonomy" with regard to hiring and firing was an adjustment for many physicians. An ER physician suggested that workers' power in the organization meant that workers were "a little bit more sensitive in terms of physicians' demands on them." And a family practice doctor acknowledged wryly, "The only people here that aren't union are the physicians." He explained, "When you're in private practice, the women there work for you. . . . You can chastise them, you can fire, you can hire, you can reassign." In contrast, he continued, "Here, you don't have any of that. And as a matter of fact, you're told up front, 'Hands off the staff because they're union.' . . . If you have a gripe, then it has to go through certain channels." He noticed great variation in the staff from different departments. While the staff in his office were "consummate professionals," those at the other end of the hall were "young, they're cliquish . . . they're shopping online, they're twittering about makeup." That being said, this same doctor recognized that "after you work with these folks long enough, they either respect you or they don't. And if they respect you, they will bend over backwards for you, whether they're union or not, whether you fire them or not." As a result, he said, he understood "which side of the bread my butter is on and I try and treat 'em well."

Several physicians and administrators also expressed concerns that labor's power within the organization meant that good care was sacrificed in the name of organizational predictability. A GroupCare administrator expressed her frustrations with union regulations. She explained, "We have an obligation to follow the contract, and so in some ways it gives us less flexibility." When she puts together committees to address patient care, for example, "I need the union to tell me who [will be on it]. I don't get to pick, I don't get to say, 'You would be great on this committee. Would you like to do it?' They tell me who is going to be on it." Furthermore, the contract meant that people did not typically work past the end of their shifts and meant that people who were "tired of nursing" waited longer to retire in order to hold out for increases in benefits. This administrator recognized the benefits of the union contract, in that rules and lines of accountability were clear: "It's very clear if it's in the contract that you have to call in and let us know that you're going to be sick two hours before the start of the shift and that's what you have to do. And that's what I can hold you accountable for." Yet she worried that employees became "so oriented to the contract that they become less professional," that working at GroupCare becomes just "a job for them," whereas she felt that the work should be "more important than just a paycheck."

A hospitalist echoed this idea when she complained that "mediocre employees" were able to "hide behind the union skirts." Moreover, she suggested, it was sometimes "hard to pull the union into having the same goals" as the organization as a whole. For example, when GroupCare began an initiative to "improve how patients perceive the service they receive in the hospital," the nurses' union refused to participate because "you can't use the word 'service' around them." In this doctor's account, the union was so bent on seeing themselves as professionals that they rejected the implication that they work within a service industry—at a time when even the doctors had begun to appreciate the service aspects of their profession.

PARTNERSHIP AND STRUGGLE

Several worker and union leaders had come to understand that the labor-management partnership was not a substitute for struggle against management but a *part* of that struggle. The very *idea* of partnership gave the union leverage. Vaughan, who was initially skeptical of the partnership, came to see, "They're saying we have true equality, and we don't have true equality. Not true equality. But we have way more than we would have if we didn't have the partnership." Phil, a chief steward, described partnership meetings by saying, "You're an equal to management when you go in there. Whether they think so or not." The partnership did not actually put labor and management on equal footing, but it gave the union an advantageous context within which to fight. Cunningham described how the union "could put pressure on managers" through the labor-management partnership process: "We didn't have any qualms going to their boss and saying, 'This person's not partnering.'" Not only was there a high cultural premium placed on the idea of the partnership, but managers were evaluated in part based on how well they worked with the union. Vaughan recalled, early in the partnership, how hospital leaders would often ask her to be a "token labor representative" at meetings. She had to work, with both herself and with GroupCare's leadership, to have a real voice. She remembered saying,

> "You're asking me to sit here and rubber-stamp something and be token labor, and I have to say, I don't agree with what this decision is." That is hard to say to a bunch of leadership, you know, when you're just . . . a nurse assistant. . . . When you're . . . in the workforce and you're working for them, [you think there is] going to be retaliation. . . . You know, you have to say what you think and your feelings. And they responded to it, and they started responding to labor. They started asking us. They would call: "What do you think about this, Susanna?"

Through advocating for herself and for labor within such meetings, Vaughan felt she was able to achieve a real say for the union. For Wells, one of the most important pieces of the labor-management partnership contract was also the most abstract—respect. She described one conversation with a difficult manager: "I actually believe we've had this conversation about respect. It isn't about you—me earning your respect. Because I don't need to earn it. You have to give it to me. It's actually page four of our contract."

Workers' power seemed to reside in their capacity to use the idea of partnership to their own advantage. Vaughan explained that many of those who had the hardest time with the partnership were the "mid-managers—people who just cannot let go of their control. . . . That's what they do—they control. It's in their blood! You know, they can't help themselves." Left uncontested, the partnership existed in name only—rhetoric from GroupCare leadership that did not influence departments' daily practice. Will, a steward at the hospital, admitted that in these instances "some of it's labor's fault, because . . . there are some stewards that are just weak. . . . I think there's quite a few stewards that are just there to have the day off—the one day off during the month that we have steward council." Yet because the leadership "really believes in this partnership," and because the partnership is "in our literature," workers had leverage against managers in order to make the partnership a reality. April said that she will "get slapped on the hand once in a while" for being outspoken within her department, but that "nothing's gonna change until you start voicing something. . . . That's why change has happened in the clinic." Far from being a *substitute* for struggle, the partnership provides a context within which workers could struggle successfully.

Cunningham explained how GroupCare's history, and the labor-management partnership contract, established "rhetoric . . . to be able to have better labor-management relationships than in other places." Still, he acknowledged, the union had to use the rhetoric "along with real power" in order for it to be effective. Behind the collaborative nature of the partnership, then, was the threat of workplace action. Among those in the union this kind of direct action was described as "going traditional," or "going contract." During one memorable instance, the janitorial staff had been asking their manager for new mops to no avail for three months. Wells called a meeting of the janitors outside the building, in plain view of administrators, where together they planned a "sticker day," on which workers would wear stickers and sing jingles demanding that they be heard. By taking action together, the janitors learned that they could make their manager listen to them. Within three days the manager gave her staff six hundred new mops. Wells thus taught workers to advocate for themselves while also coaching managers on how to listen. And disagreements that could not be resolved through the partnership did not always escalate to direct action. More often, Wells explained, when labor and management could not reach consensus they were able to fall back on the contract: "When it comes down to it, we always have the contract. And so it's black and white. So at some point, when we don't agree, we go through the process. And so I think that there are defined, distinct lines, and I think that that's what helps us—is that the partnership lets us engage [in] those conversations, but we can also say it's time to agree to disagree."

OLIGARCHY, THOUGH NOT IRONCLAD

But if the labor-management partnership did offer the possibility of more power for workers, this possibility seemed to hinge on the quality of the worker leaders in the facility. With the wrong kind of leadership, the partnership also could potentially slip into oligarchy. As the partnership began, the union appointed what was then called a "union liaison" who worked between the union and management at the facility. Vaughan recalled that the liaison "came in and started making deals, violating the contract with management," which "really pissed us off about the partnership." For Vaughan, the partnership worked well if it did not impinge at all on the contract, but "we cannot compromise the contract" without "screwing with our members."

Even at the departmental level, Cunningham described the variation among worker leaders in terms of their capacity to advocate for workers. Given the partnership, he explained, "there were a number of forums where the stewards and the managers would be taken outside of the shop and be forced into conversation . . . about how to make things better." Some stewards treated this role "as a way to get on the up-and-up," a "really nice job on their way to something else." According to Cunningham, this tendency was most common among younger stewards and among those from lower-paid departments. The younger stewards would see the role as one that might lead them into management, while the stewards from the lower-paid departments "came from a blue-collar background, and so they would get into this job and then they'd see all these various opportunities open up before their eyes and sort of lose touch with what I would see as a responsibility to be a steward." As a result they were more likely to "buddy up" to their managers and be less "accountable" to the workers they were supposed to represent. Given the intimacy with which labor and management would work together within the department team, Cunningham saw this structure as "one of the places with the greatest potential. But it's also one of the places where, you know, people began to start to gang up on their coworkers."

The line between oligarchy and representation was not clear-cut. During one conversation in the union office at GroupCare Health, Vaughan and Wells described their different approaches to negotiations with managers. At one point in the conversation, Vaughan chided Wells for her adversarial relationship with the human resources manager: "The two of them are like oil and vinegar. . . . Julia just calls her on her stuff, gets in her face." Vaughan herself, though, had "learned that if you bend a little bit, and kinda play ball with them at their level, the way they do things, when you need a favor or you need something, they're going to be more willing to say, 'Okay.'" As Vaughan mentored Wells, she had tried to teach her "to play the game." Occasionally, Vaughan admitted, they'll even change the contract slightly: "When we want to do something that's a little gray, which is what we just did, it's better to have HR on your side, so that you can work out deals that help our members, even if it's a little bit not strict by the book, but it's where you can manipulate it." Certainly, Vaughan's intentions seemed to be in the right place, her commitments to the workers she represents undiluted. Yet it did seem that her friendship with the people in human resources, her understanding of "the game," might leave her more disconnected from her constituency than she was when she started.

If HolyCare used spirituality to encourage among workers a sense of vocational subordination, GroupCare used the language and practices of "partnership" as a strategy for securing a compliant workforce. As at PubliCare, there was a certain egalitarianism among different constituencies at GroupCare. Yet where this egalitarianism was expressed at an interpersonal level at PubliCare, such as when nurses and doctors shared the same inside jokes, at GroupCare it was structured into organizational practice and enforced by a strong labor organization. Of the three hospitals in Las Lomas, GroupCare was perhaps the closest to "socialized medicine," not only in the ways it allocated care across its prepaid membership but also in the ways it allocated power across its workforce. It is especially ironic, then, that this system was also the least involved in the everyday provision of care for the poor.

Conclusion

Hospitals serve as signposts in our lives. My daughter Ella's birth at Berkeley's Alta Bates Medical Center in the autumn of 2008 is one such marker for me. I will spare the reader a minute-by-minute recounting of her entry into the world. Suffice it to say I remember my giddiness as we drove there. I remember my joy, only a few hours later, the first time I sang Ella to sleep while overlooking San Francisco Bay from our private recovery room. I remember how my stomach lurched when Ella spiked a fever in the hours before we were to be discharged, and we were transferred to the Neonatal Intensive Care Unit; my exhaustion and anxiety as we waited seventy-two hours to see whether she had a bacterial infection; my relief as we were cleared to leave. And I remember how funny Ella seemed as we strapped her into her car seat outside the hospital for the first time, her wrinkled face and furrowed brow suggesting the world-weariness of an old soul.

The hospital where Ella was born is nothing special to look at—a block of cement that seems somewhat out of place in an upscale neighborhood in Berkeley. But I am unable to drive by the building without returning to those first few days of Ella's life and to that powerful mix of feelings. Now that Ella is a walking, talking, somersaulting kid, whenever we drive by the facility I point out to her that landmark of her arrival as if it were the Statue of Liberty. But if Ella's birth was a moment of transcendence for me, it was also good business for the hospital. The costs associated with it almost never cross my mind, thanks to our good health insurance at the time. The bill was something upwards of $40,000.

In the years I have been working on this book, I have watched my daughter Ella grow from a vulnerable newborn into an exuberant, vivacious five-year-old. Thankfully, she has not had to spend any significant amount of time in the hospital since those first few days in the neonatal intensive care unit. But my family and friends have not been so fortunate. I returned to the hospital where Ella was born, not long after her birth, when a mentor of mine came down suddenly with a systemic infection. More recently, I waited at Stanford Hospital as my mother-in-law recovered from surgery on an aggressive inflammatory breast cancer.

The implications of this book are inevitably personal for all of us. We all want the best care for ourselves and for our loved ones. Those of us living in the United States are all forced to confront at least some of the contradictions in the market for hospital care. As I discuss this research with family and friends, certain questions inevitably arise. Which hospital is best? Having spent time in all three, what advice can I give them about their own medical choices? But it is difficult to give straightforward answers, even now.

In 2007, as part of an attempt to make hospital outcomes more transparent, and thus make hospitals more accountable, the California HealthCare Foundation—working in collaboration with the University of California, San Francisco—launched CalHospitalCompare.org, a service that compares hospitals on various measures of patient satisfaction and health care quality. One can thus examine PubliCare, HolyCare, and GroupCare along many specific quantitative indicators. Yet turning to the numbers, as they currently exist, is surprisingly unhelpful. According to data published in February 2012, heart attack patients at HolyCare were slightly less likely to be readmitted to a hospital after discharge than their counterparts at PubliCare or GroupCare, although patients at all three fared better than the state average. Patients with hip fractures, on the other hand, had a slightly higher mortality rate at HolyCare than they did at PubliCare or GroupCare—although, again, all had mortality rates near the state average. Patients with pneumonia fared slightly better at GroupCare than they did at either PubliCare or HolyCare, although patients in the intensive care unit fared slightly better at PubliCare than they did at GroupCare (HolyCare did not report outcomes from the ICU). Patient safety measures in surgery were deemed "superior" at PubliCare and GroupCare, while only "average" at HolyCare, although this reflected only that HolyCare followed protocols ninety-seven percent of the time while PubliCare followed it ninety-eight percent of the time and GroupCare ninety-nine. At all three hospitals, about 70 percent of patients ranked their patient experience as a "nine" or "ten" on a scale from one to ten, around the state average for aggregate patient satisfaction.

And so what these indicators demonstrate, as much as anything else, is the difficulty of distinguishing these hospitals based on available indicators alone. One might conclude that HolyCare—that state-of-the-art facility—delivered slightly inferior care compared to the other two. Yet it seems unlikely that this will diminish its market share among the wealthy. Indeed, for better or worse, in trying to determine which hospital I might use for myself or my family, the hospitals' different cultures tended to loom larger than any marginal differences in outcomes. I am relaxed by the camaraderie of the doctors and staff at PubliCare, and I support their vision of public service, even while I am alarmed at the hospital's chaos. I am seduced by HolyCare—its feeling of luxury, its state-of-the-art technology, its premium on service—even as I'm wary of physicians' incentives to overtreat and cynical about its rhetoric of spiritualism. I feel reassured by the efficiencies in the GroupCare system, at the same time I worry about becoming a cog within it. I admire the system's commitment to scientific medicine even as I worry that it may be used to justify undertreatment.

All this being said, at some point one has to choose. As graduate students at UC Berkeley, my wife and I were not offered insurance coverage for our daughter. Compelled to buy insurance for Ella on the individual market, we signed her up as a member with Kaiser-Permanente, a prepaid group practice organization a lot like GroupCare. Despite our worries about its impersonality, we liked how doctors there refused to reinforce our parental hypochondria. One summer afternoon, when Ella was not yet two years old, she climbed out of her crib during a nap and must have fallen—she came to find us in the kitchen, sobbing. She seemed fine at the time, but in the middle of that night she began projectile vomiting. We rushed her to the emergency room at Kaiser-Oakland and were seen within fifteen minutes. The doctor, gentle and relaxed, looked in her eyes, felt her neck, asked us a few questions, and sent us home in time to get another few hours of sleep. Was this undertreatment or evidence-based practice or something in between? I still don't know, but I know that we felt taken care of, and everything turned out okay. We now live in New York City, but Ella still asks about Dr. Jennifer Tenney, her pediatrician at Kaiser. Tenney's office was in a monstrous pillar of concrete abutting the freeway, the quintessence of bureaucracy. Nevertheless, we felt close to her, and we still wave from the highway every time we pass by.

We chose a GroupCare equivalent for Ella, and the GroupCare model seems on the ascendance nationwide. References to the "accountable care organizations," to "evidence-based practice," to prioritizing health care "value" over health care "volume" are everywhere. As I have argued above, the three hospitals in Las Lomas represent three different souls of American medicine; but they are also emblematic of different time periods. If PubliCare is reminiscent of the hospital's past, and HolyCare is indicative of health care's present, then GroupCare seems to anticipate health care's future.

But what is this future? On March 23, 2010, while I was in the middle of my fieldwork in Las Lomas, President Obama signed into law the Patient Protection and Affordable Care Act, the most sweeping health care reform legislation since the passage of Medicare and Medicaid in 1965. While the major provisions of the law have only recently gone into effect, it seems likely that it will mitigate some of the most objectionable dimensions of contemporary health care practice. Perhaps most significant, the law mandates that most people possess medical insurance and creates important new pathways for people to acquire it—such as the expansion of Medicaid (though some states are opting out of this provision), the creation of tax credits to lower insurance premiums for the middle class, and the structuring of new state insurance exchanges. In turn, the law penalizes individuals who do not acquire insurance and large employers that do not offer it as a benefit. As a result of these and other provisions, the law promises to expand access to care.

The law also imposes important new regulations on the insurance industry. For example, it requires that insurers spend at least 80 to 85 percent of their premium revenue on clinical services or quality improvement expenses, and mandates that insurance plans include free access to preventive care. Insurers can no longer exclude patients based on preexisting conditions or other health-related factors and can vary patient premiums based only on certain narrow criteria and only within certain parameters. They have to justify premium increases of more than 10 percent to a regulatory board and can no longer impose annual or lifetime dollar limits on essential benefits.

The Affordable Care Act also promotes and incentivizes "evidence-based" practice. For example, since the law's passage, the Center for Medicare and Medicaid Innovation has begun to develop and test different payment and service delivery arrangements; and the Patient-Centered Outcomes Research Institute has been established to conduct and promote comparative clinical outcomes research. Through several different provisions of the law, Medicare has shifted towards paying hospitals and physicians based on patient outcomes rather than on health care utilization—moving from "volume" payments to "value" payments.

These changes are worth celebrating. Without minimizing the reform, however, we should also recognize the extent to which things are likely to stay the same. While the Affordable Care Act changes the rules of the game, the game of health care in the United States is still inextricably linked—perhaps even *more* tightly linked—to the profit motive. For example, by mandating insurance coverage, yet restricting the possibilities for a "public option," the legislation ensures that large, for-profit insurance companies will become even larger. Indeed, the promise of an expanded market was necessary to convince insurers to swallow the bitter pill of regulation. Pharmaceutical companies, medical device manufacturers, physicians, hospital systems, and others also backed the reform for this reason.

And while the new legislation certainly changes the market for hospital care, it does not resolve the market's contradictions. Though many more people are covered by insurance under the Affordable Care Act than were before, the tension between hospital care as a scarce resource and hospital care as a social right is likely to remain. Most obvious, there still are groups excluded from coverage (such as undocumented immigrants) and still are people unable—for a variety of reasons—to navigate the bureaucracies necessary to obtain care. With easier access to primary and preventive care, fewer people have to rely on emergency room care for primary care services. But there are certainly still many who appear at the doors of the emergency room burdened by social problems far outside the usual boundaries of medical care. In fact, with more people granted the promise of medical insurance in an age of shrinking budgets and a frayed social safety net, we might expect *more* people to turn to hospitals (and all medical care) for help with a myriad of social needs. Yet those hospitals that accept this broad social responsibility most willingly will likely continue to be the most "inefficient" in medical terms. And as all hospitals are held accountable even more aggressively for the "value" they produce, those that respond to general social needs are likely to be driven out of the market entirely.

The tensions between the emotional, vocational dimensions of hospital care and its economic value are also likely to persist. In a competitive marketplace, hospitals will always seek to distinguish themselves based on their espoused commitments and values, and the commitments and values of the people who work within them. Most of us are more willing to pay for health services when we feel like our practitioners truly care. Yet the relationships between hospitals' economic interests and practitioners' vocational commitments will continue to be fraught. To the extent that insurance providers use measures of patient satisfaction to compare different types of organizations, we might expect hospitals to invest new energy into standardizing the interactions of nurses, doctors, and other practitioners so as to enhance these scores; yet this very standardization will likely make these interactions seem coerced rather than authentic, and threaten to undermine or degrade such efforts. Furthermore, one might expect that—in an environment of "accountable care"—government and insurance companies would be reluctant to pay for those aspects of emotional and spiritual care that cannot be quantified or linked directly to better health outcomes. As a result, one might imagine that these aspects of care might move outside the insurance market altogether, becoming even more akin to luxury goods than they are today.

Finally, the tension between individual well-being and group health will almost certainly remain at the forefront of public discussion and debate. Everyone wants rational care, but no one wants to feel like care is being *rationed* in ways that jeopardize their own health. One need only recall how images of the "death panel" nearly derailed the passage of health care reform to appreciate how violently the U.S. public recoils from discussion of allocating scarce health care dollars. Somewhat puzzlingly, the legislation establishing the Patient-Centered Outcomes Research Institute in the Affordable Care Act explicitly limits the use of quality-adjusted life years (QALYs) in determining what kind of care is recommended or to compare interventions against one another. The QALY is a metric widely used in the fields of epidemiology, public health, and health policy as standardized measure by which to understand the average value of widely varying health care interventions and policies. Yet the new health legislation seeks to avoid any hint of rationing or discrimination against different kinds of patients. As two health-policy researchers put it recently, "The antagonism toward cost-per-QALY comparisons . . . suggests a bit of magical thinking—the notion that the country can avoid the difficult trade-offs that cost-utility analysis helps to illuminate. It pretends that we can avert our eyes from such choices, and it kicks the can of cost-consciousness farther down the road."[1]

Nevertheless, one can imagine a future in which the contradictions identified in this book no longer animate hospital care. Twenty years from now, moral-market entrepreneurs may have succeeded in rationalizing the closing of safety-net hospitals like PubliCare; may have transformed HolyCare more unequivocally into a high-end health care spa; or may have made a convincing moral case for the health care rationing that takes place in GroupCare. From this perspective, the contradictions elaborated herein are merely symptomatic of a field in transition. Once the market for hospital care has been more uniformly moralized, it might be argued, the contradictory character of its commodification will fade. Of course, as Philippe Steiner points out, this may be a world in which markets drive our morality, "a society in which law and morals are increasingly overwhelmed by the market mentality."[2] An unproblematically moralized market for hospital care may be evidence both of flexibility in the relationship between markets and morals and simultaneously of the power of an expanding market to exploit this flexibility, colonizing domains previously off-limits. Yet given how long different forms of hospital organization have survived, despite extensive changes in their organizational environment, what seems more likely is that the contradictions in the commodification of hospital care will endure.

In this book I have focused on three hospitals in the same town, each of which epitomizes one contradiction in the commodification of hospital care. These hospitals, and the models of care they represent, will likely feel familiar to many readers. Each was founded in a different era in order to serve a different constituency and solve a different problem. And the landscape of U.S. health care is still littered with hospitals like them—hospitals that are places of last resort, hospitals that seem to double as four-star hotels, hospitals that aspire to the sleek efficiency of the assembly line.

One might argue that the differences observed among these three hospitals are merely a result of different organizational structures or financial incentives. To some extent, this is undoubtedly correct. For example, GroupCare's form of prepaid group practice, which combined health insurance with service provision, and integrated clinical practice with hospital services, certainly shaped its emphases on reducing medical uncertainty, providing preventive services, and reducing overtreatment. HolyCare physicians billed on an individual basis much more than the doctors at PubliCare and GroupCare, most of whom were paid on salary. HolyCare doctors were thus more likely to think of themselves as individual businessmen and -women than those at the other facilities. Yet I have sought to show that these organizational structures cannot easily be disentangled from their institutional foundations. Rather, the structures and incentives must be seen alongside the understandings and practices as constituting the "relational packages" through which care is delivered.[3] The differences in these relational packages, in turn, can only be understood by tracing their different historical lineages.

That being said, there are several models for the delivery of hospital care that are absent in Las Lomas and excluded from this study. First, while less prevalent than one might expect, for-profit hospital systems like Hospital Corporation of America or Tenet Healthcare are important players in modern hospital care, particularly in the South. These organizations are unabashed in their attempts to maximize shareholder value, and—perhaps as a result—they are also organizations consistently plagued by scandal. Future scholars might explore in more detail the relative failure of for-profit hospitals to take hold in the United States, as well as their regional concentration; they might also work to understand how these for-profit organizations navigate the contradictions I elaborate in this book.

Second, the academic medical center is in many ways the heart of modern medical care, particularly in large metropolitan areas. Nothing in Las Lomas compares with the sprawling facilities of nearby University of California, San Francisco, or institutions like it. Like PubliCare, these organizations combine medical teaching and practice; unlike PubliCare, these organizations support extensive clinical and laboratory research as well as a variety of institutes and centers of specialty practice. Ethical questions that sit six inches below the surface at PubliCare—about the exchange of poor bodies as "clinical material" for medical care—come into full bloom at these types of institutions. Volunteer subjects are the bread and butter of medical research; but the kinds of exchanges that take place in this research—who gets access to which kinds of trials, the nature of "consent" in the context of this research—needs deeper exploration.

Finally, the Veterans Health Administration runs an extensive network of hospitals, primary care clinics, nursing homes, and other health care facilities for military veterans across the country. This system, a branch of the Department of Veterans Affairs, is the closest thing to a national health system that one is likely to find in the United States. From at least one perspective, it combines PubliCare's commitment to health care as a right with GroupCare's commitment to accountable care and evidence-based practice. Phillip Longman's paean to VA health care, *Best Care Anywhere: Why VA Health Care Is Better than Yours*, makes just such a case.[4] From another perspective, however, it is easy to imagine how the VA might wrestle with both the impersonal tendencies within GroupCare and the boundless needs of patients within the PubliCare system.

Differences among hospitals in the United States might seem insignificant when one compares the United States with the rest of the world—a worthwhile project outside the scope of this book. Philip Lederer, an internal medicine doctor, is one of my closest friends from college. He has spent extensive time working on medical care in Mozambique, in Botswana, and on the U.S.-Mexico border; and he also serves as my family's off-hours doctor. In his view, the only way to solve the country's and world's health care problems is to eliminate the profit motive. How does one do that? "Cuba," he writes, only half jokingly, and he is not the only one discussing such alternatives.[5] Phil is one of a growing legion of medical leaders and practitioners in the United States who believe that a market for health care is as inefficient as it is immoral; that for the sake of justice and efficiency the United States, and the international community, must structure the provision of health care without reliance on self-interest and gain.

Until this sort of broad restructuring occurs, however, health care practitioners in the United States will have to work within and struggle against the parameters set by a market for health services. Hospitals will continue to be imbued with public purpose and yet be driven by revenue considerations. Hospitals will continue to offer compassion and emotional support, at the same time this emotional labor is incorporated into the hospital's business model. And hospitals will continue to sell care as a discrete, individualized good when the practice of medical care can only be made regular and predictable when applied to large groups. In order to survive, in other words, hospitals will have to continue to navigate the contradictions in the commodification of hospital care.

This book also raises questions that are beyond the scope of its analysis. First, I do not make any causal claim about the relationship between each hospital's historical legacy and the understandings of the practitioners who work within each. While it seems likely that practitioners have selected to work within the hospitals based on the hospitals' reputations, it also seems plausible that different work experiences help to generate different moral-market orientations. Future research might explore more explicitly the ways in which individuals' orientations towards the market are shaped by, and in turn shape, the organizations in which they work.

Second, this book treats the three hospitals of Las Lomas as independent cases, each of which struggles to reconcile previously institutionalized morals with contemporary market pressures. But one might also examine the ways in which the three hospitals of Las Lomas together constitute a field through which the class character of the contemporary hospital is reproduced. PubliCare, founded as an almshouse, continued to attract a disproportionate share of the poor despite the efforts of its administrators; HolyCare, founded for the paying patient, made spirituality synonymous with luxury, and so continued to attract a wealthy clientele; and GroupCare, founded in order to bring health care costs under control for the middle class (and their employers), continued to attract a middle-class membership base. Future research might more explicitly examine the ways in which moral-market orientations are associated with class positions or other sets of social distinctions; how "connected lives" are connected within unequal worlds.

The questions raised in this book are relevant beyond the hospital as well. The United States is a market society. More than many other countries, we are willing to entrust the allocation of a wide range of goods—from health care to education to public safety—to the principle of exchange for gain. And while this book has focused on the market for hospital care, one can easily imagine applying its lessons to other kinds of markets about which we feel ambivalent—from the market for higher education to the market for pollution credits.

Broadly, the lesson of this book is that markets do not inevitably eviscerate our social values or inexorably lead to disorganization and chaos; but neither do we easily reconcile our values with markets or bring markets under our control. On the one hand, at the macro level, institutions govern the sorts of exchanges that are permissible within markets. On a more micro level, organizations and the people within them use tremendous creativity and ingenuity to reconcile their social values with exchange relationships and use all sorts of formal and informal structures to make markets stable and predictable.

Nevertheless, despite these institutionalized rules of exchange, and despite the best efforts of organizations and individuals, the principle of exchange for gain is often difficult to reconcile with the values we attach to certain things. This does not mean that people do not try, as we have seen. But they do not fully succeed. Here I have begun to distinguish analytically among the different sorts of problems posed by the market for things like hospital care and to envision both the possibilities and perils embedded in our contradictory attempts to address them.

Acknowledgments

My greatest debts are to the doctors, nurses, administrators, ancillary workers, labor representatives, religious leaders, and community members who shared their stories and insights with me; and who let me shadow them as they went about their work. This book would have been impossible without their generosity and their trust. I have not yet met anyone who enjoys being written about. But even if no one in Las Lomas *likes* what I've written, at the very least I hope that I have done justice to their perspectives.

This project has been a long time in the making. From its inception, I have had help in shaping it from some of the best in the business. Michael Burawoy continues to astound me with his patience, wisdom, and mentorship. I don't know how he does it. I have also had the tremendous fortune of being a part of Michael's dissertation group, a community of scholars so deeply committed to one another's work that our meetings often lasted way past my bedtime. I am deeply grateful to Emily Brissette, Laleh Behbehanian, Marcel Paret, Lina Hu, Gabriel Hetland, and Julia Chuang for sustaining such a haven in the heartless world of academe. I'm a little scared of writing without them.

Others at Berkeley were also important sources of inspiration and fortitude. Among them Dylan Riley, Sandra Smith, Kim Voss, Jonathan Simon, Marion Fourcade, Neil Fligstein, Roi Livne, and Corey Abramson provided guidance at critical junctures. My officemates and good friends Gabriel Hetland and Sarah Anne Minkin were key to my thinking and to my emotional equilibrium (to the extent I had one). This book would be much weaker without my afternoon runs in the Berkeley hills with Gabe and Friday night dinners with Sarah Anne. Daniel Dohan at the University of California, San Francisco provided medical knowledge and a critical eye from across the bay.

Although I have only recently arrived at Columbia, I have already benefited enormously from the support of my new colleagues. Detailed feedback from Peter Bearman and Shamus Khan have made this work much stronger. I am trying to figure out how to reciprocate. Conversations with Gil Eyal, Karen Barkey, Diane Vaughan, Sammy Zahran, Ryan Masters, and Bruce Link have also helped me make it around the final lap. Eric Schwartz at Princeton University Press has been a consistent advocate for this project. I'm particularly grateful for the tremendously helpful reviews he solicited. I am also tremendously thankful for the production work of Ali Parrington and others at Princeton University Press, for the careful eye of my copyeditor, Molan Goldstein, and for the indexing work of Margie Towery.

I have also exploited my personal relationships in order to make this work stronger. My parents, Robert Reich and Clare Dalton, have helped me wrestle with the ideas herein. Doctor Phil Lederer, one of my closest friends, has provided me more insightful feedback than I know what to do with. I hope he forgives me for ignoring some of it (perhaps he should write a book himself). Thanks also to Ben Sigelman for his pragmatic advice, and to Dr. Michael Rhodes for his close read.

This work would not have been possible without the generous support of the Jacob K. Javits Foundation and the National Science Foundation, each of which provided me fellowships for graduate study that allowed me the time and space to immerse myself in the field. A Robert Wood Johnson Foundation Health and Society Fellowship has allowed me to finish this work and to imagine what might come next. I'm also thankful to Kathy Jackson for all of her transcription work, to Natalie Forsythe for the magical way she took care of my daughter during my fieldwork, and to Natural Home Cleaning for the bimonthly cleanings that we could not have done without.

Teresa Sharpe, my partner and friend, continues to help me think and laugh and wrestle with the big questions. This book is dedicated to my daughter, Ella Reich-Sharpe, the most visceral reason I have to work for a better future.

A Note on Methods

I did not plan to study hospital organizations when I arrived at graduate school at the University of California, Berkeley in the fall of 2005. My intention was to study the U.S. labor movement. And so when a friend introduced me to Fred Ross Jr., a well-known labor and community organizer, I jumped at the chance to work with him. Fred suggested that I get my feet wet by volunteering with a local campaign to organize a Catholic Hospital, which he was helping to lead. Between the fall of 2006 and the spring of 2008, I spent approximately fifteen hours a week as a religious and community organizer with what was then United Healthcare Workers–West (SEIU-UHW). As a result of the work, I got to know several workers at the hospital, as well as many local religious and community leaders.

The campaign was a herculean eight-year effort that I discuss in *With God on Our Side: The Struggle for Workers' Right in a Catholic Hospital*. Most compelling to me about the campaign was how both hospital leaders and workers seemed to understand their economic interests in moral terms. Both sides agreed that "the market" for hospital care was pernicious, but each saw the dangers of the market as embodied in the other. According to hospital leaders, the union threatened to degrade the "sacred encounters" on which the hospital's care was based. The union was a "third party," an outside force that would "turn covenants into contracts," channeling workers' vocational commitments into narrow economic interests. For worker leaders, on the other hand, hospital *managers* embodied the dangers of the market. These administrators were putting profits ahead of people and making it difficult for workers to deliver care as they felt it should be given. From their perspective, a union would better allow them to live out their vocational commitments to their patients by giving them a say in how the hospital was run.

The Research Question

My work with the campaign got me interested in larger questions about hospital care in the United States. Almost everyone involved in the campaign spoke about how health care had become more and more of a business—how profits were running the show. But in the same breath, many people—from workers to hospital leaders to the doctors and community leaders I met along the way—discussed how they considered hospital care, and their own involvement in the health care industry, as something that transcended the market as well.

Of course, I recognized that the ways in which people reconciled their market position and the mission of health care in the Catholic hospital were likely somewhat peculiar—a legacy of the hospital's religious history and a result of the ongoing involvement of religious leadership its administration. But I thought I had put my finger on a more general problem as well. While many people recognize how central health care is for the U.S. economy, no one seems ready to give up on its broader social purposes.

And so I broadened my lens to encompass the three major hospitals in Las Lomas. Each of the three hospitals was founded in a different era, and each originally intended to serve a different constituency of patients. By making comparisons across the three, I thought I could begin to understand differences in how hospitals—and the people who work within them—work to reconcile mission and market.

My approach differed from the prevailing field-level studies in organizational sociology. For example, perhaps the seminal sociological work on the market transformation of American health care has been *Institutional Change in Healthcare Organizations: From Professional Dominance to Managed Care*, by Richard Scott and others.[1] Directed by Scott, one of the leading scholars of the new institutionalism in organizational theory, the book demonstrates in exacting detail many ways in which market actors and market logics have come to predominate in the health care field. Yet the framework of the "field," as it was used here, seemed much better at explaining organizational similarity at any given moment in time than it was at explaining organizational variation or struggle.[2] Scott and his colleagues recognized that, in the face of market pressures, "old forms and practices coexist alongside the new."[3] To the extent that hospitals had resisted market pressures, it was because of their "strong roots in the communities they serve"[4] or because "older organizations and forms of organization exhibit substantial inertia."[5] But the particular ways in which organizational histories structured ongoing perceptions and practices differently seemed impossible to grasp at such height.

Coincidentally, the town of Las Lomas sits within the nine-county San Francisco Bay Region on which Scott and his colleagues focused. And so I began to think of my project as a complement to this more bird's-eye view. Rather than explore the dynamics of the health care field as a whole, I would focus on variation in the cultures and structures of practice that have emerged within three different hospitals in the same community. Rather than analyze the ways in which market pressures had transformed health care organizations in similar ways, I would look at how similar pressures were refracted differently through organizations with particular histories. And rather than emphasizing the power of the market to shape hospital practice, I would examine the enduring power of other social values in the hospital—and how people worked to rebuff, frame, or tame the market in relation to these values.

The Research Process

Over the course of the union campaign, I had gotten to know a rather narrow swath of health care workers in the area, as well as an array of progressive religious and community leaders. In order to undertake the larger project, however, I would need to interview workers, nurses, doctors, and administrators at all three facilities. Thankfully, my previous work had embedded me firmly enough within the city that I was able to find the people who served as informal nodes within local health care networks. There was Ted Booth, the GroupCare palliative care specialist whom I had met at a dinner party in 2007. There was the nurse director at GroupCare, who was married to a religious leader whom I had helped with an event in 2008. There was the ER doctor at PubliCare who was the friend of a lay leader I had befriended in 2006. These three—along with the workers I knew at HolyCare—introduced me to several other key doctors, nurses, and administrators, who in turn were able to introduce me to countless others. The process of organizing for the union had prepared me well for organizing my own academic project.

Through selective snowball sampling, beginning in 2009 and continuing for the next fifteen months, I conducted 106 interviews with administrators, physicians, nurses, and ancillary workers who worked within (and across) the three hospitals in town, and an additional fifteen interviews with community leaders. These interviews lasted between forty-five minutes and two hours. All took place either at the interviewees' homes or in private settings at work.

An advantage of conducting my research within a relatively self-contained community such as Las Lomas was that the three hospitals (and the people who worked within them) used the other hospitals as explicit points of comparison. I was thus able to examine both the objective position each hospital occupied in relationship to the others and the way these relationships were understood by the actors who worked within each. I was also able to analyze the trajectories of practitioners as they moved across the three facilities. Of the 106 administrators and practitioners I interviewed, thirty-two had worked at two of the hospitals in Las Lomas, and three had worked at all three.

Interviews were transcribed, imported into an electronic database, and coded systematically using the qualitative software ATLAS.Ti. I undertook both open coding and focused coding in order to determine prominent themes among the interviews.[6] In order to verify the results I obtained from interviews, I triangulated using three other sources of data.[7] First, I spent approximately two hundred hours conducting participant observation within the three hospitals. Most of this time I spent "shadowing" individual doctors within the emergency rooms and medical wards of the three hospitals. I also attended several physician and departmental meetings, as well as meetings with groups representing workers at the three hospitals. Second, I supplemented my qualitative research with quantitative data on the three hospitals collected by California's Office of Statewide Health Planning and Development (OSHPD). Finally, I drew on primary and secondary source material to understand the history of the three hospitals within Las Lomas and these hospitals' relationship to the history of hospital care in the United States more generally.

In this book I do not refer to any people, organizations, or places by their real names. While any mildly determined detective will have little trouble locating "Las Lomas" on a map, I have gone to greater lengths to preserve the anonymity of my interviewees by changing their names and making small changes in their biographical details.

Notes

INTRODUCTION

1. Portions of this book appear in Adam Reich, "Contradictions in the Commodification of Hospital Care," *American Journal of Sociology* 119:6 (2014). Used with permission from University of Chicago Press.
2. See Velthuis, *Talking Prices*, 6.
3. Stevens, *In Sickness,* 361.
4. Rosner, *Once Charitable Enterprise*; Starr, *Social Transformation*; Stevens, *In Sickness*. See also Light, "Ironies of Success," 18–20; Scott et al., *Institutional Change.*
5. Scott et al., *Institutional Change.*
6. Stevens, *In Sickness.*
7. As a cause, the passage of Medicare and Medicaid in 1965 infused huge amounts of money into health care. Somewhat paradoxically, this massive infusion of state spending attracted the attention of business entrepreneurs. As a consequence, in turn, these entrepreneurs have invested in and lobbied for the health care market's ongoing expansion.
8. Cutler, *Your Money.*
9. Anderson and Frogner, "Health Spending"; Muennig and Glied, "Changes in Survival Rates."
10. The nonprofit's prohibition from the distribution of financial surplus is understood by some scholars as a response to the problem of consumer trust (Hansmann, "Nonprofit Enterprise."
11. Sirovich et al., "Discretionary Decision Making"; Wennberg, *Tracking Medicine.*
12. Fligstein, *Architecture of Markets*. For example, the passage of Medicare and Medicaid in 1965 signaled a right to a degree of care for the elderly and some segments of the poor. Since 1972, those with end-stage renal disease have also been entitled to Medicare coverage. The Emergency Medical Treatment and Active Labor Act (1986) gives anyone in the United States the right to a basic level of emergency room treatment. Professional licensing requirements ensure, at least nominally, that health care practitioners maintain an extra-economic commitment to their work. Some states have sought to ensure that not-for-profit hospitals earn their special status. With the passage of SB 697 in 1994, for example, not-for-profit hospitals in California have had to document annually the "community benefit" they provide. Regulative oversight by organizations such as the Joint Commission and Healthcare Facilities Accreditation Program (HFAP) ensure some degree of measurement and accountability. The fact that employers and insurance companies mediate the relationship between most "consumers" and "producers" of hospital care can also be understood to ensure some accountability regarding health care cost and quality.

13. By "commodification" I mean just the process of turning hospital care into something bought and sold on a market.

14. Sirovich et al., "Discretionary Decision Making"; Wennberg, *Tracking Medicine*.

15. More analytically, I build on the work of Karl Polanyi, a mid-twentieth-century social theorist (Polanyi, *Great Transformation*). Polanyi anticipated many contemporary thinkers in that he recognized the inextricability of the market from social relationships and social life (Baker, "Networks and Corporate Behavior"; Granovetter, "Economic Action"; Powell, "Neither Market nor Hierarchy"). But unlike many more contemporary scholars, he also emphasized how "market fundamentalism" (Somers and Block, "From Poverty to Perversity") continued to pose a threat to society (and to itself!). There was never really a "free market," according to Polanyi. Rather, modern market societies emerged and were maintained "by an enormous increase in continuous, centrally organized and controlled interventionalism" (Polanyi, *Great Transformation*, 146). The problems posed by the market were all the more troubling for Polanyi because the market was a result of such extensive human planning and regulation.

   The market could never exist purely, according to Polanyi, because it depended upon the commodification of things that are not commodities—his "fictitious commodity" (ibid., 75). Granted, Polanyi's conception of the fictitious commodity was rather underdeveloped (ibid., 204). Polanyi regards commodities as "objects produced for sale on the market" (ibid., 75). He then argues that land, labor, and money are "obviously not commodities" because "the postulate that anything that is bought and sold must have been produced for sale is emphatically untrue in regard to them" (ibid.). Yet many commodities are not exactly produced for sale (e.g., fish, spring water) and function perfectly well as commodities nonetheless. More precisely, we might argue that the production of all commodities involves an interaction between human activity and a world that preexisted humans, the latter of which was emphatically *not* "produced for sale." In this light, the training of labor power and rearing of cattle, the cultivation of land and the procurement of lumber, *all* involve both a moment of intentional production and a moment of preexisting nature. Polanyi's conception of the fictitious commodity thus seems to rely on our intuitive agreement with him. We might agree that labor is not a *real* commodity in the same way that cows are; that land is not a *real* commodity in the way that lumber is. But we are hard-pressed to legitimize these distinctions using Polanyi's argument on its own. The power of Polanyi's analysis thus derived not from this concept so much as from his account of the "grave dangers to society" (ibid., 204) posed by the commodification of certain things; as well as his description of the ways that people resist these dangers and—in so doing—*re-embed* them within social relations.

16. This echoes Polanyi in his critique of the commodification of labor power. He argues that the market for labor could only be established "with the application of 'nature's penalty,' hunger. In order to release it, it was necessary to liquidate organic society, which refused to let the individual starve" (Polanyi, *Great Transformation*, 173). Polanyi suggests that primitive societies were thus "more humane," if "less economic," in that there was no "threat of individual starvation" (ibid., 172).

17. Sandel, *What Money Can't Buy*; Satz, *Not for Sale*; Walzer, *Spheres*.

18. Satz, *Not for Sale*, 95.

19. Sandel, *Can't Buy*, 21–22.

20. Walzer, *Spheres*, 89.

21. Ibid., 90.

22. This idea is core to Polanyi's critique of the markets for land and labor. Labor and land cannot be commodified, he implies, because these things are inextricably linked to social relationships and sacred values and so are debased through commodification. Labor cannot be commodified without "dispos[ing] of the physical, psychological, and moral entity 'man'" (Polanyi, *Great*

Transformation, 76). Land "invests man's life with stability; it is the site of his habitation; it is a condition of his physical safety; it is the landscape and the seasons" (ibid., 187). Turned into a commodity, and estranged from these social foundations, land loses not only its social value but ultimately its economic value (ibid., 193).

23. Titmuss, *Gift Relationship*.

24. Healy, *Last Best Gifts*. Healy acknowledges that market incentives can crowd out other sources of motivation, but he provides the important caveat that different sources of motivation lead to different results in different environmental and organizational contexts. For example, he suggests, Titmuss was writing at a time when blood sellers were more likely to be infected with hepatitis than blood donors. In the 1980s, however, blood donors were more likely to be infected with AIDS than sellers (Healy, *Last Best Gifts*, 89, 92). Moreover, the nonmarket ties between donor organizations and donors made these organizations less responsive to the AIDS crisis (ibid., 103).

25. Frey and Oberholzer-Gee, "Price Incentives"; Gneezy and Rustichini, "A Fine Is a Price"; Healy, *Last Best Gifts*, 89; Satz, *Not for Sale*, 192–195.

26. Polanyi illustrates a similar principle in his analysis of currency (Polanyi, *Great Transformation*, 201).

27. Fox, "Medical Uncertainty"; Eddy, "Variations"; Arrow, "Uncertainty."

28. Shorter, *Doctors*.

29. Bursztajn et al., *Medical Choices*.

30. Zelizer, *Priceless Child*; Cutler, *Your Money*.

31. Starr, *Social Transformation*, 14; Richmond and Fein, *Health Care Mess*, 137; Arrow, "Uncertainty," 949.

32. Healy, *Last Best Gifts*, 11.

33. Zelizer, "Relational Economic Sociologist."

34. Sandel, *Can't Buy*, 144–149.

35. Viviana Zelizer, "Human Values," 601.

36. Satz, *Not for Sale*, Chapter 6.

37. Zelizer, *Social Meaning*, 103–104.

38. Healy, *Last Best Gifts*.

39. Dimaggio and Powell, "Iron Cage Revisited"; Meyer and Rowan, "Institutionalized Organizations"; Quinn, "Transformation of Morals."

40. Organizational scholars have begun to use Bourdieu's concept of the "habitus" to capture the ways in which organizational histories and positions consciously and unconsciously shape organizational practice (Dimaggio and Powell, "Iron Cage Revisited"; Emirbayer and Johnston, "Bourdieu," 19; Vaughan, "Bourdieu and Organizations.")

41. Somers and Block, "Poverty to Perversity."

42. Ibid., 281.

43. Fourcade and Healy, "Moral Views," 293.

44. Zelizer, "Relational Economic Sociologist," 165.

45. Fourcade, "Moral Sociology," 1060.

46. Ibid., 1059.

47. The cultural dimensions of economic activity on which Zelizer and others focus may be more effective at addressing the problem of debasement than the problem of social rights or the problem of uncertainty outlined above.

48. Scholars have begun to develop the idea of institutional contradiction to describe the ways in which different institutional orders in modern society—different rules, practices, and understandings—have the potential to conflict with one another (Armstrong and Bernstein, "Culture, Power, and Institutions"; Clemens and Cook, "Politics and Institutionalism"; Friedland and

Alford, "Bringing Society Back In"; Sewell, "A Theory of Structure"). As Friedland and Alford point out, these "institutional contradictions are the bases of the most important political conflicts in our society.... A key task of social analysis is to understand those contradictions and to specify the conditions under which they shape organizational and individual action" ("Bringing Society Back In," 256).

49. Friedland and Alford, "Bringing Society Back In," 255; Emirbayer and Johnson, "Bourdieu," 22; Healy, *Last Best Gifts*, 118.
50. Fourcade, *Economists and Societies*, 15.
51. Zelizer, "Relational Economic Sociologist," 151.

PART ONE

1. Rosenberg, *Care of Stranger*, 22.
2. Starr, *Social Transformation*, 163; Vogel, *Invention*, 107.
3. Rosenberg, *Care of Strangers*, 17.
4. Ibid., 39.
5. Throughout this book, in order to protect the identities of the people and places I describe, I do not include references for historical material. However, I am able to provide citations upon request.
6. Vogel, *Invention*, 23.
7. Rosenberg, *Care of Strangers*, 27; Vogel, *Invention*, 34–35.
8. Katz, *Shadow*; Starr, *Social Transformation*, 150; Stevens, *In Sickness*, 19, 42; Vogel, *Invention*.
9. Katz, *Shadow*, 25.
10. Somers and Block, "Poverty to Peversity"; Polanyi, *Great Transformation*. In Polanyi's account, the Speemhamland Law of 1795, which guaranteed a minimum income to all men in England regardless of employment, was intended to mitigate the social destruction of industrialization but actually wrought economic havoc since "no laborer had any financial interest in satisfying his employer" (Polanyi, *Great Transformation*, 83). By the time of the repeal of Speenhamland in 1834, according to Polanyi, huge swaths of the country had been "pauperized," driven from the labor market into dependence on state entitlements (ibid., 84).
11. Legini et al., "Privatization," 27.
12. Ibid., 85.
13. Ibid.
14. Ibid., 86.

CHAPTER ONE

1. Those whose visits were categorized as either "minor" or "low/moderate" by the hospital.
2. Heart attack patients were typically taken to either PubliCare or HolyCare, since GroupCare did not have a heart catheterization laboratory. Sexual assault victims were taken to PubliCare because that was where the sexual assault laboratory was located. Trauma victims were taken to HolyCare, which was designated as the regional trauma center in 2000.
3. Malone, "Whither the Almshouse," 797.
4. Ibid., 801.
5. Ibid., 821.
6. Ibid., 816; Padgett and Brodsky, "Psychosocial Factors."

7. A "hospitalist" is a doctor who specializes in coordinating care for patients while they are in the hospital. Traditionally, primary care doctors were responsible for their own patients while they were in the hospital. Increasingly, however, primary care doctors delegate this work to hospitalists.
8. Mauss, *The Gift*.

CHAPTER TWO

1. Haskell, "Professionalism."
2. Rosenberg, *Care of Strangers*, 190.
3. Ibid., 41.

CHAPTER THREE

1. Gouldner, *Patterns*.
2. The results of such surveys, like the Hospital Consumer Assessment of Healthcare Providers and Systems (or HCAHPS), increasingly are being standardized and made available to the public in an effort to increase transparency and accountability regarding health care quality.

PART TWO

1. Rosenberg, *Care of Strangers*, 245–246; Starr, *Social Transformation*, 159; Vogel, *Invention*, 60–62.
2. Starr, *Social Transformation*; Vogel, *Invention*, p. 68.
3. Rosenberg, *Care of Strangers*, 245.
4. Ibid., 259.
5. Wall, *American Catholic Hospitals*, 55.
6. Nelson, *Say Little*, 55.
7. Ibid., 13.
8. Wall, *Unlikely Entrepreneurs*, 42.
9. Rosenberg, *Care of Strangers*, 240; Vogel, *Invention*, 101.
10. Stevens, *In Sickness*, 23.
11. Wall, *American Catholic Hospitals*, 111–112.
12. Ibid., 113.
13. Starr, *Social Transformation*, 166.
14. Rosenberg, *Care of Strangers*, 63; Starr, *Social Transformation*,163.
15. Starr, *Social Transformation*, 167.
16. Ibid., 25.
17. Vogel, *Invention*, 94.
18. Shorter, *Doctors*, 151, 159; Starr, *Social Transformation*, 11.
19. Wilensky, "Professionalization."
20. Stevens, *In Sickness*, 123.
21. Rosenberg, *Care of Strangers*, 240; Stevens, *In Sickness*, 164.
22. Stevens, *In Sickness*, 164.
23. Stevens, *In Sickness*, 164.
24. Michael Winerip, "The Vanishing of the Nuns," *New York Times*, December 2, 2012.

CHAPTER FOUR

1. Rothman, *Strangers*.
2. Hochschild, *Managed Heart*. Barbra Mann Wall makes a similar point when she observes that Catholic hospitals have in recent years been reasserting their values as a way of distinguishing the service they give from that of other hospitals (Wall, *American Catholic Hospitals*, 5)
3. Approximately twenty-five percent of Medicare spending occurs during the last year of life, a percentage that has remained consistent over the past twenty years (Hogan et al., "Costs of Care." With that said, research has also shown that end-of-life costs are only slightly higher for those who die than for those sick patients who survive—meaning that these costs are likely attributable to the "substantial disease burden" (ibid., 191) of patients whether or not they are actually dying. Nevertheless, coordination of care for the frail and dying remains one of the primary drivers of health care costs in the country.

    Palliative care professionals encourage those with serious medical conditions to consider hospice instead of expensive and intrusive medical intervention, and they are one partial solution to high costs at the end of life. It costs significantly more money to die in a hospital than it does to die at home or in a hospice facility. When surveyed, approximately 50 percent of people say they would rather die at home than in a hospital. Yet over two-thirds of people continue to die in hospitals (Fried et al., "Terminal Care". Palliative care consultations can help people come to terms with their own approaching death so as to die in a way that feel comfortable to them, and in a way that is cost efficient as well.
4. Fox, Myers, and Pearlman, "Ethics Consultation."
5. Zawacki, "Corporate Soulcraft."
6. Ibid., 40.
7. Ibid., 45.

CHAPTER FIVE

1. Keaney, *Emergency Medicine*.
2. Keaney called these administrators "kitchen schedulers," suggesting that they did little more than sit at home and schedule other doctors' work.
3. On one recent occasion, for example, it had advised doctors to have patients sign informed consent waivers when doctors decided not to give tissue plasminogen activator (tPA) after patients suffered a stroke. There had been a rash of lawsuits surrounding this decision, though most doctors agreed that tPA was overprescribed.
4. Whether this story was true or apocryphal, it demonstrated the depth of physician distrust.
5. See note 5 in part 1.

CHAPTER SIX

1. Portions of this chapter appear in Adam Reich, *With God on Our Side: The Struggle for Workers' Rights in a Catholic Hospital* (Ithaca: Cornell University Press, 2012). Used by permission of the publisher, Cornell University Press.
2. Jazwiec, *Eat That Cookie*.
3. Ibid., 2.
4. Bronfenbrenner, "Employer Behavior"; Bronfenbrenner and Juravich, "More than House Calls"; Clawson, *Next Upsurge*; Getman, *Power of Unions*; Jacoby, *Masters to Managers*.

5. Getman, *Power of Unions*, 101.

6. Given internal union politics outside the scope of this study, the system never actually negotiated such ground rules before the election took place.

PART THREE

1. Light, "Ironies of Success"; Mechanic, "Managed Care"; Starr, *Social Transformation*, 395. With a similar logic, in 1983, President Reagan signed legislation that incorporated prospective payment into Medicare, meaning that hospitals would get a set amount of money by type of diagnosis (Stevens, *In Sickness*, 324). As Rosemary Stevens suggests, this reform meant that Medicare would treat patient care "in terms of standardized 'products,' reinforcing the image of the hospital as a factory. 'Scientific management' was finally to be achieved. The question was, at what cost?" (Stevens, *In Sickness*, 324).

2. Greenlick, "Prepaid Group Practice"; Luft and Greenlick, "Group- and Staff-Model HMOs"; Somers, "Comprehensive Prepayment Plans."

3. Hendricks, *National Healthcare*.

CHAPTER SEVEN

1. See Jim Rutenberg and Jackie Calmes, "False 'Death Panel' Rumor Has Some Familiar Roots," *New York Times*, August 13, 2009, p. A1.

2. Rittenhouse and Shortell, "Patient-Centered Medical Home."

3. Gawande, "Cost Conundrum."

4. Brownlee, *Overtreated*.

5. Andriole et al., "Mortality Results"; Schroder et al., "Screening."

6. Jonsen, "Sounding Board"; Jonsen, "'Life Is Short.'"

7. Callahan, *Kind of Life*.

8. Eduardo Porter, "Rationing Health Care More Fairly," *New York Times*, August 22, 2012, p. B1.

CHAPTER EIGHT

1. Portions of this chapter appear in Adam Reich, "Disciplined Doctors: The Electronic Medical Record and Physicians' Changing Relationship to Medical Knowledge," *Social Science and Medicine* 74 (2012): 1021–1028. Used with permission from Elsevier.

2. Freidson, *Professional Powers*, 130.

3. Ibid., 154.

4. Among the many components of recent health care reform legislation, perhaps none has received as much positive attention and bipartisan support as the institutionalization of EMRs. Health policy research has demonstrated the positive effects of such technology on patient health outcomes (Hunt et al., "Computer-Based Clinical Decision Support Systems"; Institute of Medicine, *Quality Chasm*) and shown the ways in which EMRs can limit unnecessary health care spending (Wang et al., "Cost–Benefit Analysis"). The PSS is also widely accepted as important to contemporary medical practice, which puts a premium on the idea of patients as allies in the provision of care (Armstrong, "Patient's View"). Not only have patients increasingly come to assert their right to make informed medical decisions as consumers (Reeder, "Patient-Client"; Timmermans and Oh, "Social Transformation"), but practitioners have come to appreciate the

importance of this involvement for patient compliance with treatment plans and for subsequent health outcomes (Reiser, "Era of the Patient"; Hibbard, "Health Care Consumers"). Over the last thirty years, there has been an exponential increase in the number of medical journal articles addressing patient satisfaction with medical treatment (Sitzia and Wood, "Patient Satisfaction").

5. Orentlicher, "Rise and Fall."
6. Fuller and Smith, "Consumers' Reports."
7. See National Audit Office, *National Programme for IT.*
8. See Fox, "Medical Uncertainty."
9. Angell, *Drug Companies*; Krimsky, *Science.*
10. In many ways these surveys resembled the consumer reports that Fuller and Smith have observed proliferating throughout the service sector. They note, "Quality service requires that workers rely on inner arsenals of affective and interpersonal skills, capabilities which cannot be successfully codified, standardized, or dissected into discrete components and set forth in a company handbook" (Fuller and Smith, "Consumers' Reports," 3). The consumer report allows for a sort of hands-off management, a strategy that "intefere[s] as little as possible with employees' ability to exercise the amount of self-direction necessary to deliver quality service" (ibid., 4).
11. Armstrong, "Patient's View"; Armstrong, "Clinical Autonomy."
12. Hibbard, "Health Care Consumers," 61.
13. Armstrong, "Clinical Autonomy," 168.
14. Ibid., 171.

CHAPTER NINE

1. March, "Business Firm"; Pfeffer and Salancik, *External Control.*
2. Fantasia and Voss, *Hard Work.*
3. Kochan et al., *Healing Together.*
4. Ibid., 107.

CONCLUSION

1. Neumann and Weinstein, "Perspective."
2. Steiner, "Who Is Right," 105–106.
3. Zelizer, "Relational Economic Sociologist."
4. Longman, *Best Care.*
5. Campion and Morrissey, "A Different Model."

A NOTE ON METHODS

1. Scott et al., *Institutional Change.*
2. DiMaggio and Powell, "Iron Cage Revisited"; Emirbayer and Johnson, "Organizational Analysis."
3. Scott et al., *Institutional Change*, 1.
4. Ibid., 73.
5. Ibid., 113.
6. Emerson et al., *Ethnographic Fieldnotes*, 142–144; Weiss, *Learning from Strangers*, 154–156.
7. Miles and Huberman, *Qualitative Data Analysis*, 266–267.

Bibliography

Abbott, Andrew. *The System of Professions: An Essay on the Division of Expert Labor*. Chicago: University of Chicago Press, 1988.

Anderson, Gerard F., and Bianca K. Frogner. "Health Spending in OECD Countries: Obtaining Value per Dollar." *Health Affairs* 27:6 (2008): 1718–1727.

Andriole, Gerald L., E. David Crawford, Robert L. Grubb III, Saundra S. Buys, David Chia, Timothy R. Church, Mona N. Fouad, et al. for the PLCO Project Team. "Mortality Results from a Randomized Prostate-Cancer Screening Trial," *New England Journal of Medicine* 360:13 (2009): 1310–1319;

Angell, Marcia. *The Truth about Drug Companies: How They Deceive Us and What to Do about It*. New York: Random House, 2004.

Ansell, David A., and Robert L. Schiff. "Patient Dumping: Status, Implications, and Policy Recommendations." *Journal of the American Medical Association* 257:11 (1987): 1500–1502.

Armstrong, David. "Clinical Autonomy, Individual and Collective: The Problem of Changing Doctors' Behavior." *Social Science & Medicine* 55 (2002): 1771–1777.

Armstrong, Elizabeth A., and Mary Bernstein. "Culture, Power, and Institutions: A Multi-Institutional Politics Approach to Social Movements." *Sociological Theory* 26:1 (2008): 74–99.

———. "The Patient's View." *Social Science & Medicine* 18:9 (1984): 737–744.

Aronowitz, Stanley. *False Promises: The Shaping of American Working Class Consciousness*. Durham, NC: Duke University Press, 1973.

Arrow, Kenneth J. "Uncertainty and the Welfare Economics of Medical Care." *American Economic Review* 53:5 (1963): 941–973.

Baker, Wayne E. "Networks and Corporate Behavior." *American Journal of Sociology* 96:3 (1990): 589–625.

Bell, Daniel. *The Coming of Post-Industrial Society: A Venture in Social Forecasting*. New York: Basic Books, 1973.

Ben-Ner, Avner, and Benedetto Gui. "The Theory of Nonprofit Organizations Revisited." In *The Study of the Nonprofit Enterprise*, edited by Helmut Anheier and Avner Ben-Ner. New York: Kluwer Academic, 2003.

Block, Fred. "Introduction." In *The Great Transformation: The Political and Economic Origins of Our Time*," by Karl Polanyi. Boston: Beacon Press, 2001.

Bronfenbrenner, Kate. "Employer Behavior in Certification Elections and First Contracts: Implications for Labor Law Reform." In *Restoring the Promise of American Labor Law*, edited by Sheldon Friedman, Richard W. Hurd, Rudolph A. Oswald, and Ronald L. Seeber, 75–89. Ithaca, NY: ILR Press, 1994.

Bronfenbrenner, Kate, and Tom Juravich. "It Takes More than House Calls: Organizing to Win with a Comprehensive Union-Building Strategy." In *Organizing to Win: New Research on Union Strategies,* edited by Kate Bronfenbrenner, Sheldon Friedman, Richard W. Hurd, Rudolph A. Oswald, and Ronald L. Seeber, 19–36. Ithaca, NY: ILR Press, 1998.

Brownlee, Sharon. *Overtreated: Why Too Much Medicine Is Making Us Sicker and Poorer.* New York: Bloomsbury, 2007.

Bursztajn, Harold J., Richard I. Feinbloom, Robert M. Hamm, and Archie Brodsky. *Medical Choices, Medical Chances: How Patients, Families, and Physicians Can Cope with Uncertainty.* New York: Routledge, 1990.

Callahan, Daniel. *What Kind of Life?* New York: Simon and Schuster, 1990.

Campion, Edward W., and Stephen Morrissey. "A Different Model—Medical Care in Cuba." *New England Journal of Medicine* 368:4 (2013): 297–299.

Clawson, Dan. *The Next Upsurge: Labor and the New Social Movements.* Ithaca, NY: ILR Press, 2003.

Clemens, Elisabeth S., and James M. Cook. "Politics and Institutionalism: Explaining Durability and Change." *Annual Review of Sociology* 25 (1999): 441–466.

Committee on Health Insurance Status and Its Consequences, Institute of Medicine. *America's Uninsured Crisis: Consequences for Health and Health Care.* Washington, DC: National Academies Press, 2009.

Cutler, David M. *Your Money or Your Life.* New York: Oxford University Press, 2004.

DeNavas-Walt, Carmen, Bernadette D. Proctor, and Jessica C. Smith. "Income, Poverty, and Health Insurance Coverage in the United States: 2010." *Current Population Reports: Consumer Income.* Washington, DC: U.S. Census Bureau, 2011, 23.

DiMaggio, Paul J., and Walter W. Powell. "The Iron Cage Revisited: Institutional Isomorphism and Collective Rationality in Organizational Fields." *American Sociological Review* 48:2 (1983): 147–160.

Durkheim, Emile. *The Division of Labor in Society.* 1933. Reprint, New York: Free Press, 1984.

Eddy, David M. "Variations in Physician Practice: The Role of Uncertainty." *Health Affairs* 3:2 (1984): 74–89.

Elliott, Carl. *White Coat Black Hat: Adventures on the Dark Side of Medicine.* Boston: Beacon Press, 2010.

Emerson, Robert M., Rachel I. Fretz, and Linda L. Shaw. *Writing Ethnographic Fieldnotes.* Chicago: University of Chicago Press, 1995.

Emirbayer, Mustafa, and Victoria Johnson. "Bourdieu and Organizational Analysis." *Theory and Society* 37 (2008): 1–44.

Fantasia, Rick. *Cultures of Solidarity: Consciousness, Action, and Contemporary American Workers.* Berkeley: University of California Press, 1988.

Fantasia, Rick, and Kim Voss. *Hard Work: Remaking the American Labor Movement.* Berkeley: University of California Press, 2004.

Fligstein, Neil. *The Architecture of Markets: An Economic Sociology of Twenty-First-Century Capitalist Societies.* Princeton, NJ: Princeton University Press, 2002.

Fourcade, Marion. *Economists and Societies: Discipline and Profession in the United States, Britain, and France, 1890s to 1990s.* Princeton, NJ: Princeton University Press, 2009.

———. "The Moral Sociology of Viviana Zelizer." *Sociological Forum* 27:4 (2012): 1055–1061.

Fourcade, Marion, and Kieran Healy. "Moral Views of Market Society." *Annual Review of Sociology* 33 (2007): 285–311.

Fox, Ellen, Sarah Myers, and Robert A. Pearlman. "Ethics Consultation in United States Hospitals: A National Survey." *American Journal of Bioethics* 7:2 (2007): 13–25.

Fox, Renee. "The Evolution of Medical Uncertainty." *Milbank Memorial Fund Quarterly: Health and Society* 58:1 (1980): 1–49.

Freidson, Eliot. *Professional Dominance: The Social Structure of Medical Care*. New York: Atherton Press, 1970.

———. *Professional Powers: A Study of the Institutionalization of Formal Knowledge*. Chicago: University of Chicago Press, 1986.

———. *Professionalism Reborn: Theory, Prophecy, and Policy*. Chicago: University of Chicago Press, 1994.

Frey, Bruno S., and Felix Oberholzer-Gee. "The Cost of Price Incentives: An Empirical Analysis of Motivation Crowding-Out." *American Economic Review* 87:4 (1997): 746–755.

Fried, Terri R., Carol van Doorn, John R. O'Leary, Mary E. Tinetti, and Margaret A. Drickamer. "Older Persons' Preferences for Site of Terminal Care." *Annals of Internal Medicine* 131:2 (1999): 109–112.

Friedland, Roger, and Robert R. Alford. "Bringing Society Back In: Symbols, Practices, and Institutional Contradictions." In *The New Institutionalism in Organizational Analysis*, edited by Walter W. Powell and Paul J. DiMaggio, 232–266. Chicago: University of Chicago Press, 1991.

Fuller, Linda, and Vicki Smith. "Consumers' Reports: Management by Customers in a Changing Economy." *Work, Employment & Society* 5:1 (1991): 1–16.

Gawande, Atul. "The Cost Conundrum: What a Texas Town Can Teach Us about Health Care." *New Yorker*, June 1, 2009.

Getman, Julius G. *Restoring the Power of Unions: It Takes a Movement*. New Haven, CT: Yale University Press, 2010.

Gneezy, Uri, and Aldo Rustichini. "A Fine Is a Price." *Journal of Legal Studies* 29:1 (2000): 1–17.

Gouldner, Alvin W. *Patterns of Industrial Bureaucracy*. New York: Free Press, 1954.

Granovetter, Mark. "Economic Action and Social Structure: The Problem of Embeddedness." *American Journal of Sociology* 91:3 (1985): 481–510.

Greenlick, Merwyn R. "The Impact of Prepaid Group Practice on American Medical Care: A Critical Evaluation." *Annals of the American Academy of Political and Social Science* 399 (1972): 100–113.

Hansmann, Henry B. "The Role of Nonprofit Enterprise." *Yale Law Journal*, 89:5 (1980): 835–901.

Haskell, Thomas. "Professionalism versus Capitalism." In *The Authority of Experts: Studies in History and Theory*, edited by Thomas Haskell. Bloomington: Indiana University Press, 1984.

Haug, Marie R. "Deprofessionalization: An Alternate Hypothesis for the Future." *Sociological Review Monograph* 20 (1973): 195–211.

Healy, Kieran. *Last Best Gifts: Altruism and the Market for Human Blood and Organs*. Chicago: University of Chicago Press, 2006.

Hendricks, Rickey. *A Model for National Healthcare: The History of GroupCare*. New Brunswick, NJ: Rutgers University Press, 1993.

Hibbard, Judith H. "Engaging Health Care Consumers to Improve the Quality of Care." *Medical Care* 41:1 (2003): 61–70.

Hochschild, Arlie R. *The Managed Heart: Commercialization of Human Feeling*. Berkeley: University of California, 1983.

Hogan, Christopher, June Lunney, Jon Gabel, and Joanne Lynn. "Medicare Beneficiaries' Costs of Care in the Last Year of Life." *Health Affairs* 20:4 (2001): 188–195.

Hunt, Dereck L., R. Brian Haynes, Steven E. Hanna, and Kristina Smith. "Effects of Computer-Based Clinical Decision Support Systems on Physician Performance and Patient Outcomes." *Journal of the American Medical Association* 280 (1998): 1339–1346.

Imber, Jonathan B. *Trusting Doctors: The Decline of Moral Authority in American Medicine*. Princeton, NJ: Princeton University Press, 2008.

Institute of Medicine (ed.). *Crossing the Quality Chasm: A New Health System for the 21st Century*. Washington, DC: National Academy Press, 2001.

Jacoby, Sanford M. (ed.). *Masters to Managers: Historical and Comparative Perspectives on American Employers*. New York: Columbia University Press, 1991.

Jazwiec, Liz. *Eat That Cookie!: Make Workplace Positivity Pay Off . . . for Individuals, Teams and Organizations*. Gulf Breeze, FL: Fire Starter Publishing, 2009.

Jonsen, Albert R. "'Life Is Short, Medicine Is Long': Reflections on a Bioethical Insight." *Journal of Medicine and Philosophy* 31:6 (2006): 667–673.

———. "Sounding Board: Scientific Medicine and Therapeutic Choice." *New England Journal of Medicine* 292:21 (1975): 1126–1127.

Katz, Michael. *In the Shadow of the Poorhouse: A Social History of Welfare in America*. New York: Basic Books, 1996.

Keaney, James K. *The Rape of Emergency Medicine*. Santa Fe, NM: American Academy of Emergency Medicine, 1992.

Klaidman, Stephen. *Coronary: A True Story of Medicine Gone Awry*. New York: Scribner, 2007.

Kochan, Thomas A., Adrienne E. Eaton, Robert B. McKersie, and Paul S. Adler. *Healing Together: The Labor-Management Partnership at Kaiser Permanente*. Ithaca, NY: ILR Press, 2009.

Konrad, George, and Ivan Szelenyi. *The Intellectuals on the Road to Class Power*. Brighton: Harvester Press, 1979.

Krimsky, Sheldon. *Science in the Private Interest: Has the Lure of Profits Corrupted Biomedical Research?* Lanham, MD: Rowman and Littlefield, 2003.

Krippner, Greta R. "The Elusive Market: Embeddedness and the Paradigm of Economic Sociology." *Theory and Society* 30 (2001): 775–810.

Larson, Magali Sarfatti. *The Rise of Professionalism: A Sociological Analysis*. Berkeley: University of California Press, 1977.

Legini, Mark, Stephanie Anthony, Elliot Wicks, Jack Meyer, Lise Rybowski, and Larry Stepnick. "Privatization of Public Hospitals." Washington, DC: Henry J. Kaiser Family Foundation, 1999.

Light, Donald W. "Ironies of Success: A New History of the American Health Care 'System.'" *Journal of Health and Social Behavior* 45 (2004): 1–24.

Lockard, C. Brett, and Michael Wolf. "Employment Outlook: 2010–2020: Occupational Employment Projections to 2020." *Monthly Labor Review* 135:1 (2012): 84–108.

Longman, Phillip. *The Best Care Anywhere: Why VA Health Care Is Better than Yours*. San Francisco: PoliPointPress, 2007.

Luft, Harold S., and Merwin R. Greenlick. "The Contribution of Group- and Staff-Model HMOs to American Medicine." *Milbank Quarterly* 74:4 (1996): 445–467.

Malone, Ruth. "Whither the Almshouse? Overutilization and the Role of the Emergency Department." *Journal of Health Politics, Policy and Law* 23:5 (1998): 795–832.

March, James. "The Business Firm as a Political Coalition." *Journal of Politics* 24:4 (1962): 662–678.

Mauss, Marcel. *The Gift: Forms and Functions of Exchange in Archaic Societies*, translated by Ian Cunnison. New York: Norton, 1967.

McKinlay, John B., and Lisa D. Marceau. "The End of the Golden Age of Doctoring." *International Journal of Health Services* 32 (2002): 379–416.

Mechanic, David. "The Rise and Fall of Managed Care." *Journal of Health and Social Behavior* 45 (2004): 76–86.

Meyer, John W., and Brian Rowan. 1977. "Institutionalized Organizations: Formal Structure as Myth and Ceremony." *American Journal of Sociology* 83 (1977): 340–363.

Miles, Matthew B., and A. Michael Huberman. *Qualitative Data Analysis*. Thousand Oaks, C.A.: Sage Publications, 1994.

Moynihan, Ray, and Alan Cassels. *Selling Sickness: How the World's Biggest Pharmaceutical Companies Are Turning Us All into Patients*. New York: Nation Books, 2005.

Muennig, Peter A., and Sherry A. Glied. "What Changes in Survival Rates Tell Us about U.S. Health Care." *Health Affairs* 29:11 (2010): 2105–2113.

National Audit Office, Report by the Comptroller and Auditor General. *The National Programme for IT in the NHS: An Update on the Delivery of Detailed Care Records Systems*. London: Stationery Office, 2011.

Navarro, Victoria. *Medicine under Capitalism*. New York: Neale Watson, 1976.

Nelson, Sioban. *Say Little, Do Much: Nursing, Nuns, and Hospitals in the Nineteenth Century*. Philadelphia: University of Pennsylvania Press, 2001.

Neumann, Peter J., and Milton C. Weinstein, "Perspective: Legislating against Use of Cost-Effectiveness Information." *New England Journal of Medicine* 363 (2010): 1495–1497.

Orentlicher, David. "The Rise and Fall of Managed Care: A Predictable 'Tragic Choices' Phenomenon." *Saint Louis University Law Journal* 47 (2003): 411–421.

Owens, Pamela, and Anne Elixhauser. "Hospital Admissions that Began in the Emergency Department, 2003." Statistical Brief no. 1. Rockville, MD: Agency for Healthcare Research and Quality, 2006.

Padgett, Deborah K., and Beth Brodsky. "Psychosocial Factors Influencing Non-urgent Use of the Emergency Room: A Review of the Literature and Recommendations for Research and Improved Service Delivery." *Social Science & Medicine* 35:9 (1992): 1189–1197.

Pfeffer, Jeffrey, and Gerald Salancik, *The External Control of Organizations: A Resource Dependence Perspective*. New York: Harper and Row, 1978.

Polanyi, Karl. *The Great Transformation: The Political and Economic Origins of Our Time*. 1944. Reprint, Boston: Beacon Press, 2001.

Potter, Wendell. *Deadly Spin: An Insurance Company Insider Speaks Out on How Corporate P.R. Is Killing Health Care and Deceiving Americans*. New York: Bloomsbury Press, 2010.

Powell, Walter W. "Neither Market nor Hierarchy: Network Forms of Organization." *Research in Organizational Behavior* 12 (1990): 295–336.

Quinn, Sarah. "The Transformation of Morals in Markets: Death, Benefits, and the Exchange of Life Insurance Policies." *American Journal of Sociology* 114:3 (2008): 738–780.

Reeder, Leo G. "The Patient-Client as a Consumer: Some Observations on the Changing Professional-Client Relationship." *Journal of Health and Social Behavior* 13:4 (1972): 406–412.

Reich, Adam. "Contradictions in the Commodification of Hospital Care." *American Journal of Sociology* 119:6 (2014).

———. "Disciplined Doctors: The Electronic Medical Record and Physicians' Changing Relationship to Medical Knowledge." *Social Science & Medicine* 74 (2012): 1021–1028.

———. *With God on Our Side: The Struggle for Workers' Rights in a Catholic Hospital*. Ithaca, NY: Cornell University Press, 2012.

Reiser, Joel. "The Era of the Patient: Using the Experience of Illness in Shaping the Missions of Health Care." *Journal of the American Medical Association* 269:8 (1993): 1012–1017.

Richmond, Julius B., and Rashi Fein. *The Health Care Mess: How We Got into It and What It Will Take to Get Out*. Cambridge: Harvard University Press, 2005.

Rittenhouse, Diane R., and Stephen M. Shortell. "The Patient-Centered Medical Home: Will It Stand the Test of Health Reform?" *Journal of the American Medical Association* 301:19 (2009): 2038–2040.

Rodwin, Marc A. *Conflicts of Interest and the Future of Medicine*. New York: Oxford University Press, 2011.

Rosenberg, Charles. *The Care of Strangers: The Rise of America's Hospital System*. New York: Basic Books, 1987.

Rosner, David. *A Once Charitable Enterprise: Hospitals and Health Care in Brooklyn and New York, 1885–1915*. New York: Cambridge University Press, 1982.

Rothman, David. *Strangers at the Bedside: A History of How Law and Bioethics Transformed Medical Decision Making*. New York: Basic Books, 1991.

Sandel, Michael. *What Money Can't Buy: The Moral Limits of Markets*. New York: Farrar, Straus and Giroux, 2012.

Satz, Debra. *Why Some Things Should Not Be for Sale: The Moral Limits of Markets*. New York: Oxford University Press, 2010.

Schiff, Robert L., David A. Ansell, James E. Schlosser, Ahamed H. Idris, Ann Morrison, and Steven Whitman. "Transfers to a Public Hospital: A Prospective Study of 467 Patients." *New England Journal of Medicine* 314 (1986): 552–557.

Schoen, Cathy, Sara R. Collins, Jennifer L. Kriss, and Michelle M. Doty. 2008. "How Many Are Underinsured? Trends among U.S. Adults, 2003 and 2007." *Health Affairs* 102 (2008). doi: 10.1377/hlthaff.27.4.w298.

Schroder, Fritz H., Jonas Hugosson, Monique J. Roobol, Teuvo L. J. Tammela, Stefano Ciatto, Vera Nelen, Maciej Kwiatkowski, et al. for the ERSPC Investigators. "Screening and Prostate-Cancer Mortality in a Randomized European Study." *New England Journal of Medicine* 360 (2009): 1320–1328.

Scott, W. Richard, Martin Ruef, Peter J. Mendel, and Carol A. Caronna. *Institutional Change and Healthcare Organizations: From Professional Dominance to Managed Care*. Chicago: University of Chicago Press, 2000.

Sewell, William H. "A Theory of Structure: Duality, Agency, and Transformation." *American Journal of Sociology* 98:1 (1992): 1–29.

Shorter, Edward. *Doctors and Their Patients: A Social History*. 1985. Reprint, New Brunswick, NJ: Transaction Publishers, 2009.

Simons, John H. "The Union Approach to Health and Welfare." *Industrial Relations: A Journal of Economy and Society* 4:3 (1965): 61–76.

Sirovich, Brenda, Patricia M. Gallagher, David E. Wennberg, and Elliott S. Fisher. "Discretionary Decision Making by Primary Care Physicians and the Cost of U.S. Health Care." *Health Affairs* 27:3 (2008): 813–823.

Sitzia, John, and Neil Wood. "Patient Satisfaction: A Review of Issues and Concepts." *Social Science & Medicine*. 45:12 (1997): 1829–1843.

Smith-Doerr, Laurel, and Walter W. Powell. "Networks and Economic Life." In *The Handbook of Economic Sociology, Second Edition*, edited by Neil J. Smelser and Richard Swedberg, 379–402. Princeton, NJ: Princeton University Press, 2005.

Somers, Anne Ramsay. "Comprehensive Prepayment Plans as a Mechanism for Meeting Health Needs." *Annals of the American Academy of Political and Social Science* 337:1 (1961): 81–92.

Somers, Margaret M., and Fred Block. "From Poverty to Perversity: Ideas, Markets, and Institutions over 200 Years of Welfare Debate." *American Sociological Review* 70 (2005): 260–287.

Stark, David. *The Sense of Dissonance: Accounts of Worth in Economic Life*. Princeton, NJ: Princeton University Press, 2009.

Starr, Paul. *The Social Transformation of American Medicine*. New York: Basic Books, 1982.

Steiner, Philippe. "Who Is Right about the Modern Economy: Polanyi, Zelizer, or Both?" *Theory and Society* 38 (2009): 97–110.

Steinberg, Richard. "Economic Theories of Nonprofit Organization." In *The Nonprofit Sector: A Research Handbook, Second Edition*, edited by Walter W. Powell and Richard Steinberg. New Haven, CT: Yale University Press, 2006.

Stevens, Rosemary. *In Sickness and in Wealth: American Hospitals in the Twentieth Century*. 1989. Reprint, New York: Basic Books, 1999.

Stinchcombe, Arthur. "Social Structure and Organizations." In *Handbook of Organizations*, edited by James G. March. Chicago: Rand McNally, 1965.

Tawney, Richard Henry. *The Acquisitive Society*. New York: Harcourt, Brace and Company, 1921.

Timmermans, Stefan, and Hyeyoung Oh. "The Continued Social Transformation of the Medical Profession." *Journal of Health and Social Behavior* 51(S) (2010): S94–S106.

Titmuss, Richard. *The Gift Relationship: From Human Blood to Social Policy*. 1971. Reprint, New York: New Press, 1997.

Uzzi, Brian. "The Sources and Consequences of Embeddedness for the Economic Performance of Organizations: The Network Effect." *American Sociological Review* 61:4 (1996): 674–698.

Vaughan, Diane. "Bourdieu and Organizations: The Empirical Challenge." *Theory and Society* 37 (2008): 65–81.

Velthuis, Olav. *Talking Prices: Symbolic Meanings of Prices on the Market for Contemporary Art*. Princeton, NJ: Princeton University Press, 2005.

Vogel, Morris J. *The Invention of the Modern Hospital: Boston, 1870–1930*. Chicago: University of Chicago Press, 1980.

Wachter, Robert M., and Lee Goldman. "The Emerging Role of 'Hospitalists' in the American Health Care System." *New England Journal of Medicine* 335 (1996): 514–517.

Wall, Barbra Mann. *American Catholic Hospitals: A Century of Changing Markets and Missions*. New Brunswick, NJ: Rutgers University Press, 2011.

———. *Unlikely Entrepreneurs: Catholic Sisters and the Hospital Marketplace, 1865–1925*. Columbus: Ohio State University Press, 2005.

Walzer, Michael. *Spheres of Justice: A Defense of Pluralism and Equality*. New York: Basic Books, 1983.

Wang, Samuel J., Blackford Middleton, Lisa A. Prosser, Christiana G. Bardon, Cynthia D. Spurr, Patricia J. Carchidi, Anne F. Kittler, et al. "A Cost-Benefit Analysis of Electronic Medical Records in Primary Care." *American Journal of Medicine* 114 (2003): 397–403.

Weiss, Robert S. *Learning from Strangers: The Art and Method of Qualitative Interview Studies*. New York: Free Press, 1994.

Wennberg, John E. *Tracking Medicine: A Researcher's Quest to Understand Health Care*. New York: Oxford University Press, 2010.

Wilensky, Harold L. "The Professionalization of Everyone?" *American Journal of Sociology* 70:2 (1964): 137–158.

Wilper, Andrew P., Steffie Woolhandler, Karen E. Lasser, Danny McCormick, David H. Bor, and David U. Himmelstein. "Health Insurance and Mortality in U.S. Adults." *American Journal of Public Health*, 99:12 (2009): 2289–2295

Zawacki, Bruce E. "Corporate Soulcraft in Healthcare." *HealthCare Ethics Committee Forum* 12:1 (2000): 39–48.

Zelizer, Viviana. *Economic Lives: How Culture Shapes the Economy*. Princeton, NJ: Princeton University Press, 2011.

———. "How I Became a Relational Economic Sociologist and What Does That Mean?" *Politics & Society* 40:2 (2012): 145–174.

———. "Human Values and the Market: The Case of Life Insurance and Death in 19th-Century America." *American Journal of Sociology* 84:3 (1978): 591–610.

———. *Pricing the Priceless Child: The Changing Social Value of Children*. Princeton, NJ: Princeton University Press, 1994.

———. *The Purchase of Intimacy*. Princeton, NJ: Princeton University Press, 2005.

———. *The Social Meaning of Money*. 1994. Reprint, Princeton, NJ: Princeton University Press, 1997.

———. "The Social Meaning of Money: 'Special Monies.'" *American Journal of Sociology* 95:2 (1989): 342–377.

Index

Page numbers in *italics* indicate figures and tables.

academic medical centers, 195
accountability: of chaplains, 79–80; of patients, 40; peer review and peer pressure in, 156–58; of physicians, 53, 54, 56, 63, 100; privatization and, 23–24; protocol development and, 155–56; transparency of outcomes and, 190
accreditation, 5, 74, 205n12
Affordable Care Act (ACA). *See* Patient Protection and Affordable Care Act
AFL-CIO, 178
AIDS, 89, 127, 207n24
Alford, Robert R., 207n48
almshouses: hospital as, 10, 19, 22, 33–36; matron and steward of, 21, 22; physicians' role in, 73; private hospital compared with, 71–72. *See also* hospitals and hospital care; PubliCare Hospital
Alta Bates Medical Center (Berkeley), 189
ambulance. *See* emergency medical services
American Academy of Hospice and Palliative Medicine, 85
American College of Surgeons, 74
American Hospital Association, 72
ancillary staff: attempt to close PubliCare and, 68–69; direct action of janitors, 186; disciplinary regime and lack of collegiality among, 109–11; egalitarian atmosphere, 12–13, 17–18, 61; employee evaluations, 114–15, 178; integrated in GroupCare structure, 14–15, 178; interviews of, 203–4; motives for union involvement, 183–84; patients as, in early hospitals, 20; productivity goals for, 136–37; respect for, 186; responsibility shared by, 63–66; responsiveness to patients, 84; Sisters' mission supported by, 75–76; as special breed at PubliCare, 36–38; subordinated in hierarchy, 14, 17, 76, 111–17; values as terrain of struggle for, 117–21. *See also* labor-management partnership; social workers; unions
antiunionism, 118, 119–20
April (pseud.), 181, 186

Best Care Anywhere (Longman), 194
Block, Fred, 10, 206n15
blood supply, gifts vs. payments, 7, 9, 207n24
Booth, Ted (pseud.), 127–31, 203
Bourdieu, Pierre, 207n40
Brenner, Dan (pseud.), 48–50, 51
Brownlee, Sharon, 141–42
bureaucratic organizations: attempts to change, 64–66; contradictions in and conflict among, 207n48; entrepreneurs enlisted to change, 66–68; ethics of, 87–88; individuals' moral-market understandings and, 9–12; informal and collegial (indulgency) pattern in,

bureaucratic organizations (*cont.*) 59–60; organizational theory on, 202. *See also* hospitals and hospital care; managed care; standardization; *and specific institutions*

CalHospitalCompare.org, 190
California HealthCare Foundation, 190
California Nurses Association (CNA), 65, 66
care: marketing of, 11–12; models of, 16. *See also* cultures of practice
Catholic Church: conservative stance, 86, 88–89; encyclicals, 119
Catholic Hospital Association (CHA), 72
Catholic hospitals: distinctions emphasized by, 210n2; emerging market linked to, 72–75; guidance in, 82–83; non-Catholic hospital compared with, 84; preference for poor and, 89–90; religious values in, 75–76. *See also* HolyCare Hospital; spiritual encounter vs. luxury product
Center for Healthcare Reform (St. Francis Health System), 93–94
Center for Medicare and Medicaid Innovation, 192
chaplains, 78–80, 128
clinics: family practice, 127, 135, 140, 166; primary care for poor and indigent people, 89–90, 145; urgent care, 89, 91–92, 96–97
Clinton, Don (pseud.), 52
Coastal Health Net (CHN, pseud.), 100–101
collegiality: absence of, 109–11; construction of, 168–70; at PubliCare, 44, 57, 59–66
commodification of hospital care: Catholic hospital's centrality in, 72–73; consumer trust and, 205n10; context and limits of, 1–4; contracts for specialized corporations in, 95–99; contradictions in, 6–16, *11, 12*; current legislation and unresolved issues in, 192–94; emergence of, 71–72; further ques-

tions about, 196–97; managed care growth in, 124; "moralized" market understandings, 9–12; opposition to, 196; physician's critique of, 48–50; use of term, 206n13. *See also* debasement; health care as social right vs. scarce resource; market; population health vs. individualized care; spiritual encounter vs. luxury product; uncertainty
Community Health Association (HMO, pseud.), 124
computerized systems, 6. *See also* electronic medical records
Cuban medical system, 196
cultures of practice: comparisons of, summarized, 190–91, 194–97; contradictions in, 8–16, *11, 12*; differences in, 5–6; efficiencies aligned with "best care" in, 135–38, 154–55; ER contract firm and, 98–99; impact of billing practices on, 103–6; peer pressure and peer review in, 156–58; protocol development, 155–56. *See also* debasement; electronic medical records; ethics of care; health care as social right; patient satisfaction surveys; uncertainty
Cunningham, Jake (pseud.), 183, 185, 186, 187

death and dying: collusion of silence about, 85–86, 129; personal preferences in, 210n3; physicians' resistance to thinking about, 129–30. *See also* hospice and palliative care
debasement: moralizing market to overcome, 13–14; problem of, 7–8. *See also* HolyCare Hospital; spiritual encounter vs. luxury product
delivery of care, 17–18. *See also* ancillary staff; cultures of practice
doctors. *See* physicians; specialists
drug companies, 88, 156, 192
drugs and drug use: generic, 139; pain medication prescriptions and, 41; physicians' attitudes toward, 105; PSS and overprescribing potential, 163–64;

staying up-to-date on slang concerning, 35; tracking efficacy via EMR, 133

Eat That Cookie (Jazwiec), 114

egalitarianism: comparisons across hospitals, 188; emphasis on, 12–13, 17–18, 36–37, 59, 61; responsibility shared in, 63–66; teaching mandate and, 62

electronic medical records (EMRs): culture of constraint due to, 158–59; as disciplinary technology, 152–55; implementation, 44–45, 131–34; patients' access to, 133; patient satisfaction and, 161–62; peer review and, 156–57; physicians' interaction with, 169; protocols and, 155–56; used in peer pressure, 157–58; variation across departments, 166–68; widespread support for, 211n4

Emergency Medical Incorporated (pseud.), 95–99, 104–5, 106

emergency medical services (EMS): costs of, 39; point-of-entry plan on ER admissions, 31–33; specialized facilities for, 208n2; training for, 62. *See also* emergency rooms

Emergency Medical Treatment and Active Labor Act (EMTALA, 1986), 29, 205n12

emergency rooms: access to, 143–44; differences among, 51–53; electronic records access, 132; mandate to treat, 29, 40, 205n12; PPACA's impact, 192–93; stroke treatment, 210n3; uninsured patient visits compared, 29, *29*; visits by severity compared, 29–30, *30*; workloads compared, 103

—GROUPCARE: attitudes toward, 125; collegiality of, 168–69; EMR and PSS scrutinized for, 153–54, 163–65, 166–67; "fifty-one fifty" patient at, 31–32; financial incentives and doctors' metrics, 157–58; physicians' on staff, 96, 99, 150; power center in, 175–76; rational care, 136–39; triage system, 106, 150

—HOLYCARE: chaplain, 79; clinics to funnel patients away from, 89, 91–92; distinguishing paying from uninsured patients, 104–5; overtreatment, 107–8; physicians' autonomy, 103; physicians' contract, 95–99, 104–5; triage system, 106

—PUBLICARE: egalitarianism and informality, 36–37, 59, 63–64, 66; "frequent fliers," 37–38; organizational change, 64–65; overutilization, 33–35, 38–42; patient satisfaction surveys, 60–61; physicians' autonomy, 55–56; physicians' contract and financial arrangements, 52–53, 96, 99; plans to expand, 68; poor, indigent, and/or uninsured patients sent to, 30–33, 46, 51; social justice commitment of staff, 49; specialists called in, 57–58; staff communications, 44; types of physicians, 45

emotional vulnerability: hospital's guidance and support in, 7–8; nurse on management of, 4–5; spirituality as response strategy to, 76–77. *See also* hospice and palliative care; spiritual encounter vs. luxury product

EMRs. *See* electronic medical records

EMS. *See* emergency medical services

England. *See* Great Britain

Ethical and Religious Directives for Catholic Health Care Services (USCCB), 83, 86–89

ethics of care: alienation of patient as issue in, 82–83; economic interests as trumping, 93–94; economic leverage and, 117–18; in hospice and palliative care, 86–88; market incentives for physicians to overtreat and, 108; physicians' concern about, 73; spiritual dimensions of care for patients in, 83–85. *See also* cultures of practice

"evidence-based medicine": EMR linked to, 160; market and emphasis on, 131; physicians and implementation of, 151–53, 172; PPACA's emphasis on,

"evidence-based medicine" (*cont.*)
3, 192; problems of, 8, 146, 155, 176;
rationing care and, 159, 176, 191–92;
VHA and, 195

family practice physicians: GroupCare
clinic, 127, 135, 140, 166; limited scope
of practice in hospital, 149–50; on
peer review, 156–57; on PSS and EMR
scrutiny, 166; on research studies, 156;
residency program for, 36, 48–49, 51,
69, 110; vocational ethic of, 51
fee-for-service model: ethical questions in,
146; insecurity in, 149–50; misaligned
incentives in, 147–48; overtreatment
in, 136, 138, 140, 141–42; rationing
masked in, 159. *See also* HolyCare
Hospital
for-profit hospitals, 195
Fourcade, Marion, 10, 199
Freidson, Eliot, 150
Friedland, Roger, 207n48
Fuller, Linda, 212n10

Gawande, Atul, 135
GDP (gross domestic product): health
expenditures as percentage of, 2, *2*
Gleeson, Roger (pseud.), 172, 174, 176
global health spending, 2, 196
Gouldner, Alvin W., 59
Great Britain: minimum income law,
208n10; National Health System, 146,
153–54
GroupCare Health Foundation (pseud.),
172–76
GroupCare Health System (pseud.):
benefits at, 149; campus specialties in,
140; data from PSS and EMR utilized
by, 152; description, 131–34; financial
model, 16, 116, 126, 130–31, 134,
145, 178, 188, 194; hospital deaths
in Northern vs. Southern California
facilities, 130; interpersonal skills
classes of, 161; membership community, 142–46; motto ("flourish"), 134,
148–49; ongoing change in, 151; part-

nership model of, 171–72, 188 (*see also*
labor-management partnership); peer
review at, 156–57; power center in,
173–76; preventive care emphasized,
135–36, 145; protocol development
at, 155–56; as "socialized medicine,"
142, 188. *See also* "evidence-based
medicine"; labor-management partnership; managed care
GroupCare Hospital (pseud.): approach
to studying, 16–18; attitudes toward,
125–26; authority hierarchy, 63–64;
bureaucratic system, 15; chaplain,
79; contradictions in practice, 12,
12; discharge process, 138–39, 140;
disciplinary limits, 166–68; disciplinary
technologies, 45, 151–53, 169–70 (*see
also* electronic medical records; patient
satisfaction surveys); drug companies
banned, 88; efficiencies and productivity goals, 136–38; energy savings, 181;
founding, 11, *11*, 124, 125, 177–78; historical context, 123–24, 125; indigent
and/or uninsured patients not welcomed, 32–33, 36, 90; lengths of stay
compared, 140, *141*; local charitable
endeavors by, 144–45; mission, 14–15,
131, 137, 146; motto ("flourish"), 134,
148–49; other hospitals compared with,
4–6, 81, 108; other hospitals compared
with, summarized, 190–91, 194–97;
preventive care emphasized, 135–36,
145; rational care argument at, 125–26,
131, 138–42, 159; research potential
at, 133, 145, 152, 154–55; responsibility expected at, 40, 115–16; scheduling
changes as issue, 182; staff status distinctions absent, 171–72; standardization at, 51–52, 55; taming of market to
reduce uncertainty at, 14–16, 123–26,
169–70, 179; workloads at, 104, 129.
See also labor-management partnership; population health vs. individualized care
—PHYSICIANS: authority and status differences, 173–76; autonomy and, 149–50;

division of labor, 150–51; recruitment, 100, 101; salary and work ethic in, 53, 147–49, 165
—SPECIFIC DEPARTMENTS: cardiology department, 140; critical care (ICU), 52, 174; department team program, 179–80, 181–82; family medicine, 166; family practice clinic, 127, 135, 140, 166; hospital-based medicine, 167–68; obstetrics, 150; palliative care team and resources, 28, 127–31, 203. *See also* emergency rooms: GroupCare
GroupCare Medical Group (pseud.), 53, 96, 100, 101

habitus concept, 207n40
Harper, David (pseud.), 59
health and health care: assessing value of, 8; expenditures in relation to GDP, 2, *2*; further questions, 196–97; global concerns, 2, 196; nutrition and diet concerns, 21; reform, 136 (*see also* Patient Protection and Affordable Care Act). *See also* clinics; hospitals and hospital care
health care as social right: commitment to, 27–29, *29*, 37–38, 42–44, 60–61; egalitarianism in, 36–37; legislation supporting, 205n12; market as antithetical to idea of, 48–50; rebuffing market to protect, 12–13
health care as social right vs. scarce resource: contradictions in practice, 6–7, 11, *12*, 25, 28–33, 35, 58; hopes to find balance in, 23–25; moral distinctions in, 13, 38–42; persistence of problem, 192–93. *See also* almshouses; PubliCare Hospital
Healy, Kieran, 7, 9, 10, 207n24
Henry J. Kaiser Foundation, 23, 24
HFAP (Joint Commission and Healthcare Facilities Accreditation Program), 205n12
Hill-Burton Act (Hospital Survey and Construction Act, 1946), 72
HIV/AIDS, 89, 127, 207n24

HMOs (health maintenance organizations), 100, 123–25. *See also* managed care
Hoddess, John (pseud.), 175
HolyCare Hospital (pseud.): amenities, 82, 84, 101; approach to studying, 16–18; attempt to close PubliCare and, 68–69; attitudes toward, 46; authoritarian structure, 63–64, 109–13; average charge per stay, *92*; contradictions in practice, 11–12, *12*, 76–77; employee evaluations, 114–15, 178; ethics committee, 85–89; finances, 14, *83*, 85, 86, 88, 100–101, 117; founding, 10–11, *11*; free and uncompensated care by, 89–94, *90*, *91*; historical context, 71–75; indigent and/or uninsured patients not welcomed, 32–33; integrated delivery system absent, 100–102; lengths of stay compared, *141*; marketing strategy and religious identity merged at, 13–14, 80, 113–17; mission, 13, 14, 75–76, 82–85, 93–94, 108; moral distinctions made at, 38, 89; other hospitals compared, 4–6, 81, 115–16, 126; other hospitals compared, summarized, 190–91, 194–97; patient placements from, 43–44; researcher's access to, 109; SMF's role at, 66–68; social and spiritual interactions, 82–85; social services for poor absent at, 92–93, 105–6; staff interaction, 61; state-of-the-art treatment, 81–82, 106–8; strikes at, 180; trust (and its absence) at, 102, 103–6; unionization attempt and values struggle, 117–21; vocational subordination at, 111–17, 188; volunteer training of, 111–12. *See also* Sisters of St. Francis; spiritual encounter vs. luxury product
—PHYSICIANS: individualism and billing, 52–53, 99–100, 102, 103–7, 111, 149; specialists' roles, 56–58, 100–102, 111; workloads, 51, 103–4
—SPECIFIC DEPARTMENTS: cardiology, 67, 101–2; chaplaincy program, 78–80; hospitalists, 81, 102–3, 104, 106, 107–8;

HolyCare Hospital (pseud.) (*cont.*)
intensive care unit (ICU), 52; Mission
Integration and Spiritual Care, 13,
79–80; neonatal ICU, 126; palliative
care, 28, 86–88, 102, 128; social work,
27–28; trauma center (level II), 81, 91,
208n2; urgent care clinics, 89, 91–92,
96–97. *See also* emergency rooms:
HolyCare
hospice and palliative care: as "appropriate
utilization" (cost control), 130–31; development of, 85; different approaches,
27–28; ethics and support for, 86–88;
institutional resources and program
for, 127–31; Medicare's last-year-of-life
spending on, 210n3. *See also* death and
dying
Hospital Consumer Assessment of
Healthcare Providers and Systems
(HCAHPS), 209n2
Hospital Corporation of America, 195
hospitalists: attitudes toward GroupCare,
125; ER relations, 65; financial arrangements with hospitals, 52; palliative
care doctors and, 129–30; roles of, 36,
168, 209n7; specialists in relation to,
57–58, 168–69; workloads compared,
103–4
—TOPICAL COMMENTS: attempt to close
PubliCare, 69–70; cost considerations,
159; discharge issues, 42; disorganization, 44; electronic records, 132, 154;
integrated services lacking at Holy-
Care, 102; managed care, 142; market
incentives to work hard, 106; market's
influence decried, 50; number of days
on shift, 176; protocol development,
155, 156; PSS, 160; quality of life, 129;
vocational ethic, 50–51
hospital personnel. *See* ancillary staff;
managers/administrators; nurses and
nurse managers; physicians
hospitals and hospital care: amenities
described in 1887, 20–22; appearance
and reputation, 14; approach to studying, 16–18, 202–3; clientele differences,

142–43; comparisons, summarized,
190–91, 194–97; competition among,
1–2, 81, 126; emotional and spiritual
meanings, 71–72; expenditures in relation to GDP, 2, *2*; for-profit type, 195;
further questions, 196–97; future of,
191–94; "gaming the system," 41–43;
moral and social purposes, 20–21;
not-for-profit type, 3, *3*, 205n12; paradoxical place, 1; perception of quality,
160–62; pricing differences, 90–91; private ("voluntary") type, 10–11, 71–75;
private vs. public, debated, 74–75;
rationing vs. rational, 15–16, 145–46;
short-term beds, by type of control, 3,
3; as signposts in lives, 189–90; as standardized products, 211n1; symbiotic
relationship of physician to, 100–102.
See also almshouses; Catholic hospitals; commodification of hospital care;
GroupCare Hospital; health and health
care; HolyCare Hospital; PubliCare
Hospital
Hospital Survey and Construction Act
(Hill-Burton Act, 1946), 72

individuals and individualized care. *See*
middle-class clientele; patient-centered
medicine model; patients; poor people;
population health vs. individualized
care; wealthy clientele
*Institutional Change in Healthcare Organi-
zations* (Scott et al.), 202
institutions. *See* bureaucratic organizations; hospitals and hospital care
insurance industry: alternative views of, 9;
critique of, 39–40; growth of, 75; hospital negotiations with, 1–2; PPACA's
impact on, 192–93
intensive care units, 4–5, 36, 52, 54–55,
102, 126, 189–90

John Paul II (pope), 119
Joint Commission and Healthcare Facilities Accreditation Program (HFAP),
205n12

Kaiser Foundation, 23, 24
Kaiser-Permanente, 183, 191
Keaney, James K., 95, 210n2
Kochan, Thomas A., 183

Laborem Exercens (encyclical, 1981), 119
labor-management partnership (Group-
    Care): department teams central to,
    179–82; limits of, 182–85; oligarchy vs.
    representation line in, 187–88; as part
    of labor struggle, 185–87; union sup-
    port, contract, and initiatives, 177–81
labor's commodification, critiqued,
    206nn15–16, 22. *See also* ancillary staff;
    unions
labor unions. *See* labor-management part-
    nership; unions
Lacks, Sandra (pseud.), 26–28, 40–41, 42, 43
Las Lomas (pseud.): early hospitals,
    20–22; farmer's market, 135; Group-
    Care's involvement in community,
    144–45; HMOs in, 124–25; hospitals
    in, 4–6, 202–4; paying hospital patient
    problem of, 73–75. *See also* GroupCare
    Hospital; HolyCare Hospital; PubliCare
    Hospital
Las Lomas county entities: board of super-
    visors, 21–22, 23–25, 69, 74–75; county
    farm, 21, 22, 30–33, 47; county jail,
    34, 42 (*see also* prison inmates); health
    department, 81, 91
Las Lomas County Medical Association,
    124–25, 145
Lederer, Philip, 195
legislation: health-related in California, 29,
    192, 193, 205n12; health-related in U.S.,
    72, 211n1. *See also* Medicaid; Medicare;
    Patient Protection and Affordable Care
    Act
Leo XIII (pope), 119
Logan, Joanne (pseud.), 79, 80
Lombardi, Fred (pseud.), 103–4
Longman, Phillip, 194

Malone, Ruth, 33
malpractice insurance, 95, 98

managed care: "appropriate utilization"
    (cost control) in, 130–31; cost efficiency
    key to, 124–25; electronic medical rec-
    ords system, 131–33, 145–46; growth
    of, 11, 100, 123–24, 191; historical
    context, 142; inclusiveness and partner-
    ship embedded in bureaucracy of, 172;
    limits of "scientific," 145–46; ongoing
    change in, 151; physician's critique of,
    48–50; physicians incorporated into,
    148–51, 169–70; physicians' salary and
    work ethic in, 147–49, 165; undertreat-
    ment in, 140–42. *See also* GroupCare
    Health System; GroupCare Hospital;
    rational care
managers/administrators: attitudes and
    mindset, 47; employee evaluations
    by, 114–15; EMRs and peer pressure
    used by, 157–58; as management vs.
    employee centered, 63. *See also* Sisters
    of St. Francis
—TOPICAL COMMENTS: charitable endeav-
    ors of departments, 144; electronic
    medical records, 132–33; ethics com-
    mittee, 86–88; hospital's public orienta-
    tion, 28–29; integrated delivery system,
    101; labor-management partnership,
    179–81, 184–85, 186; ministry in rela-
    tion to profits, 82; patient satisfaction,
    162; physicians' autonomy, 54; physi-
    cian strategy, 100; productivity goals,
    136–37; protocols, 65; on resource al-
    location, 38–39; Sisters' mission, 75–76;
    spiritual dimensions and responsive-
    ness, 83–85
market: GroupCare's taming of uncer-
    tainty in, 14–16, 123–26, 169–70, 179;
    hospital and health care determined
    by, 1–2; ideal of, as fiction, 10, 206n15;
    "management" ostensibly antithetical
    to, 124; moralizing of, to overcome
    debasement, 13–14; Polanyi's views
    on, 206nn15–16, 22, 207n26, 208n10;
    protecting rights by rebuffing, 12–13;
    social relationships inseparable from,
    6–7, 206n15. *See also* commodification

market (*cont.*)
    of hospital care; health care as social
        right vs. scarce resource; population
        health vs. individualized care; spiritual
        encounter vs. luxury product
Martinelli, Adriana (pseud.), 60–61
martyred heart concept, 111
Marx, Karl, 10
Massachusetts General Hospital, 20
McEvoy, Matthew (pseud.), 97–98, 104
Medicaid: attitudes toward, 39; expansion
    of, 191–92; health care as social right
    under, 205n12; health care market's ex-
    pansion due to, 205n7; reimbursement
    negotiations of, 90–91; Westside Health
    lease of PubliCare and, 25
Medi-Cal (California's Medicaid), 39, 145
medical students: egalitarianism and, 62;
    paying patients spared gaze of, 71–72;
    poor as material for, 53. *See also* family
    practice physicians: residency program
    for
Medicare: health care as social right under,
    205n12; health care market's expan-
    sion due to, 205n7; knee replacement
    guidelines, 55; last-year-of-life spend-
    ing, 210n3; payments based on patient
    outcomes, 192; prospective payment
    into, 211n1; recovery audit contractors
    (RACs), 55; reimbursement negotia-
    tions, 90–91; Westside Health lease of
    PubliCare and, 25
methodology: background, 201; focus,
    202–3; process, 203–4
middle-class clientele: attitudes toward
    PubliCare, 46–47; reluctant to take
    time off, 143; standardization and cost
    efficiency for, 124; as typical Group-
    Care member, 142–46. *See also* Group-
    Care Hospital
moral frameworks: market understandings
    and, 9–12; paternalism and disdain,
    53–54; poor people evaluated via, 13,
    38–42, 89; unionization attempt in,
    118–20. *See also* values

moral hazards: debates about, 22–23; per-
    sonal responsibility and, 38–41
moralizing the market (concept), 9, 14, 18,
    120–21, 194. *See also* spiritual encoun-
    ter vs. luxury product; values

National Labor Relations Act (Wagner Act,
    1935), 73
National Labor Relations Board (NLRB),
    118–19
Nelson, Sioban, 72
Nixon, Richard, 123
not-for-profit hospitals, 3, *3*, 205nn10, 12.
    See also GroupCare Hospital; HolyCare
    Hospital; PubliCare Hospital
nuns. *See* Sisters of St. Francis
nurses and nurse managers: camaraderie,
    collegiality, and informality of doctors
    and, 44, 57, 59–66; career goals, 4–5;
    vocational commitment and creativity,
    42, 60–61; vocational subordination
    of, 111–17; wages, voluntarism, and
    religiosity of, 62–63, 73
—TOPICAL COMMENTS: atmosphere and
    patient satisfaction, 60–61; attitudes
    and mindset, 47; authoritarian work
    structure, 110–11; bureaucratic corrup-
    tion, 176; cost efficiencies vs. medical
    benefits, 140; egalitarian treatment,
    36–37; emergency room visits, 30,
    31, 34, 38; GroupCare members,
    143; HolyCare as state-of-the-art, 81;
    hospitals' differences, 5–6, 36; indigent
    and/or uninsured cases, 31–33; moral
    distinctions, 38–39; palliative care, 28;
    personal responsibility, 40; physicians
    and overtreatment, 107–8; physicians
    and un- and underinsured patients,
    104, 105; physicians' autonomy, 54–55;
    power differences and relationships,
    174–75; productivity goals, 136–37;
    protocols, 65; public perception, 46;
    scheduling changes, 182; sisters' pres-
    ence, 112–13
nutrition and diet concerns, 21

Obama, Barack, 130
"Obamacare." *See* Patient Protection and Affordable Care Act
Office of Statewide Health Planning and Development (OSHPD), 204
organ donations, 87
orthopedic care, 33, 55, 57, 58
Overtreated (Brownlee), 141–42

palliative care. *See* hospice and palliative care
patient-centered medicine model, 135, 160. *See also* patient satisfaction surveys
Patient-Centered Outcomes Research Institute, 192, 193
patient/physician relationship: emails and phone consultations, 133–34; fee-for-service billing practices and, 103–6; follow ups, 51; organization's mediation of, 150–51; as partnership, 160–61; paternalism in, 53–54; physicians' concern about, 73. *See also* electronic medical records; patient satisfaction surveys
Patient Protection and Affordable Care Act (PPACA, 2010), 3, 130, 191–92, 193. *See also* electronic medical records
patients: accountability and responsibility of, 13, 38–42; categorized by dependency, 21; distinguishing paying from uninsured, 104–5; early home care for, 20; emotional well-being of, 160–62; hospital staff vs. system navigated by, 138; indigent and/or uninsured, sent to PubliCare, 31–33; lack of information and uncertainty of, 8; medical model focused on, 135, 160; palliative care team for, 127–31; paying, facilities for, 71–75; physicians as lifestyle models for, 148–49; preventive care emphasized, 135–36, 145; records of, 44–45, 55 (*see also* electronic medical records); spiritual dimensions of care for, 83–85; terms for, 48. *See also* electronic medi-

cal records; patient/physician relationship; patient satisfaction surveys
patient satisfaction surveys (PSS): analysis and uses of, 130, 160–62, 190; consumer reports compared with, 212n10; decline of scores, 112; as disciplinary technology, 152–53; display and comparison of, 164–65; emergency room visits, 60–61, 165, 209n2; physicians' critique and ambivalence about, 162–64; physicians' interaction with, 169–70; standardization of, 209n2; variation across departments, 166–68; widespread support for, 211n4
Patterns of Industrial Bureaucracy (Gouldner), 59
peer review and peer pressure, 156–58
pest house, 21
Peterson, Tom (pseud.), 85–87, 102, 128
pharmaceutical companies, 88, 156, 192. *See also* drugs and drug use
Phil (pseud.), 185
physicians: amenities for, 171; approach to studying, 17; attitudes and mindset, 47, 125–26; authority and status, 11, 15, 50, 71, 72–73, 173–76; autonomy of, 52, 53, 54–56, 148–51; beepers vs. overhead pages, 84; billing and payment, 14, 52–53, 73, 95–99, 103–6 (*see also* fee-for-service model); camaraderie, collegiality, and informality of nurses and, 44, 57, 59–66; disciplinary technologies and, 151–53 (*see also* electronic medical records; patient satisfaction surveys); drug companies' influence on, 88; hospital appointments, 19–20, 22; individualism and billing practices of, 52–53, 99–100, 102, 103–7, 111; interpersonal skills, 161–62; malpractice insurance, 95, 98; managed care roles, 148–51; market incentives and work ethic, 106–8, 147–49, 165; paternalism and disdain toward patients, 53–54; peer review and pressure, 156–58; phone consultations,

physicians (*cont.*)

133–34; vocational commitment and creativity of, 42; vocational ethic of, 50–53; workload differences, 51, 103–4, 129. *See also* family practice physicians; hospitalists; patient/physician relationship; specialists

—TOPICAL COMMENTS: attitudes toward GroupCare, 143–44; authoritarian work structure, 111; collegiality, 59–63, 109–10; cost efficiencies and productivity goals, 137–38; cost efficiencies vs. medical benefits, 138–41; egalitarian treatment, 37; electronic records, 44–45, 132–33, 153; emergency room visits, 30, 31, 33–35; ER contracts, 95–97; HIV/AIDS, 89; HolyCare as state-of-the-art, 81; hospice and palliative care, 28, 85–87; labor contract, 184–85; market's influence decried, 48–50; personal responsibility and moral hazards, 39–41; privatization, 24; protocol development, 155–56; PSS, 162–65; PubliCare vs. GroupCare patients, 142–43; public perception, 46; reproductive health services, 89; responsiveness to patients, 84; RVU model, 99; social problems of patients, 36; staff's commitment to PubliCare, 61; staying up-to-date on street slang, 35; under- and overtreatment, 140–41; urgent care clinics, 91–92

Polanyi, Karl, 206nn15–16, 22, 207n26, 208n10

Polyakova, Alex (pseud.), 44, 50, 51, 56, 57–58, 65

poor (or county) farm, 21, 22, 30–33, 47. *See also* almshouses

poor people: almshouses for, 10, 19, 33–36; attitudes toward time off for treatment, 142; categorization of, 21; early institutions to deter poor from seeking welfare, 22–23; egalitarian treatment of, 36–37; emergency room visits, *29*, 29–35, *30*; free and uncompensated care for, 89–94, *90*, *91*; medical care

and social care boundaries unclear for, 35–36; moral evaluations of, 13, 38–42, 89; physicians' attitudes toward, 53–54, 104–6; PubliCare's commitment to, 28–29, *29*, 37–38, 42, 60–61; sent to PubliCare, 31–33. *See also* health care as social right; PubliCare Hospital

population health vs. individualized care: contradictions in practice, *11*, 12, *12*, 131; financial efficiencies and members' well-being in, 134–38; persistence of problem, 193–94; physicians' role in balancing, 147–49, 158–59; rational care argument in, 125–26, 131, 138–42; standardization and individual monitoring in, 131–34; systematization and ethical questions in, 145–46. *See also* uncertainty

preventive care, 135–36, 145, 192

prison inmates, 33

private ("voluntary") hospitals, 10–11, 71–75. *See also* Catholic hospitals

privatization, 23–25. *See also* PubliCare Hospital

profitability: entrepreneurs enlisted to improve PubliCare's, 66–68; HolyCare vs. PubliCare, 82, *83*. *See also* GroupCare Health System

protocols, 65, 155–57

psychiatric services, 31–32, 34, 137

PubliCare Hospital (pseud.): accreditation, 74; as almshouse, 10, 19, 22, 33–36; approach to studying, 16–18; attempt to close, 68–70, 88–89; average charge per stay, *92*; camaraderie, collegiality, and informality at, 44, 57, 59–66; commitment to serving poor people, 28–29, *29*, 37–38, 42, 60–61; contradictions in practice, 11, *12*, 12–13, 25, 28, 35, 58; discharge issues, 35–36; disorganization at, 44–45, 50; egalitarianism at, 36–37, 59, 62, 63–64, 188; ethics committee, 86; finances and privatization, 12–13, 23–25, *25*, 31, 68–70, *83*, 125; founding, 10, *11*; free and uncompensated care by, 89–94, *90*, *91*; GroupCare as boon for, 124; historical context, 19–23; indigent and/or uninsured patients sent to, 31–33; lack of chaplain, 79; lengths of stay compared, *141*; market's influence decried at, 48–50; mission, 12, 14, 24, 44, 46–47, 64, 68–70; other hospitals compared with, 4–6, 62–63, 81, 116, 126; other hospitals compared with, summarized, 190–91, 194–97; patient placements from, 42–43, 44; patients viewed as taking advantage of, 13, 38–42; public perception, 46–47; record system, 44–45; researcher's access to, 109; social services, 26–28, 32, 38, 46, 92; staff status distinctions at, 172; status of (1940), 73–74; strikes at, 180; as teaching hospital, 53, 61 (*see also* family practice physicians: residency program for); vocational commitment and creativity at, 27–29, *29*, 37–38, 42–44, 60–61; vocational ethic at, 50–53. *See also* health care as social right; health care as social right vs. scarce resource; Westside Health Corporation

—PHYSICIANS: autonomy, 52, 53, 54–56; financial arrangements, 52–53; as partners at, 97; specialists' roles, 56–58, 100–102; workloads, 51, 103

—SPECIFIC DEPARTMENTS: cardiology, 46–47, 54–55, 56–57, 67–68, 126, 208n2; intensive care unit (ICU), 52; orthopedic care, 33; palliative care, 86; residency program, 36, 48–49, 51, 69, 74, 110. *See also* emergency rooms: PubliCare

Public Works Administration, 74

quality-adjusted life years (QALYs), 193–94
Quan, Andrew (pseud.), 171

RACs (recovery audit contractors), 55
The Rape of Emergency Medicine (Keaney), 95, 210n2
rational care: concept, 125–26; incentives for, 123–25; informal authority and

hierarchies in context of, 175–76; lean production method and, 147; limits of, 176; model and tools of, 131, 138–42; physicians' role in, 147–49, 158–59; rationing care and debates about, 145–46, 193–94. *See also* GroupCare Hospital; managed care; standardization

Reagan, Ronald, 211n1
reciprocal obligations, 42–43
recovery audit contractors (RACs), 55
regional trauma center. *See* HolyCare Hospital
Reich-Sharpe, Ella, 189, 191
relational package concept, 9–10, 17. *See also* physicians
reproductive health services, 88–89
Rerum Novarum (encyclical, 1891), 119
residency program, 74, 110. *See also* family practice physicians: residency program for
responsibility: expectations at GroupCare, 40, 115–16; of patients, 13, 38–42; physicians' lifestyle as model, 148–49; privatization as fostering, 24; shared by PubliCare staff, 63–66; for utilization management, 1, 29, 54
Roberts, Amanda (pseud.), 78–80
Rosenberg, Charles, 19, 53, 54
Ross, Fred, Jr., 201
Rothman, David, 82
RVUs (relative value units), 98–99

Sampson, Brittany (pseud.), 39–40, 41
Sandel, Michael, 6–7, 8–9
Satz, Debra, 6, 8–9
Schmidt, Ron (pseud.), 147
Scott, John (pseud.), 138–39
Scott, W. Richard, 202–3
SEIU-UHW (United Healthcare Workers–West), 201
Service Employee International Union (SEIU), 65, 201
Sierra Medical Foundation (SMF, pseud.), 66–68
The Simple Truths of Service (Blanchard and Glantz), 112

Sisters of St. Francis (pseud.): clinics, 89–90; disengagement, 76; leadership and presence, 112–13; legacy of service, 111–12; mission, 75–76, 93–94, 108; physicians' initial attitudes toward, 99–100; scolding by, 109; training in values of, 80; unionization attempt and, 118–20; values and milieu, 117. *See also* HolyCare Hospital; St. Francis Health System

SMF (Sierra Medical Foundation, pseud.), 66–68

Smith, Vicki, 212n10

"socialized medicine," 24, 33–35, 142, 188

social rights. *See* health care as social right

social values. *See* values

social welfare: declining services, 33–34; early institutions to deter poor from seeking, 22–23; PubliCare's role, 41–44

social workers: on "frequent fliers," 37–38; on indigent and/or uninsured cases, 32–33; on "institutionalized" patients, 42; motivation and commitment, 26–28; on palliative care team, 129, 130; tasks, 26–27; on unions, 66; vocational commitment and reciprocal relations of, 42–44

Somers, Margaret M., 10, 206n15

specialists: autonomy of, 54; avoiding use of, 135, 137; on electronic records, 132, 161–62; finances, 33, 57, 100–101, 168; key in managed care, 151; lack of collegiality, 168–69; on peer pressure, 157–58, 165; phone consultations, 133; primary care physicians vs., 57, 100–102, 110; resources requested, 55, 110; silence concerning deaths, 85–86. *See also* HolyCare Hospital

Speemhamland Law (England, 1795–1834), 208n10

spiritual encounter vs. luxury product: chaplaincy program and, 78–80; context of, 71–75; contradictions in practice, *11*, 11–12, *12*, 73, 75–77; persistence of problem, 193; physi-

cians' individualism and billing in, 52–53, 99–107, 111; social and spiritual interactions reconciled with market position, 82–89, 93–94, 113–17; state-of-the-art treatment in, 81–82; values as terrain of struggle in, 117–21; vocational subordination and, 111–17. *See also* HolyCare Hospital

standardization: cost efficiencies and productivity goals in, 124, 136–38; culture of constraint in, 158–59; definition of, 134; difficulties in creating, 53; electronic medical records system, 131–33, 145–46; EMRs and peer pressure in, 157–58; inefficiency generated from, 175–76; of patient surveys, 209n2; physicians' autonomy vs., 54–55; physicians' critique of, 51–52; protocol development and, 155–56; of PSS, 209n2. *See also* bureaucratic organizations; managed care; rational care

Stanford Hospital, 190

Starr, Paul, 73, 75

Steiner, Philippe, 194

Stevens, Rosemary, 1, 73, 75, 211n1

stewardship, 85

St. Francis Health System (pseud.): Catholic values inculcated by, 76–77; Center for Healthcare Reform of, 93–94; ethics department, 86–89; "Mission and Mentoring" program, 80. *See also* Sisters of St. Francis

Strangers at the Bedside (Rothman), 82

supplier-driven demand, 8

Sweeney, John, 178

taxi vouchers, 38, 39

Taylor, Katherine (pseud.), 4–6

Tenet Healthcare, 195

Tenney, Jennifer, 191

Titmuss, Richard, 7, 9, 207n24

Toyota principles, 147

uncertainty: partnerships as means of reducing, 171–72; problem of, 8; protocol development and, 155–56; rational care to overcome, 125–26, 145–46; salaried physicians as reducing, 149–50; taming the market to reduce, 14–16, 123–26, 169–70, 179. *See also* "evidence-based medicine"; GroupCare Hospital; population health vs. individualized care

unions: attempt to close PubliCare and, 69; benefits, 65–66, 116–17, 179, 185–87; direct action of janitors, 186; economic vs. noneconomic aspects of contract, 183; HMO of, 124; lack of, 110; quality of leaders in, 187–88; strikes, 180; values struggle in attempt to form, 117–21; weakness of, 64. *See also* labor-management partnership

United Healthcare Workers–West (SEIU-UHW), 201

United States Conference of Catholic Bishops (USCCB), directives, 83, 86–89

university medical centers, 195

University of California medical facilities, 74, 194

utilization management: "appropriate" (cost control), 130–31; finances in relation to, 148; metrics for, 166–67; monitoring and reducing, 57, 102, 152, 157–59, 164, 165; responsibility for, 1, 29, 54; right to care and, 28

vaccinations, 135

values: founding goals and, 4; hospital care imbued with, 7–8; individual economic activities reflective of, 9–12; rhetoric vs. practice, 113–15; self-sacrifice inspired by, 116–17; as terrain of struggle, 117–21. *See also* health care as social right; spiritual encounter vs. luxury product

Vaughan, Susanna (pseud.), 183–84, 185–86, 187–88, 200

Veterans Health Administration, 194

voluntarism: administrative hierarchy and, 109–10; ideal of, 72; religious nursing staff and, 73, 76–77; vocational subordination and, 111–17

vulnerability. *See* emotional vulnerability

wages and salaries: differences among hospitals, 62–63; nurses and ancillary staff, compared, 73, 171, 177; PSS useful in context of, 165. *See also* fee-for-service model; physicians; unions

Wagner-Murray-Dingell bill (1943), 72

Wall, Barbra Mann, 72, 93, 210n2

Walzer, Michael, 7

wealthy clientele: attitudes toward PubliCare, 46–47; level and type of care for, 53, 81–85, 86. *See also* HolyCare Hospital

Wells, Julia (pseud.): background and motive for union involvement, 177, 182–83; on energy savings, 181; knowledge of contract, 178; on labor contract, 185–87; negotiation style of, 187–88

Westside Health Corporation (pseud.): benign neglect of PubliCare, 64; care for poor not in mission, 90; decision to close PubliCare, 68–69; entrepreneurs enlisted by, 66–68; layoffs by, 61; lease and terms, 23–25, 34, 53; mentioned, 32, 125; organizational preferences of, 59–60; paper to electronic records shift, 44–45; paying patients sought by, 46–47; public distrust of, 69–70. *See also* PubliCare Hospital

Westside Medical Foundation (pseud.), 52, 100, 101

What Money Can't Buy (Sandel), 6–7

Why Some Things Should Not Be for Sale (Satz), 6

Will (pseud.), 186

With God on Our Side (Reich), 201

women's issues: health care access, 69; reproductive health services, 88–89; surrogacy, 87

workers. *See* ancillary staff

working class. *See* middle-class clientele

Zelizer, Viviana, 9, 10, 17, 207n47